How to Read This Book

The book you just opened is history in the making. And if you are praying, contributing to Bike for Haiti, or reading this book—you are a part of it.

Its two-sided design will give you insight into one man's calling, brought to life by two bike rides.

This first side holds *Lessons From the Road: Moving from the Mundane to the Miraculous* as written in 2012. In it, Guy Melton will take you on his first Bike for Haiti journey—a trek that spans 1,500 miles and two countries. You will laugh. You will weep. You will finish this first account a changed person.

Then, you can turn the book to its second side to enjoy *Devotions from the Road*, a collection of reflections from his second bike ride: a trek from California to Florida, spanning 3,200 miles. These are daily entries and insights that include a biblical nugget. Both books will inspire you to keep moving forward into the eternal purpose for which God has wired us all.

Pastor Guy Melton's journey from the mundane to the miraculous is a reality I have witnessed in Guy since we were young teens growing up 44 years ago in the same church. The miracles related in this book are as real as the man who lived them. I believe the story he tells of "God Sightings" while biking between Miami and New York are all true because the pure in heart really do see God.

Reading the story of how his compassion for the children of Haiti has taken shape and inspired him to risk so much has touched me as deeply as any book I have ever read. This is a book I want in the hands of everyone I love and everyone who wants to love.

Bud McCord
Missionary to Brazil and President of Abide International Ministries

Pastor Guy Melton's heart for the Lord and for people is inspiring. The Lord has used him to challenge scores of people to obey Christ in tangible ways that profoundly impact others.

Eric Geiger
Vice President LifeWay Christian Resources

Finally, someone with courage gives us his personal testimony about the tragedy in Haiti and how it motivated him to get involved. *Lessons From the Road* calls us to rethink how we apply the gospel to a broken third-world country. "Actions speak louder than words," and this book will transform our good intentions into genuine, lasting change and action.

Dr. Jean Ulrick Moise, President and CEO, Palm Beach Baptist Theological Seminary – W.P.B., Mosheh Theological Seminary - Haiti, Mission Evangelique Baptiste Mosheh --Haiti.

With the humble, homespun charm that defines his sermons, Oasis pastor Guy Melton has written a book that will take you up and down the East Coast, into Haiti and even back through time -- to Melton's own childhood and his often difficult, ultimately victorious relationship with his abusive, alcoholic father.

This inspirational book was 1500 miles in the making, the distance Melton was willing to ride a bicycle to raise money for the children of Haiti. Come along for a spiritual sightseeing journey from Mount Vernon to Ground Zero, from Savannah to South Florida, with more than a few peeks at our Father in heaven -- "God Sightings," as Melton calls them. And they happened all along the East Coast, where Melton was never too far from the ocean ... or from God.

Gregg Doyel , CBSSports.com columnist

© 2012—Guy Melton
Lessons From the Road… Moving From the Mundane to the Miraculous

ISBN 978-0-9883311-0-5
Printed in the United States of America.
All rights reserved under International Copyright Law. Contents, cover, or any portion of this book may not be copied, stored, or used in whole or in part in any form without the express written permission of the publisher, except for brief quotations in critical reviews or articles.

Published by Oasis Productions
12201 SW 14th Street
Pembroke Pines, FL 33025
www.bikeforhaiti.com/
www.visitoasis.org/

Unless otherwise noted, scripture quotations are taken from the *Holy Bible, New International Version*®. © 1973, 1978, 1984 by International Bible Society. Used by permission of Zondervan Publishing House. All rights reserved. "NIV" is a trademark of International Bible Society.

Scripture quotations marked NASB are taken from the *New American Standard Bible*. © The Lockman Foundation 1960, 1962, 1963, 1968, 1971, 1972, 1973, 1975, 1977, 1995. Used by permission.

Scripture quotations marked The Message are taken from *The Message*. © 1993, 1994, 1995, 1996, 2000, 2001, 2002. Used by permission of NavPress Publishing Group.

Scripture quotations marked KJV are taken from the Holy Bible, *King James Version*, Cambridge, 1769.

Edited by Gina Lynnes
Cover design by Corey Melton
Layout and interior design by Scott Shaffer

Author Contact Information:
Guy Melton
Oasis Church
12201 SW 14thStreet
Pembroke Pines, FL 33025
www.bikeforhaiti.com/
www.visitoasis.org/

LESSONS FROM THE ROAD

MOVING FROM THE MUNDANE TO THE MIRACULOUS

Guy Melton

Oasis Productions
Pembroke Pines, Florida

DEDICATION

To Tonia who has supported me through 37 years of marriage and more of the craziest endeavors and faith adventures than any one woman should have to endure: You have always loved me. You have quietly, and not so quietly at times, supported me behind the scenes. You are a great wife, mother, daughter, sister, daughter-in-law, mother-in-law and grandmother. I love you more today than ever.

To my mom who raised four children mostly on her own and never ceased to encourage, love, and support us all even when we didn't deserve it: You worked two jobs seven days a week to put food on the table and a roof over our heads. You might not have supported me in the beginning of this ride but you were there at the end when I arrived in New York City. I love you, Mom.

To my sons, Jim, Nate, and Corey: You guys have made me proud to be your dad. You have all followed your hearts and your own paths as adults and I am proud of the men you have become. All I ever wanted as a father was to be your friend when you became adults and to know that you love the Lord. You have honored me with both.

To Jenni and Sabrina: You are the two most wonderful daughters-in-law I could have ever asked for. I began praying for you when your husbands were just babies. God gave me the perfect girls.

To my grandchildren, Gavyn, Caleb, Selah, and Raelynne: Until the day I held you in my arms I didn't understand how much I could love a baby I'd just met. Until that moment I didn't know it was possible to love someone else as much as your own children. I love you more than I can put into words. My daily prayer as I mounted my bike during the ride was that I would see you again. I have, and now my greatest desire is to leave a godly heritage to you. I want you to know me as the Poppy who loves you unconditionally and who loves God more.

To my father-in-law and mother-in-law , Gil and Yvonne Gilmore: You have loved me and supported me since the day I met you. I fell in love with you Yvonne even before I loved your daughter. The gift of your car and your camper for the Bike for Haiti ride was the most generous gift made during this whole journey. Your love was displayed more in your great sacrifice than in words. I love you both. I am forever grateful for the gift you gave to me 37 years ago when you granted me the hand of your precious little girl.

LESSONS FROM THE ROAD
MOVING FROM THE MUNDANE TO THE MIRACULOUS

TABLE OF CONTENTS

Table of Contents:
Chapter 1: It's Never One Thing	1
Chapter 2: Blind Eyes	7
Chapter 3: No Escape Hatch	13
Chapter 4: The Power of Preparation	17
Chapter 5: Launch Day	21
Chapter 6: A New Attitude	25
Chapter 7: The Bridges of Brevard County	29
Chapter 8: Eye of the Storm	33
Chapter 9: Living in the Downdraft	37
Chapter 10: Teaming Together	43
Chapter 11: The Road More Traveled	49
Chapter 12: The Bisiklet Boys	55
Chapter 13: What a Difference a Day Makes	63
Chapter 14: Cool Winds and Hot Coffee	69
Chapter 15: Friday the 13th	75
Chapter 16: The Secret of Contentment	81
Chapter 17: One Child at a Time	87
Chapter 18: Survival…of the Blessed	93
Chapter 19: Little Foxes	101
Chapter 20: Listen Up!	107
Chapter 21: A Nation Under God	113
Chapter 22: The Second Century	119
Chapter 23: Love Doesn't Look Away	125
Chapter 24: The Longest Ride	131
Chapter 25: The Big Apple	137
Chapter 26: No Recession in God's Economy	145
Chapter 27: A Fork in the Road	153
Lessons From the Road	159
Endnotes	207

ACKNOWLEDGMENTS

To Oasis Church of South Florida—the only church family I have ever pastored and ever hope to pastor: You supported me in this journey from the time you heard me share my vision. I would have never been able to accomplish, or even start this without your support financially, your prayers, and the time you allowed me to take on a sabbatical. I am honored to serve you.

To Johnny Guimaraes, Nathan Lamberth, Eric Weachter, and Taylor Leischman for your coaching and encouragement: You were with me from day one. Without the support and help you supplied I would have never made it to launch day. I am forever grateful. You were all great mentors in your own right.

To the staff of Oasis Church: Well, what can I say? I know from the start you rolled your eyes behind my back and murmured, "There he goes again." Or at least that's what I imagined. But you supported, encouraged, and picked me up throughout the process. When I pedaled out of the parking lot that Sunday, May 1st I knew you had my back during my journey and I never worried if our church family would be cared for. I can't begin to recount in this small space all the extra time and effort each of you put forth to make Bike for Haiti a success. I love you guys. You're a great team. Thanks for letting me follow my "Radical Call."

To the guys I called my mentoring group, Joel Collins, Ben Windle, John Adams, and Luke Windle: In the end you mentored me. When I asked you to pray for this "Radical Ride" you did. When I asked you what you thought, you gave me your full support. You were the first guys I shared this with after my own family. Then each of you joined our support team and went a week with me on the ride, supporting me, setting up the camper, driving, taking care of the details, and keeping me alive along 1500 miles of highway. Guys, I will never forget your support and friendship. Thank you.

To Jeremy Higdon who spent a week supporting me on the roads of Georgia, South Carolina, and North Carolina: What a great week! We not only worked hard but reminisced, laughed, cried, and experienced the miracle meeting outside Charleston with the Bisiklet Boys. Thanks to you and Oasis Church of North Florida. I'm proud of you.

To all of you who prayed, wrote words of encouragement both before and during the ride: I felt your prayers and support each and every day on the bike. I am forever grateful for all of you—from the child who gave his hard earned $20, to the families who gave hundreds and even thousands of dollars—who have helped touch one Haitian child, one Haitian family at a time.

Finally to the people of Haiti for whom God has given me a love which is beyond words: What you have to live daily to survive is more than any human should have to endure. But you persevere and you look for the day when your beloved Haiti will become what it can be. You are the reason there is a Bike for Haiti. You are the reason this book was written—the book I said I would never write. You have challenged me by your love and friendship, and you are the reason this book is a reality.

FOREWORD

Don't you dare put this book down, and don't thumb through it for the next few minutes looking for some juicy tidbit or statement. Don't do it!

Just begin! If you will just read the first chapter, you will be hooked and you will read the whole book. This book is fascinating…action-oriented…and has a message that can change your life. So before you finish this paragraph, plan to just read the first chapter. If you're not hooked by then, you maybe "unhookable."

You'll not only read about Guy Melton's bicycle ride from Fort Lauderdale to New York City, you'll enter his world…think his thoughts…face his doubts…shiver at his fears…and even laugh at his mistakes. This book will bounce you through every emotion in your heart.

Guy Melton's bicycle ride up the East Coast will make you think about your own ride through life, all the fears and dangers you face, all the dreams you embrace. They are all there. Every emotion of life is found in this story. And you'll see how God answers prayer for Guy Melton, and how He'll answer your prayer as you are on your roller-coaster ride called Life.

Reading this book is like watching *Mission Impossible* on television. Even before the program began you knew the plot. You knew your heroes would accomplish the goal, and live happily ever after (at least that's what they seem to do on television after the program is over). Guy Melton made the trip; we know that. Guy Melton raised the money; we know that. So why should you read this book?

For the same reason you watch *Mission Impossible*.

We all watch that program to see how the caper was solved, or how the death threat was averted, or how the villain was caught. So read this book not to see if Guy Melton will make it. He did! Read this book to see how he made it. Learn what God was saying to him on those long lonesome stretches of highway. See his strength increase, and watch what happens when he faces his sudden fears.

I laughed…cried…and at times wanted to pray for Guy Melton in his difficulties—even knowing the experience was over a year old. We can't pray for past events to happen differently, I realize. But nevertheless I wanted to pray because as a 15-year-old kid, I once rode my bicycle from Savannah, Georgia, to Waycross, Georgia. Beginning at 4:30 in the morning, I arrived at 11:00 in the morning, just in time for a Presbyterian youth rally I attended. Why did I ride my bicycle such a long way? I wanted to walk in, sit on the front row, and have all the girls of the church stare at me and say, "My hero!"

The next summer I rode my bicycle 154 miles from Savannah, Georgia, to Sardinia, South Carolina. Two days later I rode 120 miles to Statesboro, Georgia. The next day I rode 50 miles back to Savannah. I know what Guy means when he talks about those long rides across the empty southern roads…blistering hot days…cold mornings…and lonesomeness. So I like this book because I have been there before in a small way.

I praise God for Guy Melton and what he accomplished.

May you enjoy this book as much as I did, and may you too take your spiritual "bike ride"—not from Miami to New York, but as you teach a Sunday school class, or serve on a church committee, or try to win a loved one to Jesus Christ. May you become stronger, wiser, and better equipped for your journey because you read this book, and because you learned lessons not just from Guy Melton, but from God.

Sincerely yours,

Elmer Towns
Co Founder, Liberty University
Lynchburg, Virginia

CHAPTER 1
It's Never One Thing

Catastrophic change is never caused by just one thing. I didn't wake up one morning as a 55-year-old man with a heart condition and simply decide to turn my world upside down by pushing the envelope of every aspect of my life: physical, mental, emotional, and spiritual.

I'm not brave. I'm not a risk taker.

Having written those words, I must confess that they're not altogether true. Not anymore anyway. They were true of the man I was until God upset the comfortable paradigm of who I am, why I'm here, and what I'm supposed to be doing with my life.

But I'm not the same man today. I have developed an appalling level of courage, and risks no longer leave my palms damp or my mouth dry.

How do I explain the change?

That's what I mean when I say it's never just one thing.

Think back to the wars in Iraq and Afghanistan. It's too simplistic to say that the horrific attacks on September 11, 2001, caused them. Yes, the cataclysmic events on that fateful day threw us headlong into war, but religious and political ideologies had been warring for decades before they erupted in fireballs that brought down the Twin Towers and destroyed the Pentagon.

While I'm not comparing the change in my life to war, there are a few subtle similarities. Situations on the global and national scene had festered for years before erupting in my life to a degree that required me to battle my own apathy. But once that eruption took place, everything changed.

I realized I had to break out of the limitations that had stopped me cold—my health, my age, my fear, my finances, and the economy. I had to step out of the mundane and allow the wind of the Spirit to sweep me into the miraculous, limitless life that God planned for each believer to live.

I had to leave my comfort zone and do something so radical that… *somehow*…it might make a difference in the world.

I didn't realize that it would also make such a difference in *me*.

Financial Meltdown

One of the simmering situations nationally was the recession. Florida, a kind of Ground Zero for foreclosures and unemployment, had been one of the hardest hit areas in the country. It also happened to be where I live and pastor Oasis Church.

On the heels of 15 years of financial growth of 5 to 25 percent, our congregation had been shell-shocked by four grueling years of recession. I'd lived in Florida all my life and experienced three other recessions, but nothing like this one. Although the church continued to grow, many of our members lost jobs, cars, and homes in the financial meltdown.

Most of our staff hadn't gotten a raise in four years. For three straight years we'd made cutbacks that included cutting 15 part-time employees, slashing beloved ministries, suspending one of our church campuses, and hacking $160,000 from our annual budget.

To say the situation was grim is a gross understatement. As the economy in Florida floundered like a beached whale, many wonderful pastors simply had to close their church doors. I grieved for each of them. Aware that

I was no better pastor than they were, I wondered why our church was still viable and how long we would last.

Against that backdrop, I left the office one sunny afternoon and drove home with a burden for members of our congregation who were struggling to survive. I prayed for the wisdom to lead them through such turbulent times.

"Hi, Babe!" I said as my wife, Tonia, wrapped me in a welcoming hug. I stood there letting her presence ground me, as it always did, helping me transition from the office to home.

"Not a problem. I can get you an 11-year-old girl, but a 15-year-old might be better because she'd be more developed."

I had no sense that God was up to something—no pang of premonition—when I clicked on my computer and decided to watch *Nightline* later that evening. But the topic of the program did raise the hairs on the back of my neck: How to Buy a Child in 10 Hours.[1]

My heart sank. *Surely not.*

Buying a Child

I watched as, in an unsettling undercover operation, a reporter left New York City's Upper West Side for Kennedy Airport and caught a flight to Port-au-Prince, Haiti. By 4:45 p.m., the reporter, wearing a hidden camera, sat poolside at a nice hotel, meeting with a former member of parliament.

"If I would like to get a child to live with me and take care of me, could you do that?" the reporter asked.

"Yes, I've done it many times. A boy or a girl?"

"A girl."

"How old?"

"Maybe 10 or 11."

"Not a problem. I can get you an 11-year-old girl, but a 15-year-old might be better because she'd be more developed."

"I won't have any trouble from her parents?"

"No, and when I give you the child, I will train her for you."

"I'm a little nervous. I want to make sure I'm not going to get into trouble."

"I can guarantee my service. I can get your girl as early as tomorrow."

"How much will it cost?"

"The last one I gave was $300."

"I have a friend who got one for $50."

"No."

"What about $100?"

"$150."

"I accept."

Negotiating Another Deal

By 5:00 p.m., 10 hours after leaving his office that morning, the reporter had negotiated to buy a child for $150. He met with another human trafficker who asked $10,000 for an 11-year-old girl.

Why so much?

She was pretty and came with fake papers making it easier to get her into the U.S. There was another incentive offered. "It doesn't matter what happens to the kid."

"So for $10,000 I can have a child and do anything I want?"

"Definitely."

Feeling sick at my stomach, I learned that as horrifying as selling children into slavery is, it is customary in Haiti for parents to simply *give them away.* Very poor families give their children to slightly less desperate families who promise to feed and educate them. Instead, the children work as slaves.

According to *Nightline*, UNICEF estimates there are 300,000 child slaves living in Haiti. Called *restaveks,* a Creole term meaning "stay with," these children work long hours, are often uneducated, underfed, beaten, and sexually abused. The reporter interviewed a child slave only 8 years old, filming her scars and recording her story for the world to see and hear.

Sickened, I turned off the computer and stepped outside for fresh air. The breeze off the bay rustled the palm trees as I tried to make sense of the show I'd just watched.

Haiti was our neighbor, less than 750 miles away. It took less time to fly to Haiti from South Florida than it took to fly to Atlanta. But since Haiti was the last place on earth I wanted to visit, its proximity had never mattered to me.

Until now.

Puzzle pieces fell together in my mind as I thought about how long I'd struggled wondering how God wanted our church involved in mission work. Our congregation crossed cultural lines with people from 84 different nations as members. Many of them came from Haiti. Somehow I'd always known that when God set our course in missions, it wouldn't be the norm.

Could this be what He had in mind?

I rehearsed again the facts from the *Nightline* exposé.

The Haitian parents interviewed hadn't given their children into slavery because they didn't love them. They didn't do it because they were bad people. They were desperate.

Their problem was grueling, unrelenting poverty. Haiti was the poorest county in the Western Hemisphere. Parents who couldn't afford to feed their children were strung along by promises of a better life for them. Most would never sell or give away their children if they could meet their most basic needs. So the answer to the problem boiled down to one thing.

Money.

The one commodity our church didn't have.

Although nobody in my congregation had sold their children into slavery, many were unemployed and fighting to put food on their own tables.

There was nothing we could do.

I tossed and turned that night. A deep uneasiness disrupted my sleep.

I suspected that God didn't think my answer was good enough.

CHAPTER 2
Blind Eyes

The burden I felt about children being sold into slavery because their parents couldn't afford to feed them felt like a weight I couldn't shake. Like my shadow, it dogged me, more visible in the light of day. But even in sleep it never left.

The Lord must want me to pray.

I'd prayed over different nations and hot spots in the world, but I hadn't prayed for Haiti.

Why?

Probably for the same reason I'd never wanted to set foot on the island. I didn't know where to start. The problems in Haiti were overwhelming—both spiritually and in the natural: Witchcraft and voodoo were pervasive there. The economic and environmental devastation defied description. And conditions were made worse by the country's corrupt government.

The investigative reporter for *Nightline* had met with a government official to report the beating and abuse of the child slaves he'd interviewed.

"That's not acceptable," the woman responded on camera. With the camera off, nothing was done and his phone calls weren't returned.

You'd think that since Haiti was born out of a slave revolt. the situation would be different. Having thrown off the tyranny and oppression of slavery on a national scale, it seems the leadership would be fiercely protective of individual freedoms. Yet they turn a blind eye.

Many Haitians even justify child slavery by claiming it's a solution to the poverty problem. It's a lie, of course. Small children being sexually molested, sold, raped, beaten, starved, and forced to work from dawn to dusk isn't a solution, it's a crime.

Government officials, however, don't care. Acting as enemies of their own people, they have a long history of keeping humanitarian aide out of the hands of those it's sent to help.

Hopeless Situation

The situation appeared hopeless. The only thing that made sense to me was that God wanted me to pray. So I spent the next two years praying over the situation in Haiti.

Deep inside, I knew God wanted me to do more than pray. But I felt frustrated. There was nothing I could do. Didn't He get that?

Haitians needed *money.* God had to know that Florida was in the midst of economic implosion. Yet I kept sensing He wanted me to raise money for Haiti.

Flashing back, I remembered how I'd once raised money by riding a bike for 100 miles. *Get real,* I thought, *that was 10 years ago!*

I hadn't ridden more than a mile on a beach cruiser since I finished those 100 miles. Besides, I wasn't a great athlete. I'd played a little sports in high school and college but I'd ridden a desk and pulpit since then.

I was about to turn 55 and was babying a heart condition.

I was out of shape.

I had *no desire* to climb back aboard a bike and I *hated* the outfits that bikers wore.

Petrified that God would ask it of me, I reminded Him of all my responsibilities as a pastor, mentor, husband, father, and grandfather. Besides, there were so many impoverished kids in Haiti, and only one of me. Their problems were overwhelming.

One person couldn't make a difference.

Courage to Try

A chill rippled up my spine. Was that the same reasoning that allowed Germany and most of the world to look the other way during the Holocaust as the ashes of six million Jews, along with the people who were caught helping them, rose from the crematorium ovens?

Had Oskar Schindler wondered what difference one man could make in a world gone mad?

What about Sir Nicholas Winton? He saw war on the horizon and decided he had to do *something*. In 1939, just before World War II, he arranged for eight trains to depart from Czechoslovakia and travel to Britain. He filled the trains with 600 Jewish children. Although most of their parents died in the Holocaust, Sir Winton saved the children.

> ***The ashes of 6 million Jews, along with the people who were caught helping them, rose from the crematorium ovens as a testimony against them.***

What would I have done if I'd been alive and living in Europe then? I shuddered to think. It was easy to judge the people who tried to play it safe and protect their own lives and families.

How many things had I turned a blind eye to in my lifetime?

What if Corrie ten Boom and her family had looked the other way?

In God's eyes, was it any different to turn a blind eye to Hitler than to turn a blind eye to Haiti?

I thought not.

Reluctant Heroes

Oskar Schindler, Sir Nicholas Winton, and Corrie ten Boom refused to play it safe. They lived by the old saying, "Save a life, save the world."

I didn't know *what* I could do to change the situation in Haiti. I had no illusion that I could change the world. But maybe I could change the world for one child. Then perhaps for another.

Still, I felt like Moses whining to God that He'd picked the wrong man. There was a big difference between Oskar Schindler, Sir Nicholas Winton, Corrie ten Boom, and me. They used their own finances to help the Jews. God wanted me to help save some Haitian children from a fate worse than death, but He seemed to have forgotten one small detail.

I didn't have any money.

Seemingly unconcerned that we were in the worst recession in 30 years, He'd told me in no uncertain terms, *I want you to do something for Haiti.* And He wouldn't leave me alone about it.

Finally, I agreed. Gasping at the amount, I said, "I'll try to raise $10,000."

That's not enough.

"What?"

Raise $50,000.

I couldn't even comprehend that kind of money.

"I guess I can fail to raise $50,000 as easily as I can fail to raise $10,000," I said.

Clearly, faith had been a long, ongoing work of progress in my life. One I couldn't deny. I thought of my upcoming 55th birthday and decided to one up God.

"Okay, if I'm going to ask for $50,000 just before my 55th birthday, why don't I fail even bigger and go for $55,000?"

My sarcasm was met with what sounded like a satisfied silence.

What could I do to raise that much money?

I was on a flight from New York City to Florida when I had a conversation with myself.

I wonder how far it is from South Florida to New York City?

Looking it up on a map I discovered it was 1500 miles. Roughly the same distance as a round trip to Haiti.

That's it, then. I'll ride a bike to New York City.

Petrified at the prospect, I let myself have the last word.

You're an idiot.

CHAPTER 3
No Escape Hatch

I stepped into the sanctuary for the first of our four services the weekend of February 14, 2011, feeling my heart beat a staccato rhythm in my chest. Wiping sweaty palms on my pants, I admitted the truth.

I was scared speechless to stand before the congregation and say some version of, "Listen, I know many of you have lost your jobs, your homes, and your cars, but I'm going to ride a bike to New York City and I need you to give money so we can help the Haitians."

Really, Guy? You're going to do this?

I wondered what they'd think if they knew the whole situation had me talking to myself. Maybe if I told them, my secret wish would be fulfilled. Maybe someone would stand up and say, "Stop this insanity! Don't do it!"

I felt a lot like Abraham must have felt as he raised the knife to sacrifice his son. Except it was *my life* on the altar. Each time I took another step toward the ride, I hoped that God would send a huge angel to say, "Whoa! Stop! You're willing, so now you're off the hook!"

When I finally confided in Tonia what God had put on my heart, I was as nervous as I'd been when I proposed.

What would she say?

Casting the Vision

Although I wanted her blessing, I'll admit I might have felt a hint of relief if she'd put her foot down and told me to wake up and act my age. But she didn't. She didn't offer to join me either.

"God isn't calling me to ride from Miami to New York City," she said, making her position clear. "But I'll pray for you, help you, and support you 100 percent."

I love Tonia for so many reasons, and one of the biggest is her loyal support. In her quiet way, she has supported me in everything I've done over the years. She didn't always participate in my adventures. She didn't always agree with them. She didn't always remain quiet. But her love and support have never wavered.

My next step was to open my heart and share my burden for Haiti and my plans for the ride, with my sons. I respect those men, and honor them. So I asked them to pray and they did. Like Tonia, they gave me their blessing.

I always want my family's counsel regarding big decisions. But this one was even more important to share with them because of the risk involved. I could be injured, disabled, or killed in a heartbeat riding a bicycle alongside traffic for 1500 miles. They had the right to make an informed and prayerful decision about something that could affect our family forever.

I suspected that He'd called me to ride a bike to raise money because it was something I would never choose to do. It wasn't out of the ballpark of my comfort zone; it was out of the stratosphere.

Once Tonia and our sons were on board, I knew I had to talk to my mother. I dreaded the conversation. I assumed she would respond like I would if one of my children came up with a harebrained idea that would put them in mortal danger.

My assumption was correct. "Find a safer and more logical way to accomplish your mission," she said.

That was the rub. God was requiring this of me.

I suspected that He'd called me to ride a bike to raise money because it was something I would *never* choose to do. It wasn't out of the ballpark of my comfort zone; it was out of the stratosphere.

Next I took my plans to the men I mentor and our ministry leaders. Both groups prayed and gave me their support.

Except for my mother, all the key people in my life gave their approval. Still, some expressed reservations. This wasn't a good time to ask the church for money, they said. And with families in crisis, it wasn't a good time for me—the senior pastor—to be gone on sabbatical. The congregation needed me here.

Normally it would have been wise counsel. But God had spoken. The time to help Haiti was now.

Call to Action

I rolled up the church bulletin and twisted it until it was an outward manifestation of my churning emotions. I tried to remember the last time I felt this nervous. It was on the night before we started the church 20 years ago. We had a tiny trailer parked on Florida swampland. No electricity. No bathrooms. No parking.

My son, probably 12 at the time, said, "Dad, you know nobody will be here except our family."

That's what I figured too.

Like I said, faith is an ongoing journey for me.

The next morning, somewhere around 300 people showed up. God had brought a congregation of people.

Was I about to lose them?

Stepping to the podium, I took a deep breath and told the story of the previous few weeks. Starting with the night I'd watched *Nightline*, I left nothing out as I shared what I believed God was requiring of us.

"For the first few years of the recession we focused on the jobs and homes that we lost," I said. "We focused on budget cuts and all the things we've been forced to give up. Now, God is redirecting our attention to those who have so much less."

Supernatural Response

In closing, I shared 10 things that I asked them to pray about, beginning with a new bicycle. As I stepped off the platform after the service, I faced a stampede of people. Converging on me from every direction, they stuffed their grocery money into my pockets.

"This is to go toward your bike!"

"Here's some money for your equipment."

"This isn't much, but I want you to use it for your trip."

Emotion choked me and I could hardly speak.

In addition to providing the cash for my bike and equipment, that weekend the members of our congregation pledged to give more than $50,000 over the next year.

Unable to sleep that night, I stepped outside to walk off my restlessness.

Their response wasn't typical. Our motto was, "Life's a journey not a sprint." We're a steady-eddy kind of church.

Tears streaming down my face, I looked up at the stars twinkling in the night sky.

Without a doubt, God was in this.

Blinking away my tears, I felt a shiver of anxiety. Fear gripped my throat and tried to take me down. I'd made my plans public. I'd announced to the church that I was going to ride a bike from Miami to New York City.

Now I had to do it!

God help me!

CHAPTER 4
The Power of Preparation

I'm not big on planning and preparation. I'm more of a See-A-Goal-And-Tackle-It kind of guy. I enjoy skipping as many steps as possible if it will get me to the finish line faster.

This time was different. It wasn't a matter of pride. It wasn't just about success or failure.

This time it was about life and death.

The most dangerous thing I'd ever done, this adventure could result in serious injury or death if I didn't adequately prepare for it. I couldn't afford any shortcuts.

My age and overall lack of conditioning by themselves would have been enough of an issue. But they weren't my only concern. A year earlier I'd been diagnosed with coronary artery disease. Doctors had inserted a stint that was about to get tested by fire. So I scheduled an appointment with my cardiologists and set up a stress test.

Cleared for takeoff, I started training by riding around the neighborhood. Each week I increased my longest ride by five miles. The way I mapped it out, I would complete a long ride of 70 miles before I left for New York City on May 1.

The sound of screeching brakes and someone screaming caused me to swerve, almost hitting a grandmother as a red Toyota bounced the curb into my path.

Confession is good for the soul, so I'll admit the truth. The traffic scared me so much that for the first month I stuck to the sidewalks. They were bumpy, uneven and often crowded with pedestrians, but they gave me a sense of security. I thought for sure I'd be safe there.

I was wrong. The tourists in South Florida make even the sidewalks dangerous in winter when the snowbirds travel south.

The sound of screeching brakes and someone screaming caused me to swerve, almost hitting a grandmother as a red Toyota bounced the curb into my path. I lost count of the cars that almost hit me as I wove my way between pedestrians. A mind-numbing number, I felt shell-shocked by the time I parked the bike back home.

Shaking in the saddle, I finally forced myself into traffic.

Success Is in the Details

Preparing involved much more than pedaling. The details threatened to overwhelm me: planning my routes on old highways and back roads to keep me off the interstates; deciding where to park the camper each night; organizing a support vehicle and drivers; food, equipment, clothing…it never ended.

What's more, I still had sermons to prepare, worship services to plan, and meetings to conduct. I couldn't just stop my life and ministry while I trained.

I flew off my bike, my head bouncing off asphalt path three times before I skidded to a stop on my right side.

Each night I spent hours reading articles and blogs to learn what I needed to know about long distance rides. In the wee hours of the morning, I dropped into bed exhausted, knowing I had another full day awaiting me.

Wipe Out

The first week in March I rode to South Beach in Miami. The day was gusty with 30 mile per hour winds whipping inland off the ocean. As I pedaled along a bike path, a gust of wind hit a 6-year-old boy on a bike.

He panicked and turned into me, head-on.

I flew off my bike, my head bouncing off the asphalt path three times before I skidded to a stop on my right side.

While the boy scrambled back onto his bike, I lay sprawled on the ground gasping in pain. His mother stood over me yelling that I should watch where I was going.

She finally awoke to the fact that her son was fine but I was not. Apologizing, she tried to help me up. Unable to move, I gasped, "Just let me lay here."

The pain in my hip was so intense that I knew I'd broken it. Even as I wondered if my grand ride had ended on such a pathetic note, I thanked God that Tonia had insisted that I wear a helmet. Without it, I would have been dead or in ICU.

After awhile, I moved my leg without passing out. Eventually I pulled myself up, brushed off my bruised pride, and limped to my bike.

Clipped

The further I progressed in my training, the more I learned to appreciate the right equipment. Even the spandex shorts with the padded bottom were a blessing.

Russell, a pastor friend of mine, had badgered me about getting clips on my bike and shoes. "I know you don't need them here in Florida where it's flat," he said,. "but when you're riding up and down steep hills and bridges, they'll make a big difference."

Convinced he was right, I bought a pair. I watched videos—both hilarious and gruesome—showing what happens to bikers who forgot to unclip when they stop. Having heard all the horror stories, I was cautious but determined: It was my last week of training for a ride that would tax me beyond anything I'd ever known. If the clips helped me succeed, I would wear them.

> **Pain screamed through my body. It felt as though I'd torn something in my knee.**

Stopping to refill my water on the Hollywood Beach Broadwalk, I rolled onto the ramp. Without warning, my wheels slid out from under me. Unable to get my shoes unclipped from the pedals in time, I fell hard—my head hitting the side rail before I landed on my shoulder, my knee twisted under the bike.

Pain screamed through my body. It felt as though I'd torn something in my knee. Looking up at the blue, cloudless sky, I wondered for the millionth time what else would happen to me over the next 1500 miles.

Closing my eyes against the pain, I shot a two word prayer up to God. *Really, Lord?*

CHAPTER 5
Launch Day

What was I thinking? I thought as I smiled for our local news station NBC6. Hundreds of people milled around snapping pictures and signing my bike and helmet.

Every time I looked at a name on my bike, salty tears burned my eyes as I tried not to cry. Not only had I dealt with a thousand details getting ready for a 1500-mile bike ride, I'd also preached all three messages that Sunday morning. I hadn't pedaled my first mile but I felt as though I'd ridden an emotional roller coaster.

Still bruised and sore from my last fall, I said goodbye to my friends and family. Hugging Tonia, our son, Jim, and my mother goodbye, I swallowed hard against the lump in my throat.

Would I ever see them again?

I'd almost been run over by cars, been hit by a 6-year-old, and slipped with my clips—and my ride hadn't even officially started. Anything could happen on this trip. Unable to stem the tide, tears streamed down my face as I waved goodbye and pedaled out of the parking lot.

Thanks to the recommendation of Nathan, a missionary to Belize and long distance rider, I'd lined up several people to ride with me that day. "The first day was the hardest of the entire trip," Nathan had told me, remembering his own long ride. "I felt so alone I almost quit."

Five people—Johnny, Jose, Ben, Luke, and Stephanie—started the ride with me. Excited about the adventure, none of us expected the wind to shift. Emotionally exhausted and mentally spent, I lowered my head and pedaled against the worst wind I'd yet to experience.

Riding through my home neighborhood on U.S.1 in Hollywood, I paused as friends held up signs and dashed into the street for a quick hug. I needed all the hugs I could get.

As we entered West Palm Beach, another couple of friends appeared out of nowhere to wave and shout. Each surprise gave me a burst of energy.

The Fight for Faith

Eventually there were no more cameras. No confetti. No signs. No surprises. Just mile after grueling mile pedaling into the wind.

The butterflies had stopped fluttering in my stomach.

Reality had set in.

There would be no reprieve. No chance to climb down off the altar of sacrifice.

No matter what happened, I couldn't quit. If I did I would not only fail God and myself, but hundreds of people who'd by now pledged $100,000 to the children and families in Haiti.

$100,000!

I'd been stretching my faith past the point of no return when I told the Lord I would try to raise $10,000.

How could so many people who had so little pledge so much?

They had faith. Far more than I did.

I was already exhausted and I hadn't made it a single day. How was I going to handle long treacherous days back-to-back?

The afternoon sun climbed higher in the sky but the wind refused to give us a break. One by one, those who started the ride with me peeled away. Battered by an unrelenting wind, they turned around and let it push them toward home. Toward their families. Toward their beds.

Finish Well

I was already exhausted and I hadn't made it a single day. How was I going to handle long treacherous days back-to-back?

Don't go there.

I forced myself to focus on this day. This ride. This goal.

The road stretched ahead of me into an uncertain future. Who knew what I would find on the other side of the horizon?

For years I'd prayed that God would help me finish well. I'd seen so many people start life well with the wind of the Spirit at their backs. I'd watched many of them let the wind of adversity drive them off track.

Lord, help me finish well.

I tried to relax my grip on the handlebars. The youngest riders, Ben, Luke, and Stephanie had turned back. It was just us old guys now: Johnny, Jose, and me. Our goal was West Palm Beach.

The wind slapped and fought us every inch of the way. My muscles burned from the effort. My emotions felt raw, as though buffeted against the wind.

Think about something else.

I let my mind wander back to September 2010. My mentoring group had been reading a book entitled *Radical*. As we finished it, I felt inspired to set a goal: Spend a week in Haiti.

That same month I'd boarded a plane and flown over the sapphire water of the Caribbean. A local Haitian pastor met me at the airport in a beat-up old pickup. We'd driven only a mile when he pulled onto a terrible dirt road.

One Day at a Time

The road potted and bumpy, we bounced inside the pickup. Ahead of us I saw a dump truck overflowing with garbage. While dumpster diving in the U.S. might be profitable, garbage in Haiti was nothing but refuse.

Shocked, I watched two Haitian boys about 10 years old digging through the stench for something—*anything*—to eat.

Gritting my teeth, I pedaled harder. If I could make a difference in the lives of those boys, or others like them, it didn't matter how hard the wind blew or how treacherous the journey. I wouldn't quit.

> ***Shocked, I watched two Haitian boys about 10 years old, digging through the stench for something—anything—to eat.***

Minutes faded into hours as I pedaled.

Looking up I saw the sign: West Palm Beach.

Pressing on, we rode as far as we could go before hitting the inlet to Riviera Beach. We'd ridden 68 miles. After dinner I fell exhausted into bed.

Only 1,432 miles to go.

God help me.

Prayer before Launch with Mom, Son, Jim and Tonia

CHAPTER 6
A New Attitude

"I've never ridden more than 60 miles two days in a row," I confided to John Adams as we ate cereal and packed up the camper.

I had no idea how I would do today. I'd ended the first day numb with exhaustion. After a short night, John and I had hitched the camper to Tonia's parents second car, which they lent me to use as a support vehicle. Equipped with flashing lights for safety, the car would be manned each week by a different volunteer driving behind me at a snail's pace.

It must be like watching paint dry, I thought as I looked in my rearview mirror and watched John pull onto the road behind me. My muscles felt tight and painful as I started the day at Riviera Beach.

Can I survive another long day pedaling?

Then another?

And another?

I had no idea, and that was the jaw clincher.

Watching my odometer, I pedaled for a mile.

Two miles.

Three miles.

At four miles I experienced an epiphany. The pain was gone. My muscles had warmed up and relaxed. The butterflies were gone.

Tears ran in rivulets down my cheeks.

I think I can do this.

At four miles I experienced an epiphany. The pain was gone. My muscles had warmed up and relaxed. The butterflies were gone.

It had been two years since I'd watched the *Nightline* program which set this whole thing in motion. During that time, I'd prayed, wrestled with God, bargained, and finally submitted to His will.

Compounded Energy

In all that time, today, May 2, 2011, was the first time I felt as though it might be doable.

"Lord, we can do this!" I said, grateful to be alone with my emotions.

I'd adopted my life's verse as a skinny seventh grader, memorizing and quoting it. "I can do all things through Christ which strengtheneth me," (Philippians 4:13, KJV). As often as I'd said those words, I had never envisioned applying them in such a radical way. God had asked me to do what I couldn't have imagined…until now.

I might just make it!

With each passing mile, instead of feeling weaker, I felt stronger. I'd been told it would happen that way, but I'd never experienced it.

God said that everything reproduces after its kind.

With each passing mile, instead of feeling weaker, I felt stronger.

Without a doubt, energy reproduces energy.

I left Riviera Beach behind.

I passed Hobe Sound.

Fort Pierce.

To achieve my goal, I had to stay focused on the purpose behind the grueling hours on the bike: Haiti. Now my mind wandered to Haiti's long and treacherous history.

A Hard History

Located on the island of Hispaniola in the Caribbean Sea, Haiti occupies the western third of the island. The Dominican Republic occupies the eastern two-thirds.

The two nations had not enjoyed a peaceful coexistence. Twice Haiti has occupied the Dominican Republic. Once, people from the Dominican Republic massacred Haitians living near the border.

No larger than the size of Maryland, Haiti was ruled from 1957 to 1986 by the brutal dictatorship of Francois Duvalier (Papa Doc) and his son, Jean-Claude Duvalier (Baby Doc). In 1986 the Haitians revolted and overthrew the Duvaliers, tossing the country into a long struggle for control by various factions.

After the revolution, peasants who owned land divided it among their sons. As the population grew, plot sizes diminished. The people, untrained in protecting the environment, burned off topsoil, over-planted crops, and chopped down the forests for firewood. The deforested land allowed the topsoil to wash into the sea, leaving millions of Haitians malnourished and hungry.

Eventually, the little nation that had once been one of the richest colonies in the history of the world became one of the poorest countries in the Western Hemisphere—a place ripe for the slave trade that flourishes there today.

Earth Shattering

Soon after the Lord put Haiti on my heart, the country took another near fatal blow.

On Tuesday, January 12, 2010, the world watched in horror as an earthquake registering 7.0 on the Richter Scale toppled buildings and destroyed what was left of the country. At least 300,000 died. Unidentified bodies stacked in the heat were buried in makeshift graves dug by bulldozers and dump trucks.

Of the people who survived, a million were displaced. Hundreds of thousands of them left Port-au-Prince causing already poor and overpopulated villages to double overnight.

The world ran to Haiti, as it should have. Our church, along with thousands of others, sent aid and money. This was triage; necessary, but not our ultimate goal. It didn't begin to meet the real needs.

At least 300,000 died, and unidentified bodies stacked in the heat were buried in makeshift graves dug by bulldozers and dump trucks.

Even now, two years after the quake, very few Haitians have electricity, running water, or bathrooms. They live under tarps and in pup tents.

Picturing that sea of blue tarps fueled my efforts. I pedaled past Vero Beach and ended the day at Sebastian Inlet.

I'd ridden 84 miles—my longest ride.

Somehow, I was already a day ahead of my schedule.

Back in the camper I fell into bed with a smile on my face.

I think I can…I think I can…

CHAPTER 7
The Bridges of Brevard County

The vistas were stunning as I pedaled along the Banana River with the wind to my back. Waves lapped the shore and gulls flew in lazy circles overhead. The sun felt warm on my face, but chills raced up my spine.

Today I would face one of my greatest fears.

The bridges of Brevard County.

There's something about riding a bike over long expanses of water that bothers me. I don't like being hemmed in by the bridge on one side and speeding traffic on the other. It doesn't seem…*healthy.* Tourists, anxious to get shots of the water, often pay more attention to the view than to their driving. And older bridges offer no shoulder; no place to ride to escape reckless drivers.

I put on my game face for Eric Weachter who rode alongside me. I'd started the day at Sebastian Inlet. From there I'd ridden about 20 miles to Indian Harbour Beach where my son, Nathan, and his family lived. Eric, who'd attended our Oasis Hollywood campus back when we started it, had relocated here, and he and Nathan attended the same church.

One of my mentors for this journey, Eric was a beast on a bicycle. I glanced at him and then at the bridge ahead. Eric was an expert rider who knew what he was doing. I felt certain that he wasn't intimidated by the bridges.

Taking a deep, cleansing breath, I rode onto the Banana River Bridge. Head down, all business, I pedaled as though my life depended on it.

Instead of a comfortable office, my reality was the sun, wind, and the ache of muscles that I'd never known existed.

Back on land, I felt my grip loosen and my shoulders relax. There were so many firsts on this journey. Life as I'd known it had been stripped away. Instead of a comfortable office, my reality was the sun, wind, and the ache of muscles that I'd never known existed. Most days, without Eric beside me, my constant companions were…

Solitude.

Uncertainty.

Fear.

Fatigue.

Boredom.

Facing Fear

Resisting the downdraft from passing trucks that threatened to pull me off course, I pedaled onto the next in a long succession of bridges in Brevard County. I felt more courageous with Eric beside me. Like the tourists, I was drawn to the expanse of water that rolled in waves below. It reminded me of the clear aquamarine water of the Caribbean that sparkled in the sun the day I flew into Haiti…

From the air, the island had appeared mountainous and lush. But climbing out of the plane onto a broken airstrip, I stepped into a third world country. The main terminal of the airport had been destroyed in the earthquake and had not been rebuilt.

Grabbing my bag at the hangar in sauna-like heat, I saw hundreds of displaced people living plastered along the fence on each side of the runway.

Grabbing my bag at the hangar in sauna-like heat, I saw hundreds of displaced people living plastered along the fence on each side of the runway.

Half the population of Haiti is made up of children under the age of 15, and 500,000 of them are orphans clinging to life in the middle of a society that has collapsed.

In Port-au-Prince the scene was even worse. As we approached the city I saw acres of blue tarps—homes for a million people.

Half the population of Haiti is made up of children under the age of 15, and 500,000 of them are orphans clinging to life in the middle of a society that has collapsed. Less than half the adult population is literate, and the life expectancy—for those who, having survived the earthquake, don't starve or fall victim to crime—is 62 years of age.

In my mind, Florida's blue coastal waters morphed into an ocean of blue tarps.

I can do this!

For them, I faced the bridges of Brevard County.

For them, I conquered my fears.

I finished the day by riding 74 miles.

Back in Indian Harbour Beach, we met Tonia, Nathan, my daughter-in-law Jenni, and our grandsons, Gavyn and Caleb, for dinner. We ate at our favorite Thai restaurant on the beach. During the meal, my youngest grandson, Caleb, looked at me with his beautiful eyes and biggest smile. Again and again he wrapped his arms around me and hugged with all his strength.

"I love you, Poppy," he said.

That was the medicine my soul needed.

That night, I fell into a restless sleep, dreaming of bridges that stretched thousands of miles and linked me to an ocean of blue tarps.

The next day I headed toward Daytona Beach. Each day a different part of my body ached. I suffered chafing from the constant friction, a knee that throbbed, a shoulder that cramped. Even my feet hurt.

But not enough to stop.

A Storm Brewing

Pressing on, I worked out the sore spots and my muscles loosened and settled into the rhythm. It seemed impossible that I could ask this of my body, but each day after hours of pedaling, I felt stronger.

I saw a storm brewing in the northwest. Keeping an eye on it, I pedaled toward it even as it advanced toward me.

When we met, it felt like I'd ridden into a brick wall. The temperature dropped more than 10 degrees and a frigid north wind whipped me. Shivering, I pedaled past quaint cottages and multimillion-dollar homes in Ormond Beach, Flagler Beach, and along other beachside towns.

Covering 70 miles, I ended the day after dark at Anastasia State Park, grateful to be warm at last.

Dinner with Son Nathan and his family, Indian Harbour Beach

Eric Weachter, Indian Harbour Beach

CHAPTER 8
Eye of the Storm

I snapped on my helmet and shoved off to great morning weather. My shoulder ached but, thanks to Biofreeze—which had become my friend and companion—it was manageable, as was my skin that had baked to a dusty, reddish brown in spite of 100 percent sunblock.

It had been five days since I launched from Pembroke Pines. It seemed an eternity. A lifetime ago.

Looking behind me, I saw a puff of smoke huff from under the hood of the SAG (support and gear) wagon. John pulled off to the side of the road and stopped.

"What's wrong?"

"I think it overheated."

Wiping sweat off my face, I identified.

Daylight burned as we dealt with the car. Although it slowed our progress, the camper and support vehicle were the first line of defense for my safety. They freed us from the hassle of searching for a motel each night, and allowed us to have supplies on hand.

Waiting for the car to cool, I thought of the children in Haiti who wait each day hoping for food. As hard as this was, it was nothing compared to life in Haiti.

North of Port-au-Prince, heading toward St. Marc, are mounds where 300,000 people were buried in mass graves.

After the earthquake, bodies had lain decaying in the tropical heat. There had been no database for identifying them. Some members of my church have never seen or heard from their loved ones since the day of the earthquake.

They're presumed dead.

North of Port-au-Prince, heading toward St. Marc, are mounds where 300,000 people are buried in mass graves. When we pass them I wonder, *Are they there? The missing mother, father, aunt, uncle, niece, nephew, and grandparent?*

Rotting Containers of Food

When God first gave me a burden for the Haitians, most of the world had grown cynical about helping them. The reason was simple: Haiti's corrupt government prevents most of the aid donated from reaching the people it was sent to help. Food and water containers often rot or are sold on the black market.

He sent supplies to help 90,000 people during the cholera epidemic, but they were held hostage for an insane amount of money.

Fox News did a special report on the supplies that Franklin Graham sent to Haiti through Samaritan's Purse. He sent supplies to help 90,000 people during the cholera epidemic. But the supplies were held hostage by government authorities who demanded an insane amount of money for their release.

That's why our ministry teams buy their supplies in Haiti. We found we can buy anything there with enough money. People warned us in advance that we'd pay more for such purchases—and they were right. We once spent $600 on a pump in Haiti that we could have bought at Home Depot in Florida for $250. But if we'd bought it at home, by the time we shipped it to Haiti and paid the bribes to get it out of customs, the price would have been about the same.

What's more, purchasing the pump locally offered a major advantage: We knew it arrived at the intended destination because we delivered it ourselves.

Making a Difference

Kelly Byard knows what it's like to make such deliveries. A physician's assistant who belongs to our church, six years ago she was a single mother with a brain tumor. Today the tumor has been removed and she works for a dermatologist.

> *"I knew that God didn't help me overcome a brain tumor and become a physician's assistant just so I could laser off spider veins for the rest of my life."*

"When Pastor Guy cast the vision for Haiti," Kelly remembers, "I knew that God didn't help me overcome a brain tumor and become a physician's assistant just so I could laser off spider veins for the rest of my life.

"The trip to Haiti cost $350. I didn't have the money so I signed up to take part in a clinical study that paid $300. I was nervous about going to Haiti. I'm not black. I don't speak Creole, and I didn't figure spider veins were a big issue there.

"I went with a medical team from the church a few months after the earthquake. Driving past the squalor of tent cities, I saw children trying to bathe in a bucket of water. At that moment I knew that whatever we did would make a difference. In the middle of that devastation, I realized I was in the center of God's will for my life."

Back on the road after the SAG wagon started working, I knew that, like Kelly, God had pried me loose from the norm and set me on an adventure.

I felt as though I was in a whirlwind—the eye of the storm.

But I was also in the center of God's perfect plan.

CHAPTER 9
Living in the Downdraft

Incredible. I started day six on the Florida/Georgia state line. In my wildest imagination I never dreamed that in five days I would have ridden the length of the longest state on the East Coast.

My excitement about being ahead of schedule was tempered by a deep sense of dread. During my scout trip by car, I'd checked the routes I'd planned to ride. Today I started the part of the journey that I'd dreaded the most.

The two-lane highway had a posted speed limit of 55 miles per hour. Whizzing past me were logging trucks, 18-wheelers, pickups with rebel flags and gun racks in the back window. The downdraft as they passed made me feel like I was being sucked into the vortex of an invisible hole. Fighting against that whipping wind, I gripped the handlebars for dear life, struggling to stay out of harm's way.

> ***Whizzing past me were logging trucks, 18-wheelers, pickups with rebel flags and gun racks in the back window.***

John rode my bumper, keeping a prayerful watch over my progress. Just when I thought things couldn't get any worse, another of my fears materialized: With a great rumble, the clouds opened up and baptized me in a downpour.

I'd never been cold and sweating at the same time. Already soaked to the skin, each passing truck splattered me with mud. My goal to help the people of Haiti may have been lofty but, like most things in life, the effort to meet it was drudgery.

With a great rumble, the clouds opened up and baptized me in a downpour

A passing semi hosed me with a horizontal fountain of water and mud. The Bible says that those who are willing and obedient will eat the good of the land.

I was obedient to this plan.

At this particular time, however, I wasn't very willing.

Exposed to the Elements

Wiping the mud off my face with my sleeve, I remembered thousands of Haitians who'd lost everything they owned in the earthquake. They'd been so grateful for the pup tents that gave them a bit of shelter from the elements. But then the rains came, driven by horizontal winds that blew their tents away.

Countless Haitians lived year round like I was living now. Unprotected from the elements. Baked by day; chilled by night. Soaked to the skin; splattered with mud.

They didn't have soap and a shower at the rest stop. They didn't have the luxury of a good meal at a restaurant. They didn't have a camper and a bed.

Forgive me, Lord, for whining in my heart.

The tedious time ticked by. Tired. Cold. Sweating. Muddy. Trucks flying by.

I thought of Susanna Aponte and a group of our youth who had recently traveled to Haiti. Susan had been astounded by the positive attitudes of the children there.

"In one of the villages, we played jump rope and sang for hours with kids in the neighborhood," she said. "The courtyard was filled with rubble, but the kids didn't mind.

"It started drizzling and then it rained. We played in the rain until it fell in such torrents that we had to go inside.

"Katia gave us wipes to clean off the mud and we gave some to the children. I looked down and a 5-year-old girl was using her wipe to clean *my* feet! I glanced around and realized that all the Haitian children were using their wipes to clean our feet!"

I lifted my face to the rain and pedaled past Jekyll Island….then St. Simons.

God must have approved of my attitude adjustment because He had a surprise in store. One I couldn't have planned if my life depended on it.

The Gift

At noon we arrived at one of my favorite restaurants: The Georgia Pig. Inside I used a wet paper towel to wipe off the mud. Grateful that I could afford the calories, John and I enjoyed barbeque that had been featured in *Southern Living*. Willing and obedient, I ate the fat of the land.

By the time we finished lunch, the rain had stopped. It was still muddy and messy, but the weather had cleared.

When I stepped out of The Georgia Pig, I had no idea that I'd stepped into a miracle. Although there was no way to know it at the time, over the next 1110 miles, I would never ride in rain again.

It was spring and almost every day of my trek along the East Coast, weather forecasters predicted a 30 to 70 percent chance of thunderstorms. They weren't always wrong. Sometimes it rained—but it always stopped before I arrived, or started after I left.

All around me, tornadoes ripped through the Midwest and Deep South. The southern states suffered some of the worst tornadoes in history. But none came near me. Like the Red Sea, the weather parted leaving me a clear path to New York City.

What a God.

What a gift.

Alone Again

That afternoon, I pedaled through historic little fishing villages. Behind me, I could feel John's excitement as we neared the end of the day just 58 miles south of Savannah. His time with me was finished and he was eager to fly home to his family. After pedaling 62 miles, I drove him back to the airport in Jacksonville and dropped him off.

Driving away with an empty passenger seat beside me, I had to battle something worse than wind, rain, and mud.

Loneliness settled over me like a shroud.

I stopped at a huge Wal-Mart to pick up some supplies. Hundreds of people pushed baskets down the aisles but I didn't know anyone.

This was much harder than I expected. It was harder than pumping those bicycle pedals for hours on end. I missed Tonia. I missed my sons. My grandchildren. My mother. My Oasis family.

Home.

I drove back to the camper and tried to cheer myself up. In six days I'd pedaled 419 miles! Sure, I'd ridden through rain and mud, but I was ahead of schedule and there hadn't been a single accident. I'd gotten to eat at The Georgia Pig. God was smiling on me.

So why did I feel so alone?

Turning out the lights, I lay in the dark and stared at the ceiling. I'd given myself two months to complete my journey.

How could I do this for two more weeks, much less months?

Georgia/Florida State Line

CHAPTER 10
Teaming Together

A blinking yellow light flashed on the SAG wagon behind me and a banner read, *"Caution: Bike Ahead."* Jeremy Higdon, having replaced John, drove the car half on and half off the road to buffer me from the 18 wheelers that barreled past.

I felt myself baking in the blazing Georgia sun on U.S. 17. This—the seventh day of my journey—was also the end of my longest week. For the remainder of the trip I would take a Sabbath rest on Sunday.

One of my biggest concerns had been how my body would handle back-to-back days riding 50 miles or more. Guess I had my answer: aches and pains, but getting stronger with each passing mile.

The SAG wagon overheated again and we had to stop in the middle of nowhere and wait for it to cool down. I knew the stop would eat up precious moments of daylight and interfere with the number of miles I could ride, but there was no choice. I wasn't about to brave U.S. 17 without Jeremy at my back. The car finally cooled and we got underway as Jeremy nursed it along.

Excited to find something local instead of fast food, we stopped at what looked like a little shack and ate some of the best barbeque I'd ever tasted. The up side of riding 1500 miles was that I needed all the calories I could get. That perk alone was almost worth the trip.

In South Newport, Georgia, I stopped in surprise to see something I'd read about in books and magazines but never seen in person. Climbing off my bike with a huge grin, I pulled out my camera.

The smallest church in America!

It may be small, I thought as I snapped pictures, *but it's sturdier than the one we saw in Haiti made out of banana leaves.*

The little church reminded me of how inexpensive it is to build in Haiti. All it takes is a little money and a lot of teamwork. Two churches working together can easily put up a decent building. We'd done it. Oasis had bought the cement for one Haitian pastor whose congregation had teamed up to stack rock.

I loved playing with a team in football and basketball although my coaches tried to get me to run track. They told me I had the body type for it, which meant that I was a skinny little kid who ran fast. I tried it for a few years but I hated it. I needed my team; it was too solitary.

Working with a team is an amazing experience. I've always relished it. Although I admire people whose talents and gifts can carry them to victory alone—like my sons who enjoys surfing—such solitary sports are not for me.

Even as a youngster I didn't excel in them. My coaches tried to get me to run track. They told me I had the body type for it, which meant that I was a skinny little kid who ran fast. I tried it for a few years but I hated it.

I loved playing football and basketball.

I needed my team.

When I decided to obey God and make my 1500 mile bike journey for Haiti, I would have done it alone. I would have done it without the camper or the SAG wagon. But, thank God I didn't have to, because I don't know if I would have made it without my team.

Looking behind me, I waved at Jeremy, grateful that he had my back.

I shot up a prayer of gratitude for everyone who had my back either physically, like those driving the support vehicles, or spiritually, like those who lifted my name before God each day in prayer.

Clash of Cultures

Riding the historic streets of Savannah, I pulled to a stop in front of the Haitian Revolutionary War Monument. Until a friend on Facebook had alerted me to it, I'd had no idea that Haitians fought alongside our soldiers in the Revolutionary War.

Looking at the monument of Haitians and Americans working together, reminded me of a woman in our church named Rose Toussaint. One of the first people I talked to about the call to help Haitians, she was born and raised in Haiti. She moved to the U.S. when she was 16 and went on to earn a degree in social work, taking her unique understanding of her native culture into her profession and into our church.

Rose's perspective had helped me better understand the myriad of difficulties the Haitians face. She'd also confirmed what I'd learned on *Nightline*.

"There are so many people living below the poverty line in Haiti, they simply can't afford to take care of their children," she said. "They give them to other people who promise to feed them. The children live as indentured servants, being physically and sexually abused.

"The dynamic that works in their culture doesn't work in ours. For example, when Haitian children get into our social services system because of abuse, the parents do what is expected of them in Haiti. They pretend that nothing happened. Only that doesn't work here and they often end up losing their children."

"Slavery, along with physical and sexual abuse of women and children, is rampant in Haiti, but nobody ever talks about it. It isn't that the parents don't care, they do. But most of them were abused themselves, and just learned to deal with it.

"Nothing changes because in Haiti even the police and those in governmental office are abusers. The people's mistrust of authority is so ingrained in them that it goes with them wherever they live."

The dynamic that works in their culture doesn't work in ours. For example, when Haitian children get into our social services system because of abuse, the parents do what is expected of them in Haiti. They pretend that nothing happened. Only that doesn't work here and they often end up losing their children.

"There are so few people who understand the culture and know how to help that a friend of mine started an organization called Word in Action. Part of what we do is train people to understand the culture and how to help the families."

Climbing back on my bike, I took one last look at the monument before riding away. As the miles clicked by, I thought about all the things Rose had told me.

I ended the day with 50 miles behind me. The ride had been shortened by the overheated vehicle. But, even so, with 469 under my belt, I was 111 miles ahead of my goal.

Just before I fell into an exhausted sleep, I pictured the Haitian War Monument.

They'd been there to help us.

Now it was our turn to help.

Haitian War Memorial, Savannah, GA

Brunswick, GA

CHAPTER 11
The Road More Traveled

Sweat ran down my forehead and into my eyes, stinging and blurring my vision. Afraid to loosen my grip on the bike for even a second, I tried to rub my face on the sleeve of my shirt as an 18-wheeler sped past.

The muscles in my legs burned as I pedaled in the blistering sun. In addition to the heat, the humidity steamed me like a lobster over a pot of boiling water.

Until now, launch day riding against the wind had been the hardest. This stretch of U.S. 17 in South Carolina, however, had trumped it. Another semi flew by almost blowing me off the bike. I hadn't experienced much southern hospitality among drivers today.

We'd started the day waiting for the mechanic to replace the radiator fan motor in the SAG wagon. The coolest part of the day had long since given way to intense heat by the time I'd started riding at 2:45 in the afternoon. This was our latest start and the hottest weather coupled with the toughest 15 miles of the entire trip so far.

The worst roads. The worst traffic.

This highway seemed to go forever.

I tried swatting the thought away but, like the stubborn heat, it refused to go away.

I'll be on U.S. 17 for almost a third of my journey.
Lord, help me.

Looking back, I saw dozens of trucks speeding toward me. Looking ahead, the road stretched like a ribbon into a seeming eternity of miles.

A Cool Drink of Water

Desperate for a drink of water to cool my parched throat, at the first opportunity I pulled off the road for a quick break. Guzzling the water like a dying man, I drank and then drizzled some over my head. The icy drops ran down my face and neck leaving a trail in the dust, sending a quick chill through my body that lasted for only seconds.

Taking another deep drink, I closed my eyes in appreciation.

Water.

Necessary for life, it's something most of us take for granted here in America. It's free. It's available almost anywhere. Many of us, choosing bottled water, even look down our noses at the tap.

But clean water is a luxury many people in third-world countries don't enjoy.

Richard Stern's book, *The Hole in Our Gospel* drove that fact home for my youngest son, Corey. A professional photographer, husband, and father trying to support his family, Corey has a lot on his plate. But after reading Stern's book, he decided to add to it the mission of bringing clean water to people who didn't have it.

After researching the situation, he found a company in Oklahoma who sold the necessary equipment. So he went there and learned how to use it. Then, after raising the money, he traveled to Kenya and trained people there how to drill for water manually.

While in Africa, Corey saw hundreds of wells that couldn't be used because no one had bothered to teach the people how to repair and maintain them. Even worse, he found that people died from drinking contaminated water from such wells.

> **"They don't need wells dug as much as they need people to fix the existing ones,"** Corey said pointing out broken pumps everywhere.

Repairing the Wells

To be honest, watching Corey convicted me when I was dragging my heels about helping Haitians. In the deepest recesses of my heart I heard God whisper, *Your son has ADHD and no money. His heart is so big that there's no excuse for your letting the recession stop you from doing anything.*

That's one of the reasons I took Corey with me on my second trip to Haiti. Together we toured through the heartbreaking desolation there, checking the water sources. Corey pointed out broken pumps everywhere. "They don't need wells dug as much as they need people to fix the existing ones," he said.

Drilling water wells around the world in places where clean water doesn't exist is a wonderful ministry. But neglecting to teach the people the skills needed to maintain them has been a serious oversight.

> **In Haiti if you're fortunate enough to be admitted to the hospital, you're only given the medication you can afford to buy.**

We saw just how serious the consequences can be when one of the churches we'd helped in Haiti had an outbreak of cholera. Parents and children alike wasted away and died because they couldn't afford a $2 trip to the hospital by motorcycle. Many who did make it to the hospital died because, once there, they were denied the necessary medication.

Needless Death

An infection of the small intestine caused by bacteria, cholera occurs in places with contaminated wells, poor sanitation, crowding, famine, and war. Those infected with the disease suffer severe abdominal cramping, dry mouth, and excessive thirst. With rapid dehydration from diarrhea, their sunken eyes grow glassy as they become weak and nauseous.

As the dehydration worsens, a sick child can't even cry due to the lack of tears.

The World Health Organization developed an inexpensive solution of sugar and electrolytes to rehydrate those infected with cholera. Yet because in Haiti hospital patients are given only the medications they can pay for, people still die in masses because they don't have the $8 to $10 needed to buy the solution.

Shuddering, I remembered that during the cholera epidemic that followed the earthquake, the supplies needed to treat 90,000 cases of cholera had been held for ransom by the government. How could anyone be that heartless?

On the Road Again

Finishing my water and rested from the brief break, I climbed back on my bike and onto U.S. 17. The wind had picked up and I felt whipped by the wind-driven dirt and sand. Even my eyes felt gritty.

Willing myself to pump the pedals for mile after bleary mile, I calculated that for every 60 miles I rode we could raise enough money to dig a well for a village in need of clean water. Despite my late start, the heat, and my fatigue, I made a personal goal. I wouldn't stop until I'd ridden 60 miles.

Already exhausted, I looked down at the words my son, Nathan, had written on my bike: *Every pedal stroke provides a meal.* That reminder gave me the spurt of energy I needed to press on.

Another meal.

Another meal.

Another meal.

Another meal.

The first nine days had been a lesson in letting go. I had to let go of my creature comforts. I had to let go of my wife and family. I had to let go of my congregation. I had to let go of my plans and my agenda. Looking down at my hands on the bike, I saw that my grip was so tight my knuckles were white.

I forced myself to relax my hands. One by one, I lifted each finger, wiggling it in the hot breeze of passing trucks.

That's what I've done with my life.

Free to Be

I'd held onto control of my life until God had pried my fingers loose. Pondering that, I had a revelation.

It felt good!

Why do we wrestle so hard for control when trusting God is such an adventure? I figured it must be fear. Fear of the unknown. Fear of failure. Fear of not measuring up.

I'd been most afraid that I might die.

Instead, for nine days, God's grace had made me strong in my weakness.

The odometer on my bike rolled over to 60 miles for the day. It was 7:00 p.m. as I took a deep sigh of relief and pulled to a stop.

After eating dinner, we reached the campground around 10:00. I showered, posted my blog for the day, and finally crawled into bed after midnight.

I'd ridden a total of 500 miles. One third of the 1500 miles were behind me.

But that wasn't what put a smile on my face as I closed my eyes to sleep. In spite of a long, hard day with bad roads, rude drivers, blistering sun and wind, I'd ridden 60 miles. I'd raised enough money to drill a well in a village without clean water.

Life doesn't get much better than that.

South Carolina State Line, Hardeeville, SC

CHAPTER 12
The Bisiklet Boys

This is going to be a stressful day.

That had been my first thought when I opened my eyes on the morning of day 10. I hadn't thought I would face the challenges before me until much further into the trip. But I was so far ahead of schedule that one of the rides I dreaded most was already here.

Back on the dreaded U.S. 17, I climbed on the bike about 40 miles south of Charleston, South Carolina. The first 7 to 10 miles were under construction, creating extra traffic concerns and stress. The next 30 miles would take me right through the heart of downtown Charleston where I'd face even more traffic. If that weren't bad enough, my route also included one of the tallest, if not the tallest, bridge on the East Coast.

The very thought of it chilled me.

Pedaling up the bridge wasn't my concern. The problem was the insane drop going down the other side. What if I picked up so much speed that I lost control of the bike and spilled right into traffic?

"I might have to skip the bridge," I said to Jeremy over breakfast. "If it doesn't look safe, I'll have you drive me over it and make up the miles later."

Riding through construction, I thought of the guys I'd starting calling the *Bisiklet* Boys. (*Bisiklet* is the Creole word for bicycle.) A new friend on Facebook had introduced me to them via cyberspace. Three young doctors riding from San Diego to Charleston, they too were on a mission to raise money for Haiti.

Still in their 20s, they'd decided to do something radical with their lives while in college—so they'd started a medical clinic in Haiti. Two of them, Kyle and Jeff, had finished their internship in the U.S. and traveled back and forth to work in the clinic. The third, Clayton, lived in Haiti and served as the primary physician at the Cloud Forest Medical Clinic.

In addition to starting the clinic, the trio was funding it as well. So the purpose of their ride was to raise $30,000 to hire a Haitian doctor for the clinic. What an incredible group of guys.

"They're finishing their ride in Charleston and it looks like you'll be there around the same time," my Facebook friend had written the night before. "Why don't you meet up with them?"

Divine Encounter

"It's not going to work," I wrote back.

I told him about the car overheating, the changes in our schedule, and the challenges of the day ahead. I didn't tell him I was stressed to the max and couldn't put one more thing on my plate.

"I'm just trying to survive one day at a time," I'd said. "I can't really focus on anything else." The day had enough stresses built into the route; I didn't need to add another one.

***"This is a godsend for us!"** one of the men said pulling up next to me. "We lost our support car and were scared about riding in this traffic without it."*

After less than an hour riding, I was finally leaving the construction zone, but not looking forward to the traffic going into Charleston. Just as the construction ended, U.S. 17 merged with South Carolina 64. The converging streams of trucks and cars made me nervous and I looked back to make sure Jeremy was behind me with the lights flashing.

As I merged into traffic, I heard someone shout, "Hey, it's that Bike for Haiti guy!" Looking to the west, I saw five bikers headed my way. I recognized their jerseys from Facebook photos. It was the Bisiklet Boys!

Like the speeding cars, we merged together, never missing a beat or stopping our bikes, at the exact spot 30 miles south of Charleston where the two highways met. One of the guy's father and another friend had joined them for the last leg of their journey, making five bikers who joined me.

"This is a godsend for us!" one of the men said pulling up next to me. "We lost our support car and were scared about riding in this traffic without it."

New Friends

I watched them take a collective sigh of relief as Jeremy pulled up behind all six of us with lights flashing.

It was so fun to have someone to talk to that I felt like I was riding on air. One of the guys pulled alongside me and we swapped stories for about half an hour. Then he fell back and another one pedaled alongside me and we visited. In that type of rotation, I got to know them all.

If the ride wasn't exciting enough, one of the doctors was getting married the following week. This was their last day of a 3100-mile ride that had taken them from California to South Carolina.

> **It was about three o'clock in the afternoon and in all the excitement I'd forgotten to stop for lunch.**

Having only been introduced on Facebook, we all felt an instant bond when we met. To a man, we had all dreaded this leg of the trip and the traffic into Charleston. The miles melted away as we laughed and talked nonstop. We pedaled through the beautiful and historic streets of downtown Charleston enjoying both the scenery and our stories.

Arriving at City Hall, I stood to the side while they met the vice mayor and were interviewed by the media. After the ceremony ended, they told me they had one more thing on their agenda: Before they left California, they'd dipped their tires in the Pacific Ocean; now they wanted to do the same in the Atlantic.

I felt honored when they asked me to ride with them to Sullivan's Island to witness the event.

Peer Pressure

It was about three o'clock in the afternoon and in all the excitement I'd forgotten to stop for lunch. I'd ridden 40 miles with no food since early morning. In addition, it was hot and the wind was against us.

The Bisiklet Boys' journey was over and they were soaring with excitement. I, on the other hand, felt every minute of my age.

Still, it sounded fun so I swallowed my last gel energy pack and headed for Sullivan's Island with them.

Then we reached the bridge.

> *"Look, their journey is over but you have another thousand miles to ride! Safety should be your first concern!"*

I took one look at the height and told them I was riding across it in the car and would meet them on the other side. They, however, wouldn't hear of my missing the bridge.

Neither would they take no for an answer.

I don't normally fall under peer pressure, but I felt like a wimp in front of them. I was scared out of my mind when I agreed to ride across that bridge. Jeremy looked at me as though I'd lost my mind. Pulling me aside he said, "Look, their journey is over but you have another *thousand miles* to ride! Safety should be your first concern!"

He was right of course. Everything in me wanted to duck inside the SAG wagon and snack on something while we rode over the bridge. But the friendship, camaraderie, and excitement were too much to resist.

Scared stiff, I climbed on my bike and started up the incline that seemed to go vertical into the clouds.

Facing Fear

Although my heart was doing the cha-cha in my chest, I gasped at the view of the bay and the Atlantic Ocean. It was one of the most stunning sights of the entire trip. Pumping up the incline was a cinch and it helped that the bridge was new and offered one of the best bike paths I'd seen.

We stopped at what felt like the top of the world and posed for pictures.

It was an incredible moment—a God Sighting.

After enjoying the view, we started down.

Everything was more fun with friends. And, as I flew down that bridge, I realized I was enjoying myself! I reached the bottom exhilarated and in one piece.

Reaching Sullivan's Island, I watched the Bisiklet Boys dip their tires in the Atlantic and celebrate with family and friends. Afterward my stomach reminded me that it was dinnertime and I hadn't eaten since breakfast. Saying goodbye, I stopped at the first restaurant I found.

If I had spent months planning, I could never have pulled off the Bisiklet Boys and me merging into traffic at the same time at the same place.

After dinner, I rode another 14 miles. Still psyched from the day I remembered how apprehensive I'd been that morning. What a waste it had been to worry! Nothing about the entire day had been stressful except my own fear. God had taken all my apprehensions and blown them away like dust in the wind. I'd had the time of my life!

If I had spent months planning, I could never have pulled off this meeting with the Bisiklet Boys. I was more than 150 miles ahead of schedule on my trip, but behind schedule two hours that day. Yet at the exact same time and place, we'd merged in traffic as though it had been orchestrated by a divine hand, and ridden 50 wonderful miles together.

What were the odds?

Higher than being hit by lightning in a summer thunderstorm in Florida!

Higher than winning the $100 million Powerball lottery!

Only God could have done this!

Although I've experienced God's presence in many ways, He's never been more real to me, or more tangibly present, than He was that day.

Words failed me as I talked to Tonia on the phone, and reported the day's events on my blog.

What could I say?

Riding with the Bisiklet Boys had been a gift from God. It had been His way of thanking me for my obedience to the journey. It had also been a reminder to let go and let Him give me moments of breathless joy.

Oh, what a God!

Bisiklet Boys, Charleston, SC

CHAPTER 13
What a Difference a Day Makes

The trouble with mountaintop experiences is that when you climb down from them you find yourself in a valley. My divine encounter with the Bisiklet Boys, riding together the last 50 miles of their journey, participating in their celebration, and pedaling to the top of that bridge had definitely been a mountaintop experience.

The next day felt as though I'd ridden into a valley of dry bones. By far the hardest part was being alone again. Sure, I knew Jeremy was right behind me, but for mile after lonely mile I pedaled with no one to talk to.

Yesterday we rode with a tail wind.

Today I rode alone against a headwind.

Yesterday, the day I dreaded for so long turned into a party. Now alone, fighting against blustering headwinds, riding on blacktop roads through pine forests, with logging trucks for company, I felt lonely and bored. It wasn't the same.

An old song played a loop in my mind. *"One is the loneliest number..."*

> ***Now alone, fighting against blustering headwinds, I felt lonely and bored.***

Day 11 will also go down in the books with another record. It seemed as though every time I looked up I saw another bridge. Good thing I'd conquered my fear on the tallest bridge yesterday. Today I would cross more bridges than on any day since leaving home.

Although anxiety wouldn't be a factor, monotony would. It drove me to distraction as the dreary miles slid past, repeating the same theme.

Blacktop roads.

Logging trucks.

And bridges.

Blacktop roads.

Logging trucks.

And bridges.

Blacktop roads.

Logging trucks.

And bridges.

A Bit of Dignity

I tried to imagine how monotonous life must be in Haiti. How did the people deal with day after day of details and desperation? I thought about a young man on the Oasis Church staff, Joel Collins. Like all of us, Joel felt overwhelmed by the devastation in Haiti after the earthquake.

"We went to St. Marc one afternoon," he said. "Walking through the presidential garden, I could imagine how beautiful it must have been. Now a tent city stretched as far as the eye could see.

"Shacks stood back-to-back around the big square. Visually striking because of the diversity, it was like seeing a collage of colors from every texture.

"It was inexplicable that human beings could survive in such devastation. Then I saw something I will never forget. A mother sat in the dirt next to the stench from a porta-potty and a dumpster. A little girl sat on her lap as the woman focused on fixing the child's hair.

"I felt overwhelmed at the resiliency of people trying to scratch out a life in such conditions. It spoke volumes to me of the human condition. It seemed as though the woman was saying, 'Look, I lost my home. I lost members of my family. But we're the lucky ones. We survived. My child may not have a home. She may not have a bed. She may not have a table laden with food. We may live in filth. But I can fix her hair. I can give her that dignity.'"

A mother sat in the dirt next to the stench from a porta-potty and a dumpster. A little girl sat on her lap as the woman focused on fixing the child's hair.

Terminal Boredom

In every life there's a mundane monotony that, if we let it, can rob us of the miraculous. For me that day it was pressing through, head down, pedaling the next mile and the next and the next.

For others it might be something totally different. Get the kids off to school. Do the laundry. Fix dinner. Put in another mindless eight hours at work. Write one more paper. Make another sale.

Watch TV.

Sleep.

Start all over again.

All of us, as we deal with the day-to-day-ness of life, can lose touch with its significance; with the dignity of doing the smallest things, like fixing a child's hair.

Day 11 of my journey reminded me of this. It came to represent what may be the greatest problem facing Christians today: *boredom.*

We've watered down the gospel to make it a thing of convenience instead of the most explosive world-changing event in the history of the world. Instead of taking God at His word, we've opted for comfortable lives—which translates into boredom, not only for us but for Him.

Can you imagine how dull it must be at times for God – the One who hung this sun, the moon, and the stars in place – to dwell in us?

It's one thing to think of how Jesus left His throne and came to earth as a man; it's another to imagine Him going from a life of walking on water, raising the dead, messing up funerals, multiplying a child's sack lunch, and turning water into wine...to living the life of a couch potato Christian.

Now *that's* boring.

God's Divine Design

No wonder God is trying to break us out of the box we've created for ourselves! No wonder He wants to bring down the walls of doubt, unbelief, fear, and apathy we've built to make ourselves comfortable. Those walls have become a prison. They've kept us from living radical, adventurous lives in Christ. They've made us look like a carbon copy of the world, except that we are headed to heaven.

That, however, is not our spiritual DNA. We're made in God's image. We're made for excitement, for adventure.

You are created by God to do amazing things.

If what you're doing with your life is possible in your own strength, you haven't tapped into His divine design.

God may never call you to ride a bike from Miami to New York City. He may never give you a lifelong mandate to help Haitians. But I can guarantee you He has a seemingly impossible mission for you if you choose to accept it.

He will show you a grand view of the world, perhaps not from the highest bridge on the East Coast, but from someplace uniquely designed to inspire you.

The thought of that mission might tempt you to chew your fingernails down to the nub. But, once you discover it, if you'll press forward, you'll find yourself on the adventure of a lifetime.

Some days God will show up for that adventure in such a powerful way that it takes your breath. He'll show you a grand view of the world, perhaps not from the highest bridge on the East Coast, but from someplace uniquely designed to inspire you.

There will be days like this one too: days of loneliness and boredom.

In the midst of the mundane days, you might remember the dignity of a woman in Haiti determined to help her child be the best that she could be. Then, like me, you'll realize that you are fulfilling your destiny. That you've kicked out the walls of the box that confined you.

You'll look up at the blacktop road and logging trucks and laugh with the joy of being alive.

CHAPTER 14
Cool Winds and Hot Coffee

"Pawleys Island!"

That was my first thought this morning. While there were routes I had dreaded, like the one through Charleston, I'd been looking forward to Pawleys Island, South Carolina. Located 70 miles north of Charleston and 25 miles south of Myrtle Beach, it's one of the oldest summer resorts on the East Coast. Famous for its locally made rope hammocks, the island promised a delightful stretch of wide beach and sand dunes.

The morning sky sparkled sapphire blue as the sun glinted on the water. The ride through Pawleys Island and up the coast was as wonderful as I'd imagined. But the real jewel of the day, one of my favorite spots on earth, was Myrtle Beach. A man-made island separated by intercostals waterways, Myrtle Beach boasts 60 miles of sandy beaches known as the Grand Strand. It is stunning.

Inhaling the salty sea air, I enjoyed the sights and sounds around me…until I was almost run over by a clueless driver. Shaken, I watched the traffic and tried to keep my distance, experiencing one near miss after another. Instead of a relaxing and enjoyable ride, I felt as though I was fighting for my life.

Note to self: Until you put on spandex shorts and ride a bicycle in this traffic, you haven't begun to understand the word *vulnerable*.

Although I never lose my temper and yell, I screamed at a woman who would have sideswiped me if I hadn't dodged her in the nick of time. She stared at me as if to say, *"Why are you here?"*

Instead of a relaxing and enjoyable ride, I felt as though I was fighting for my life.

Looking back, I was grateful that Jeremy had gotten lost in traffic and missed my meltdown.

As I clenched the handlebars with white knuckles and teeth grinding, I realized that all the stress I'd expected in Charleston and riding up the tallest bridge had hit me today, on what I imagined would be my favorite part of the journey. I heaved a deep sigh of relief when I left Myrtle Beach behind and crossed over into North Carolina.

Sea Breezes

The wind was forecast to be at my back, but it shifted from the North and I ended up pedaling against it. On the upside, I rode under a cloud cover that cooled me until I almost felt chilled. I stopped for a steaming cup of Dunkin' Donuts coffee, shivering with delight.

In North Carolina, there were no more north-south roads like we had in Florida. The roads meandered around, winding in every direction. I constantly rode in and out of the wind as I passed through beautiful little ocean towns like Calabash, Ocean Isle Beach and Shallotte. Although the route wasn't especially efficient, Jeremy and I enjoyed the scenery, the great seafood, and the southern hospitality.

Passing children playing on the beach, I remembered seeing children in Haiti standing in a dirt yard in front of a mud house, stark naked because they had no clothes.

Pedaling along the wandering roads, I did what I did every day. I prayed for the children of Haiti. Keeping their beautiful little faces in my mind, I pictured the 5 and 6-year-old children who walked a mile carrying 5-gallon jugs. Lined up at an old hand pump, they waited their turn to get water for their families.

As I rode past children playing on the beach, I remembered seeing children in Haiti standing in a dirt yard in front of a mud house, stark naked because they had no clothes.

I prayed for them every day.

Keeping Priorities Straight

Even now, over two years after the earthquake, there are a half million Haitian people still living in tents and under tarps. Jessenia Vargas, one of our young adults at Oasis, spent time ministering among them. She came back with heart wrenching stories about how desperate the conditions are—especially for the littlest ones.

"We were able to collect clothes and coloring books to take to the kids," she said. "For a few hours we met with a group of orphans and visited their classroom. It consisted of a tarp strung over four sticks where one lone woman attempted to care for them.

"The kids, aged 2 to 12, didn't have anywhere to sleep. No beds. No blankets. No pillows. Knowing their situation, we raised enough money to give each of them a sleeping bag. They were so excited...but when we returned to Haiti on our next trip, none of the sleeping bags had been opened. We asked why and they said they didn't want to mess them up."

After praying for the children, I prayed the second part of my daily prayer. I asked God to help me remember that this ride was about the people of Haiti.

It wasn't about Guy Melton.

I could easily lose sight of that. After all, I'd had more attention from the media and from people around the world who followed my progress on Facebook and Bike For Haiti than I've experienced in my entire life. What's more, I was up to my eyeballs in the details of the journey—the physical challenge, the image, and even raising the money.

But while I was the face of the mission and it was my 55-year-old body climbing on the bike each morning and pedaling toward New York City, I didn't want to lose my purpose and zeal for the real reason I was here. I wasn't risking my life for a photo op or to build a name for myself.

My single, driving goal was to keep the children of Haiti from being forgotten. Even riding a bike for 1500 miles was leagues easier than the life those children were forced to endure.

The Grace of Joy

I remembered watching a group of Haitian kids playing ball with a tin can, shouting with laughter. Many of them hopped on one leg – the other having been amputated after the earthquake. Using sticks as makeshift crutches, they made the most of their situation. Joy bubbled up in them as they played.

Lord, forgive me for murmuring, even in my heart.

I finished the day in Shallotte, North Carolina, just 33 miles shy of Wilmington. Today I pedaled another 73 miles, putting my total at 726.

After relocating the camper, Jeremy and I looked at one another and grinned. We were in total agreement about where we wanted to eat dinner. We climbed into the car and drove all the way back to Calabash for seafood.

I ordered a big plate of fried shrimp. My doctor back home had put me on a low cholesterol diet, one that didn't include fried shrimp. But riding a bike 60 and 70 miles a day, I burned so many calories that I could afford to indulge.

I could hardly wait to get home again. I longed for quiet evenings with my family.

But I will forever miss Calabash fried shrimp.

North Carolina State line, Calabash, NC

CHAPTER 15
Friday the 13th

Friday the 13th began with a leak in the toilet just after midnight, but hey, I'm not superstitious.

The evening before, Jeremy and I had scouted our route into Wilmington and decided that U.S. 17 was just too dangerous. We opted instead for a short ferry ride and an alternate route which took us through some beautiful little ocean towns.

Enjoying the ride, I pedaled toward the sleepy little town of Carolina Beach. As I rode past the welcome sign, I look down at my odometer. At that moment, it clicked to 750 miles.

750 miles! It's a good thing I wasn't superstitious because that was one of the magic numbers I had dreamed about since beginning the journey. Gripped by emotion, I felt tears sting my eyes.

Just then, my cell phone rang. *Tonia!* Hearing Tonia's voice, I lost it. I motioned for Jeremy to stop and wondered what the locals thought about a guy in spandex sobbing by the welcome sign.

After my conversation with Tonia, Jeremy and I pulled out the Cheerwine, a nonalcoholic beverage sold in North Carolina. We'd put it on ice for this momentous occasion.

I'd made it halfway.

It's all downhill from here, I thought.

Not literally. Most of the hills and bridges were still ahead. But mentally, this was such a milestone that it made the rest of the trip feel as though it would be downhill. If I could ride 750 miles, surely God would help me finish well.

Most of the hills and bridges were still ahead. But mentally, this was such a milestone that it made the rest of the trip feel as though it would be downhill.

The welcome sign, Tonia calling, and finishing 750 miles all at the same time was what I call a God Sighting. Too often in my life, I'd missed them. On this trip, however, I had been out of my comfort zone and unusually sensitive to them.

I believe those manifestations of His presence were God's way of reminding me He was with me every pedal stroke of the way.

My emotions tumbling like the ocean waves, I couldn't stop the tears that streamed down my face as I pedaled through Carolina Beach.

God and Family

Since the day my sons were born, I prayed that they would love God – and that we would be friends for life. What they achieved has never mattered to me. But I have always cheered their success the way that God was cheering mine.

I wanted my sons to be happy, and to love God and their family.

God and family. That's what I prayed would be the hub around which the rest of their lives would turn.

I prayed as I rode, mentioning each member of my family by name. When I prayed for my mother, my voice hitched with emotion. I wouldn't be here today if not for my mother's strength and her prayers. She was the one stabilizing force in a family wrecked by alcoholism

My dad was a wonderful man...*sober*. Drunk, he was dangerous. Some of my earliest memories centered on his drinking.

Mom worked two jobs seven days a week, but we still lived in poverty because Dad drank away all the money. He had a strong work ethic, which he passed on to all four of his kids. But after work when he hit the bottle, we lived in fear. We children walked the streets at night too afraid of him to go home. He threatened to kill our mother almost every night of our lives

Needless to say, we moved around a lot.

Things were so bad by the time I was in seventh grade that our pastor was afraid for my mother's life. He urged her to get out while she was able. For me, their divorce was the only way out of our nightmare.

After the divorce, Dad disappeared from our lives. Home became a peaceful place. Fear faded and laughter began to erupt in the family. Instead of walking the streets, we went home to our own beds.

Meeting My Dad

Years later, I was a freshman in college sitting in my dorm room and some guy knocked on my door. "Your dad's on the phone," he said. "He wants to talk to you."

Sure he'd made a mistake; I explained that the call wasn't for me. He insisted that I take the call and I answered with a tentative hello.

It was my dad. He wanted to see me.

I was 18 when I met him at a bar and sat down to talk to him. I explained that God had called me into the ministry and I was earning a degree in theology.

"Don't ever forget what I've done to you all," he said. "Teach people what alcohol does to a life and maybe you can save someone else from this."

He looked broken, ashamed.

But he hadn't stopped drinking.

> *"Don't ever forget what I've done to you all,"* he said. *"Teach people what alcohol does to a life and maybe you can save someone else from this."*

I didn't hear from my father again until several years later. Tonia and I were married and expecting our second child when he called. He was in downtown Miami outside the bus station.

Homeless.

Tonia had never met him, so I took her to downtown Miami at 11:00 p.m.

That part of Miami was dangerous; no place to take a woman who is eight months pregnant. But Tonia was game. She wanted to meet her child's grandfather. Besides, neither of us knew if we would ever see him again.

Bus Station Reunion

When we arrived, it took awhile for me to recognize my father. He was bloodied and hurt. It was a terrible thing to see.

"As long as you're drinking, you can never come into my home."

Those were difficult words to say, and harder for him to hear. But man-to-man, he understood: I would protect my wife and child.

He said he was headed to the Keys because he'd found a job. I don't know what happened to him then, but he called not long after that asking for transportation. I drove him to the Keys late one Saturday night and dropped him off at the side of the road.

Years later, I pulled all three of my sons out of school for the day and took them to meet their grandfather. He was in rehab in Fort Lauderdale.

He was a heartbreaking sight. In addition to the cirrhosis he suffered from years of alcoholism, he'd been diagnosed with cancer of the esophagus. Doctors urged him to stop smoking and drinking, but he said he'd lost everything else. Those were the only two things he had left.

I'd always known I would never be able to minister if I didn't forgive him. As I matured in the Lord and studied the Bible, I realized that not forgiving was much more serious than I'd imagined.

Mark 11:25-26 says, "And when you stand praying, if you hold anything against anyone, forgive them, so that your Father in heaven may forgive you your sins." The entire gospel hinges on forgiveness. God forgave us. We must forgive others.

Ending Well

By God's grace, I was able to forgive Dad for what he'd done to our family. I forgave him for not being a father to me. That didn't mean I had to let him disrupt the peace of my home. God expected me to hold appropriate boundaries to keep my family safe. So I loved my dad right where he was.

During the last two years of his life, I drove to visit him every month or two. I took him to lunch where we laughed and talked and I shared my heart with him.

We ended well.

I wanted more than anything to finish this journey of faith well.

Having completed more than half of my ride to the Big Apple, I called it a day a little early. Tonia and her mother, Yvonne, were joining me for the weekend.

As I celebrated my success I knew that my Father was cheering me on, thrilled with my progress. I suspected my dad would have been pleased too.

Half way point, Carolina Beach, NC

Tonia and mother in law Yvonne Gilmore, Wilmington, NC

CHAPTER 16
The Secret of Contentment

This experience was changing me.

The physical changes alone were staggering. After riding an average of 60 to 70 miles a day, six days a week, instead of growing weak and tired, I had grown stronger with every passing mile.

But while I'd expected some physical changes, I was surprised at how I had changed spiritually and emotionally. Conquering my fear, for instance, by riding across the tallest bridge, had solidified my faith that God will strengthen me in my weakness.

Looking at them collectively, the sum total of "firsts" on this journey had been incredible. I rode out of Wilmington reflecting on those firsts as I pedaled. Starting with the moment I'd agreed to make this journey (a decision that had almost scared the socks off my feet) I thought of all the times I'd felt like I was facing Goliath.

Asking the church to give to Haiti.

Saying goodbye to my family.

That terrifying day I rode away from life as I knew it.

Grueling hours spent pedaling against a headwind.

The bridges of Brevard County.

Logging trucks.

18-wheelers.

Riding through Charleston.

Riding up—and sailing down—the tallest bridge.

Facing the loneliness and learning to lean on God in a whole new way.

Changing and rearranging my plans countless times a day.

Facing the unknown every moment and every mile of my journey.

Every conquered fear had changed me. Every conquered adversity had changed me. Every conquered mile had changed me.

Salute to Heroes

Was that why God had insisted on this radical ride? I suspected it was.

Somehow I'd experienced a spiritual revolution. I was more sensitive to God's presence. I recognized His fingerprints on my life and appreciated them in a deeper way.

Every conquered fear had changed me. Every conquered adversity had changed me. Every conquered mile had changed me.

I was learning to trust Him more. Rely on Him more. Lean on Him more. Talk to Him more.

In Jacksonville, North Carolina, I rode around the outskirts of Camp Lejeune Marine base. I'd hoped to ride through the base, but the recent death of Osama bin Laden had tightened security around the military. Although I was disappointed, I applauded the heightened security measures. No amount of protection for the men and women in uniform and their families could be too much.

How could I bemoan the loss of creature comforts when those heroic men and women were battling terrorism in places like Iraq and Afghanistan?

I rode past miles of fence around the base where families had posted banners and homemade signs welcoming marines returning from war. Pulling to a stop, I read the messages from some of the families, choking on my emotions. The messages reminded me of the sacrifices not only of those killed or wounded in battle, but the incredible sacrifices of their families.

How could I bemoan the loss of creature comforts when those heroic men and women were battling terrorism in places like Iraq and Afghanistan?

I prayed for our troops and their families. Afterward, saluting, I rode away.

The Ultimate Sacrifice

The trip around Camp Lejeune produced yet another change in me. It hardened me to my own difficulties, and softened me even more to pray for our troops and for their heroic families.

They're Christ-like in their sacrifice.

Jesus died so that we might have eternal life. They fight and die so that we can enjoy freedom every day.

Thank You, Lord, for our military.

Leaving Camp Lejeune, I was heading north toward Morehead City when I saw someone flagging me down. Pulling over, I met Lenny, a former member of Oasis Church who'd relocated to North Carolina. We chatted a few minutes on the side of Highway 24, and then Lenny said he wanted to pray over the rest of my trip.

The moment Lenny put his arm around my shoulder and prayed, I knew that this was more than a happy coincidence. It was a divine appointment. A benediction. A blessing from God.

A powerful reminder of all the people who prayed, keeping me safe and well for 16 days, it summed up what this trip was all about.

Pedaling on, I entered the little town of Cape Carteret, North Carolina. There, I saw something that took my breath away—50 acres of the most beautiful flowers I'd ever seen.

I lay down in the middle of the flowers.

I don't say that lightly. I've seen the tulip fields in Washington State. I've admired hundreds of acres of stunning roses in Ecuador. But the blossoms in Cape Carteret surpassed them all.

A Changed Man

Although I'd already ridden 60 miles and had further to go, I climbed off my bike. For a few minutes I just drank in the beauty. Then I did something the old me would never have done.

I lay down in the middle of the flowers.

I closed my eyes, drank in the scent, my senses alive to the sound of bees buzzing nearby and the feel of the sun kissing my cheeks.

I felt God smiling.

Today, tired, sweaty, and covered with road grime, I refused to miss the opportunity to enjoy this gift from God.

This, I realized, was another God Sighting. I wondered how long He had waited, wanting to pry my fingers loose from the life I held so tightly, so that I could experience this.

Lying in a field of flowers in Cape Carteret, North Carolina, I was positive of something few of us ever know for sure: *I was in the center of God's perfect will.* Of all the places on earth I could have been, of all the things I could be doing for God—preaching, speaking, expanding the kingdom—this was where God wanted me to be.

The God of the universe, the God of Abraham, Isaac, and Jacob wanted me to see this. Even more, He wanted me to slow down and *experience it.*

Slow Down and Enjoy the Ride

Two weeks ago, I would've ridden past this paradise. I might have noticed it; perhaps not. Today, tired, sweaty, and covered with road grime, I refused to miss the opportunity to enjoy this gift from God.

I looked up at the beautiful cloudy sky and just basked in God's goodness. Most of my life I'd been in a hurry, always with a goal or destination in sight. Drunk on the flowers' sweet perfume, I admitted that I'd spent most of my years on the expressways of life.

If I had a single regret, it was for all the times I didn't stop to smell the flowers.

Don't get me wrong; I enjoy the Magic Kingdom in Disney World as much as anyone. But it isn't real. The Busch Gardens can't compare to the organic beauty here among this field of flowers.

If I could give you one piece of advice, it would be this: *Go where you've never been. Get off the expressways of your life and lie in a field. Enjoy the beauty of God's handiwork.*

True Contentment

According to the Bible, Paul found the secret of contentment. He said, "I know what it is to be in need, and I know what it is to have plenty. I have learned the secret of being content in any and every situation, whether well fed or hungry, whether living in plenty or in want, (Philippians 4:12).

Paul found contentment in total submission to and fellowship with God.

That's paradise.

That's what brings real happiness, and that's what God wants for each of us.

Find your radical ride, whatever that is.

Do it.

Live it.

And most of all—*enjoy it.*

I pulled myself out of the flowers and stretched. It hadn't been a long break, but I felt so refreshed. Back on the road, the miles flew by. Looking at my odometer, I realized I had set a new record.

86 miles!

What a perfect end to an epic day.

Prayer with friend Lenny outside Camp Lejeune, NC

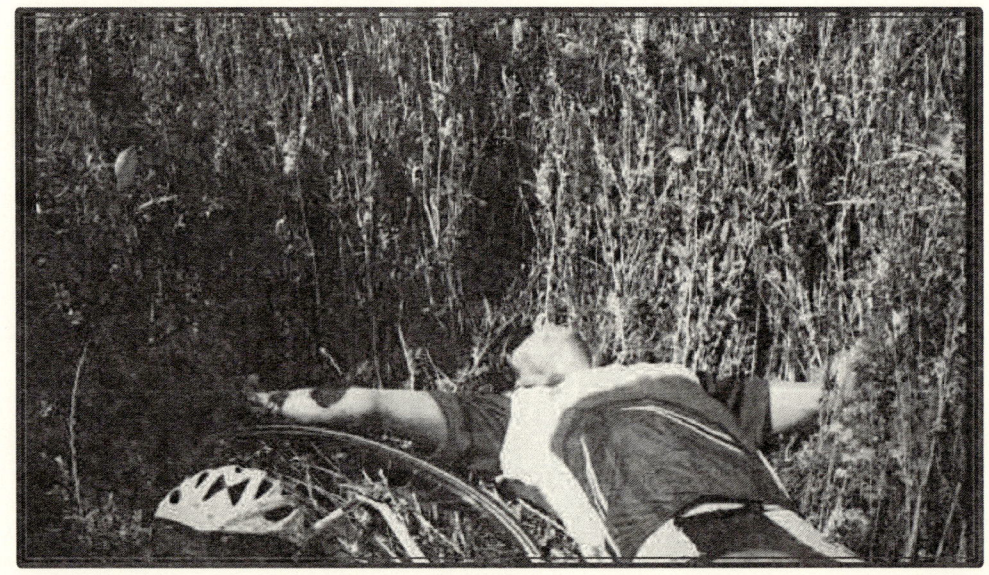

Wild Flower R&R, Cape Carteret, NC

CHAPTER 17
One Child at a Time

Success has a price. I re-learned this principle almost daily.

My epic 86 miles yesterday had changed everything. Having overshot my goal, we had to reposition the camper further north and re-plan tomorrow's route, which in turn changed all our plans for the rest of the trip.

When the week ended, I waved a fond farewell to Jeremy as he returned home to resume his life. Sunday evening, I picked up Luke Windle from the Wilmington airport, thanking God once again for my support team. I couldn't imagine attempting this without their help.

Pedaling toward Cedar Island, North Carolina, I had an ear bud in one ear listening to worship music. My other ear stayed tuned to traffic and the hum of the SAG wagon behind me. Knowing that Luke had my back comforted me.

Even with music, the ride was long and lonely. Denny, an old friend from the early days of Oasis Church broke the monotony by joining me for part of the day's journey. Denny had retired and moved to New Bern, North Carolina. He was preparing for the oldest and largest bike ride in the nation and opted to do his training ride with me.

My heart sang as Denny rode alongside of me. We discussed bikes, equipment, and compared war stories of our training experiences. We shared tips and caught up on our families and mutual friends. The miles melted away like butter in the hot sun as we laughed and talked. I treasured every moment of the experience, knowing it was a gift from God.

Denny rode with me 15 miles. Cheered by the visit, I headed for the ferry that would take Luke and me to Ocracoke Island, the southernmost of a string of barrier islands off the coast of North Carolina known as the Outer Banks.

Further by Ferry

The ferry ride was a long one – over two hours. It put a dent in my riding time and left me with miles to make up later in the day. The old me might have been frustrated with the delay, chomping at the bit to reach my destination. The new me relaxed every moment of the journey.

Luke and I talked and enjoyed listening to the waves lapping against the side of the ferry and the call of gulls. I drank in the distinctive scent of sand and water and fish. Relaxing, I let the sway of the boat rock me like a babe in his mother's arms.

Luke, an avid surfer, talked about the wind and the waves and the thrill of catching a big one and riding it to shore. I'd studied the route for the next day and knew the roads along the Outer Banks were safe and held no surprises. I decided right then to send Luke ahead to ride the waves.

Since bikers were practically invisible in daylight, I imagined that the road would seem more ominous, the trucks bigger, and the experience lonelier after dark.

Offloading the SAG wagon from the ferry, we raced 11 miles north to catch another one. The second ferry took 40 minutes and I fought not to pace. I felt like I'd been sitting all day. Actually, I had, first on the bike and then on the ferry rides.

Finally back on land, I hopped on the bike, not wanting to lose another moment of daylight. I rode hard and pedaled fast, keeping an eye on the sun as it sank toward the horizon.

My family had asked me not to ride in the dark, and I agreed with their wisdom. Since bikers were practically invisible even in daylight, I imagined the road would seem more ominous, the trucks bigger, and the experience lonelier at night.

As the day wore on, I pushed myself to make up some of the miles I'd missed that afternoon. The sound of my tires on gravel seemed louder, the incessant racket of insects grew quieter. The shadows grew longer as the sun dipped lower in the sky.

Living in the Darkness

There was something about the encroaching darkness that drew my thoughts to Haiti. The nation had been under shadow of darkness for much of its history.

The people had been shrouded in the darkness of slavery.

The country had been torn apart by war.

It had been decimated by greed.

It had been raped by poverty.

It had been sold into slavery by corruption.

One young woman in our church, Amina Dubuisson, had witnessed many of those things firsthand. Born in Haiti, her parents immigrated to the U.S. when she was 19. After earning a degree in nursing, she had married and had three children before going back to school to earn her master's degree. Afterward she became a regional director of clinical operations for Greystone Healthcare Management.

When I stepped off the airplane, it was like stepping into a war zone. There was so much blood. I'd seen a lot of things in my career, but nothing prepared me for the sheer volume of blood that soaked into the hot Haitian soil.

"I'd always wanted to do medical missions to Haiti," she said, "but I didn't know where to start. Then someone told me about the Haitian American Nurses Association and I joined the organization.

"In October 2006, I went on my first medical mission trip. Haiti was a different country back then. People couldn't ask to see a doctor. They often died because they couldn't get to the hospital on time. Or they died because after they got to the hospital, they didn't have the money to buy their medicine.

"I took a medical mission trip to Haiti every year after that, but nothing prepared me for what I saw following the earthquake in 2010. The country was totally devastated.

Blood Cries From the Soil

"Among the first medical teams to arrive in Haiti after the earthquake, I stepped off the airplane into a veritable war zone. There was so much blood. I'd seen a lot of things in my career, but nothing prepared me for the sheer volume of blood that soaked into the hot Haitian soil

"There was no hospital at the time, as it had been destroyed. I was among 70 nurses working in tents set up at the airport. There was a tent stacked with bodies of people who had died. They had a generator to keep it cool, but I was there for a week and when I left the bodies were still there.

"On that first trip after the earthquake, I worked primarily in triage and starting IVs. One day someone took me downtown to Port-au-Prince. It was horrible! Bodies stacked in piles, decaying in the heat. Blood everywhere!

"I went to Haiti seven times that year. On one trip I was assigned as team leader over wound care. During rounds, I was introduced to a little 7-year-old girl who had to be taken to the operating room or heavily sedated in order to clean her wounds and change her dressings.

"I woke early the next morning curious to know if I could find a way to do the job without subjecting her to all that sedation. I couldn't help but wonder which was worse, her pain or her terror.

"I asked her to tell me about the earthquake and describe what had happened to her leg. Then I told her I was going to change the dressings, but that I had a very bad memory and needed her to help me.

To Shine a Light

"I described in detail everything I was going to do and showed her things I needed her to hand me. Her chocolate eyes wide and trusting, she memorized the procedure. I dressed her in a gown just like mine and the first time I pretended to forget something, she reminded me of what I was supposed to do.

"With everyone watching, I cleaned the wound and changed her dressing without her taking so much as the Tylenol. It became clear to us all that her terror had accelerated her pain. Giving her a job to do and keeping her mind busy made the dressing change tolerable.

"I continue to go to Haiti regularly. The problems seem insurmountable. I can't fix the problems in the society but I can help the people – one child at a time."

Thinking about Amina and all the wonderful medical teams working in Haiti made the race against sunset bittersweet. All I wanted to do was raise enough money to shine a little light in the darkness.

With night beginning to settle over Ocracoke Island I finally stopped after 54 miles. Although disappointed that I hadn't logged more miles today, I marveled over the exactly 900 miles I'd ridden since leaving home.

My journey wouldn't raise enough money to save the world. But like Amina, I could help change the life of one child at a time.

Haitian Children in St. Marc, Haiti

CHAPTER 18
Survival...of the Blessed

I felt a spring in my step as I walked to my bike and shoved off, sending Luke ahead to enjoy the day. Inhaling the salty sea air, I released a contented sigh. The Outer Banks offered the most beautiful scenery along the entire East Coast.

The waves lapping against the sand dunes and perfect cool weather made this the kind of experience that quickened all my senses. The incredible ocean vistas created a day so perfect that I spent the first two hours worshiping. It was one of those mornings when the glory of God's creation moved me to lift my face to the warm sun and sing.

I prayed.

I quoted Scripture.

I delighted in God and in the work of His hands.

Until two days ago, I hadn't been sure I could take this route along State Road 12. Although the views were amazing any day of the year, the winds on the Outer Banks could exceed 40 mph. It would be impossible for me to ride any distance against that kind of opposition. After tracking the winds for weeks and praying that they would shift, watching them change on the weather map had prickled my skin with excitement.

Today the winds blew from the southeast at 18 mph. With the help of that tail wind I averaged 20 to 22 mph. I clocked one stretch at 31 mph, the fastest speed of the entire trip.

It was scary…*and exhilarating.*

Eighty miles of gorgeous seashore and sand dunes beckoned to me. I refused to pressure myself to ride a certain number of miles each day because I didn't need the added stress. I wanted the freedom to set a comfortable pace and enjoy my journey.

Life Unscripted

Still, with the tailwind at my back, I hoped to ride the entire 80 miles today before having to turn back to the mainland. I felt God's presence in such a palpable way that it reminded me of my oldest son, Jim.

Jim used to live in Seattle where he worked for Habitat for Humanity. Whenever he needed peace and solace, he climbed a mountain. From those heights and surrounded by stunning beauty, Jim always felt closer to God.

Not much for outdoor worship myself, I believed him, but couldn't identify with what Jim described.

Until now.

You can't script a day like this.

Approaching a construction zone, I looked up and thought I saw a mirage.

Surely not.

The worship I'd been enjoying stuck in my throat as I read the sign that explained the sight: Herbert C. Bonner Bridge. Somehow in all my planning, I'd missed this bridge on the map.

It looked like the bridge from hell. Stretching for what appeared to be miles across open water, it rose above the waves like leviathan. A serpent in my garden of God's glory, it snaked its way across the expanse.

I gazed at its tallest peak and noted the small railing blocking travelers from dropping to their death.

I would be afraid to drive across this bridge!

My mouth went dry as dust and my palms felt sweaty. I had ridden many bridges, including the one I crossed with the Bisiklet Boys. But I hadn't ridden one like this. The majority of bridges had a bike lane, or at least a sidewalk. If not, they were usually short with very little traffic. In those cases, I always had the SAG wagon at my back. But today I didn't.

It can't be that bad.

"God, let there be a bike lane!"

There was no bike lane.

Luke was miles ahead of me pulling the camper. He might be surfing. Maybe I should wait for him to come back for me.

Bridge From Hell

It may have been the lure of an 80-mile day that caused me to make a very unwise decision. It may have been the joy of the perfect morning that lulled me into a false sense of security.

Nothing could go wrong.

As I pedaled onto the bridge, I realized the belated truth. I would be afraid to *drive* across this bridge!

Built in the early 1960s, the bridge had been designed to last 30 years. Traversed by more than 2 million vehicles a year, on a scale of one to 100, with 100 being the safest, it had been officially rated at two.

Although posted a 55 mph, I was in the same lane as 18-wheelers passing at a teeth-rattling 70 mph.

To its credit, the bridge, which spanned the joining of the Pamlico Sound with the Atlantic Ocean, offered a breathtaking view. But my breathing stopped before I saw it…when I realized the bridge had no bike lane and no shoulder.

None.

Suddenly I was in the same lane with 18-wheelers that, defying the posted 55 mph limit, rumbled past me at a teeth-rattling 70 mph.

Over the span of that two and a half mile bridge, I saw more dump trucks than I saw the entire 1500 miles.

> ***I felt as though any second I would be hit by a speeding truck and hurled to my death in a watery grave below.***

Why is this bridge still open?

Dance With Death

Fear sucked all the moisture out of my body, licking it up like flames from the fires of hell. In moments I went from worshiping to begging God to spare my life.

It wasn't just my hands that held a death grip on the bike. My entire body cramped into a single spasm of terror.

Don't look down!

Don't look down!

God help me!

I felt as though any second I would be hit by a speeding truck and hurled to my death in a watery grave below. Hair stood on the back of my neck as I rode hugging the side of the bridge, feeling trucks pass so close I was sure that each breath would be my last.

I've never been so scared in my life.

Trembling from the adrenaline rush, I finally pedaled off the bridge certain that I'd aged a good 10 years.

When I met Luke for lunch, he admitted that pulling a camper over the bridge from hell had been no picnic either. He had considered turning around and coming back for me but turning around with a camper in tow would've been difficult on the narrow road. Certain he would have passed me going the opposite direction, he had continued on.

After lunch I headed toward the extreme north end of the island while Luke stopped to mail something.

Catching up with me, Luke decided to pass and move ahead. As he passed, the road narrowed and the camper mirror missed my head by mere inches. The camper, being pulled by the SAG wagon, swerved and I ran off the road to avoid being hit.

Lord, help!

"The lady in there said to be careful," Luke reported when he came out of the office. "She said there are bears and bobcats in the woods you'll be riding through."

Pressing On

This had gone from one of the most perfect days of my life to a fight for survival. I prayed with a desperation born of fear and, within an hour, I finally reached the north end of the island. Reading the sign, I realized I'd missed something else besides the bridge.

There were wild horses roaming free all over this end of the Outer Banks!

By now, I had ridden more than 80 miles, most of it with a tailwind. With energy to spare, I wanted to try for a 100-mile day. To ride the additional 17 miles I'd have to break my safety rule and ride after dark.

Luke dashed into the campground office while I finished staging the camper. As I climbed back on the bike, he reappeared with a disturbing report. "The lady in there said to be careful. There are bears and bobcats in the woods you'll be riding through."

Bears and bobcats!

Could this day get any more dangerous?

The Century Mark

Heading north toward the Virginia border, the sun dipped out of sight. Although I'd decided that safety would be my top priority on this ride, I now found myself pedaling through woods filled with bears and bobcats—in the dark. The night pitch, the only light shone from the headlights of the SAG wagon following along behind me as I counted off the miles.

85.

86.

87.

I rode on adrenaline.

90.

91.

92.

93.

94.

95.

96.

Muscles screaming, I watched my odometer click to 97 miles. Without warning, my body decided it had had enough. I felt as though I couldn't walk another step much less pedal for three more miles.

I'm done!

No, I'm not done! I didn't care if I died on that road. I didn't care if a bear ate me – I was going to finish 100 miles.

98.

99.

100!

I made the century mark! I actually rode 100 miles!

Looking at my odometer, I stared as though it were a mirage. When I hit the 100 mile mark, I also hit the 1,000 mile mark for the journey. *What were the odds?*

Only 500 miles separated me from New York City.

I was alive and whole. I had ridden my first "Century."

My first Century Ride, 100 Miles. Outer Banks, NC

CHAPTER 19
Little Foxes

I'm alive!

Stepping outside the camper, I stretched in the morning sun. *Alive!* If I had been a betting man, I wouldn't have given a dollar yesterday for my chances of climbing back on the bike today.

Grateful I'd survived, I had a revelation: I was prepared to meet my Maker but I had a good deal of unfinished business before I departed this good earth. As much as I looked forward to bowing before the throne of God, it could wait.

I wanted to hug my wife.

I wanted to spend time with my sons.

I wanted to watch my grandchildren grow into adulthood.

Even after God told me to make this journey, I never imagined I would ride 100 miles in a day. If called to the witness stand to give expert testimony regarding my ability to do so, I would've borne witness against myself.

I wanted to preach the good news of the gospel. But more than anything, I wanted to ride this bike into New York City and finish my assignment.

One hundred miles! It was still hard to believe. I'd known of people who had reached the century mark, but even after God told me to make this journey, I never imagined I would ride 100 miles in a day—especially at my age. If called to the witness stand to give expert testimony regarding my ability to do so, I would've borne witness against myself.

Instead of being exhausted, I felt alive in every molecule of my being. Part of my joy came from having survived the previous day. But most of it came from the startling changes I continued to see in myself with each passing day.

> **I'd had no idea that before a single life in Haiti had changed, my own life would be radically altered.**

My leg muscles were bulking up. My endurance was increasing and I felt a spring in my step. Instead of dreading the ride, my body yearned for the exertion.

What's happening to me?

I thought this experience was designed to help the Haitians.

I'd had no idea that before a single life in Haiti had changed, my own life would be radically altered, while at the same time the faith and vision of the members of Oasis Church was growing in a new direction.

God was amazing at multitasking.

Another Milestone

I started the day just a few miles from the Virginia border. I had mixed feelings as I crossed it. It seemed as though I'd been riding across North Carolina forever, but the scenery and southern hospitality had been spectacular.

Waving a fond farewell to North Carolina, I rode into Virginia with the excitement of passing another milestone along my path to New York City.

I was one state closer to my destination!

I pedaled past marshes and wheat fields ripening in the sunlight. I rode past row after regimented row of corn. As the sun rose in the sky, I passed lush rolling green fields surrounded by white fences and dotted with grazing horses.

I would've missed all this bucolic beauty in a car. Speeding along the interstate, I would've never seen these fields and horse farms. Worse, I never would have known what I'd missed.

By afternoon, I arrived in Virginia Beach. Feeling as though I'd unwrapped a surprise gift from God, I rode toward the beach and gasped in delight.

For a moment it seemed as though I was back home at Hollywood Beach. Waves lapped the sandy shore as gulls scavenged for fish. The boardwalk wide and inviting, it even offered a bike path.

Luke walked the beach, salivating at the surf, while I rode along the bike path. I coasted up the boardwalk admiring the incredible ocean view. Distracted while I slowed to a stop, I waited a heartbeat too long before clicking out of my pedals.

Grimacing in pain, I lay flat – slabbed across the boardwalk like a side of beef – my bike on top of me.

The Fall

Stunned, I watched it happen but was powerless to stop it. Unable to disconnect my shoes from the pedals, I felt my heart sink in hopelessness as I fell. Hitting the ground hard, still attached to the bike, my shoulder screamed from the impact.

Then my hand.

My knee.

My head hit the hard concrete with full force, bouncing in my helmet from the jolt of the fall. Grimacing in pain, I lay flat – slabbed across the boardwalk like a side of beef – my bike on top of me.

Pain raced through my body like speedboats through water. One big throbbing pain, I grimaced, unable to isolate what might be broken.

"Did you have a heart attack?"

Prying my eyes open, I squinted against the sun. Several old ladies stood over me, straddling bikes outfitted with little flower-decorated baskets.

"What?" I asked.

"Did you have a heart attack?" One of them repeated, inspecting me like fresh fruit on a roadside stand. I felt sure she would poke me at any moment.

"No, I didn't have a heart attack. I fell," I said, gasping in pain.

How embarrassing!

"Do you need us to help you up?"

I wasn't sure if they could lift my bike, much less my body.

"No, thanks, I need to lie here a moment and get my bearings."

They pedaled away leaving me to my misery.

Little Things

"Hey! Do you need some water?"

Looking up, I saw a buff young man and his wife standing on a hotel balcony. They had seen the whole thing.

Awkward!

"No! I have water! I just need to rest a minute! But thanks!"

Glancing around, I sighed with gratitude that Luke and his video camera were nowhere in sight. I felt so stupid. I'd ridden 1,050 miles on bridges and highways with 18-wheelers and dump trucks trying to run me off the road.

Then I fell on a boardwalk coasting at 2 mph.

I wasn't sure what hurt worse, my body or my pride.

This was my third fall, and in each case it had been something a little that tripped me up.

The screaming pain died down to a growl as I felt my body for broken bones. I didn't feel any. After disconnecting my shoes from the pedals, I stood and dusted myself off. My body hurt, but I could move.

Limping to a bench, I rested. This was my third fall, and in each case it had been something little that tripped me up.

Attention to Detail

I thought of the words of Solomon, "Catch for us the foxes, the little foxes that ruin the vineyards, our vineyards that are in bloom" (Song of Songs 2:15).

So often the little foxes are what make us stumble. We get so busy with the big picture that we fail to pay attention to the little details—like the needs of our spouse, our relationship with our children, or how high on our priority list we place God.

In biking, little pieces of sand and pebbles barely visible to the naked eye can ruin the day and ruin the ride. In life, moments misspent or small opportunities neglected can ruin everything.

I collapsed into bed that night with aches, pains, skinned knees, and bruises. I'd only ridden 50 miles and then I'd fallen; a far cry from the mountaintop experience of riding 100 miles yesterday.

Once again I thanked God for His protection. I could've fallen on the highway. I could've broken a bone, dislocated a shoulder, or torn the ligaments in my knee. None of those things happened.

I closed my eyes whispering a prayer in my heart.

Lord, what little foxes do I need to catch to keep from falling short in life?

Virginia Beach, VA, just before my only fall

CHAPTER 20
Listen Up!

Bruised and sore from my boardwalk fall, I finished the evening working with Luke to reposition the camper much farther north. Passing over the Chesapeake Bay Bridge and through two tunnels, we'd ended up on the Delmarva Peninsula.

Luke, tired of riding on U.S. highways, searched the maps on his phone and discovered something called Seaside Road. Imagining that the road would take us on a scenic journey along the coast, we decided to take it.

Climbing onto my bike the next morning, I realized I'd left my earbuds in the camper, positioned 40 miles away. Music had kept me sane and reduced the boredom of the past 1,000-plus miles. I couldn't imagine a day without it.

After some discussion, Luke and I decided to start riding and stop at the first convenience store along the route and buy a new pair of earbuds.

I could live without music for an hour or two.

The first hour seemed an eternity. In addition to no music, Seaside Road hadn't lived up to its name. I hadn't glimpsed the ocean once. Instead, I rode past cornfields, wheat fields, marshes, and a variety of little family farms. There wasn't a single store, restaurant, post office, or gas station in sight. I'd never ridden a more deserted road.

A second hour passed.

A third hour.

After 40 miles, I still hadn't seen a single business of any kind. And I was hungry.

In addition to the boredom, patches of the road weren't even paved. Instead they were covered with small rock.

Pebbles.

The kind that can spin a bike tire out from under you in a heartbeat. Nervous, I concentrated on not falling.

Disconnected

Muscles aching from yesterday's fall, I unclipped my shoes from the pedals. Without them, riding up the hills was much harder.

I saw a lone car about every 15 to 20 minutes. Looking back, I waved at Luke. I couldn't imagine how bored he was. The monotony was merciless. Finally, with nothing else to do, I relaxed and noticed what I'd been missing.

A lot of hills.

There was also a lot of peace and quiet.

As mile after mile passed, I received download after download from God. I couldn't remember the last time I'd gotten such a rush of revelation.

Riding onto another patch of rocks, I felt stressed. Afraid of falling, I was also hot, tired, and hungry. I'd eaten my last energy bar and drank the last of my water.

I waved Luke forward, and riding beside him, I reported what I'd learned from the Lord. To preserve the messages, I asked Luke to text them to me.

By afternoon I took stock of my situation. I was tired, hot, and hungry. But I was no longer bored. Waving Luke ahead, I gave him another message and asked him to text it to me. Thoughts flowed like a swollen river.

Alone on mile after lonely, isolated mile, I could no longer dismiss the thought that had buzzed around my head like a pesky fly for the past 20 days. I'd tried swatting it away, but it wouldn't leave. My heart sank as I realized I might be trying to swat away my next assignment.

Riding onto another patch of rocks, I felt stressed.

I was afraid of falling. My mouth felt dry as cotton. My stomach was growling. And I'd eaten my last energy bar and drank the last of my water.

Sign of the Crosses

Groaning, I hit one of the most difficult hills of my journey. Without using my clips, it felt like climbing a mountain. My muscles burned as I pedaled up...and up...and up. Cresting the hill, I was worn out and ready for a break.

Ahead, I saw what appeared to be miles of cornfields. To my right, I saw a break in the fields and the tree line.

Finally, I glimpsed the ocean.

In the middle of the cornfield, next to the ocean view, were three crosses.

I freeze framed the scene in my mind.

I would cherish that moment for ever.

It was a God Sighting.

At that moment, I yielded my heart to Him anew. In words too deep to utter, I agreed to take on my next assignment. After riding a bike 1500 miles, it was the last thing I would ever want to do.

God had asked me to write a book.

Allowing God to move me from the mundane to the miraculous was an adventure I never wanted to miss again.

Throughout the ride, the thought had dive-bombed me from every direction, but I'd ducked it, certain that God would never ask it of me. After all, He knew my limitations: I'd grown up with what some believed was attention deficit disorder. I had difficulty spelling. English had been my hardest subject. I could verbalize my thoughts but I couldn't write them.

A book? The old me would've spent a couple of years wrestling with God about it; reminding Him of all the reasons He called the wrong person. The new me understood that I could do it.

Allowing God to move me from the mundane to the miraculous was an adventure I never wanted to miss again.

Motioning for Luke to join me, we stood together overlooking the crosses. "I need you to pray for me," I said. "God has asked me to write a book."

Standing together on that dusty road, I had an epiphany. *Forgetting my earbuds had not been an accident.*

It had been a divine design.

A New Assignment

I rode the rest of the day without seeing a single store or restaurant. Luke and I both needed food. Searching his maps, Luke located a little fishing village down a country lane.

We arrived at Wachapreague, Virginia, just after 5:00 p.m. An old guy who looked like he'd spent the last 20 years on the beach welcomed us to town.

"Where can we get a bite to eat and pick up some snacks?" I asked.

"The general store," he said pointing across the street. "But it's closed."

"Oh, no!" I said looking at my watch. It closed at 5:00. It was now 5:07.

"You might try the bait and tackle store down the street," he offered. "They might have crackers."

Thanking him, I rode to the bait and tackle shop.

Closed.

Not sure what to do, Luke and I pondered the situation. A few minutes later, an older man rambled up. He took one look at my biker shorts and jersey and knew we weren't from around there.

We explained our problem, and the old man nodded and pulled out a set of keys. He owned the bait and tackle store. Opening the store, he welcomed us inside where Luke and I loaded up on cheese crackers. Nothing ever tasted so good.

Dog Attack

I asked Luke to stop and take a picture of an old post office while I rode on ahead. I'd promised myself that I wouldn't get separated from him again, but what could happen on these deserted roads?

I spotted the dog in a backyard before he spotted me. I put on the turbo, pedaling faster than I dreamed possible. By the time he realized he was seeing fresh meat in spandex, I was gone.

Still, that was my first close call with a dog so I paid more attention.

Less than two hours later, Luke was behind me again when a 100-pound Doberman pinscher tried to eat me for dinner. Turning the turbo back on, I sped ahead until the giant canine, tired of chasing me, went after Luke in the SAG wagon.

Inside the safety of the car, Luke snapped a picture of the dog. When I looked at it later I felt confused.

It was a 10-pound rat terrier.

I suspected the size of the dog depended on the perspective. From the bike, it looked huge.

Luke and I had experienced a lot of firsts together. The first near brush with death, the first 100-mile ride, the first ride through bear-infested woods, and the first dog encounter.

Ending the day, I understood that God had needed me to unplug from my earbuds so that I could hear His still, small voice.

This day had been another gift from God.

It was specially wrapped for no one but me.

I crawled into bed with a smile on my face.

Seaside Road, Northern VA

The decision to write this book happened here

CHAPTER 21
A Nation Under God

I gazed past the lush, green lawn to the fountain of water and onto the white portico with an American flag high atop it. My journey had brought me to the most famous address in the nation: 1600 Pennsylvania Avenue.

The White House.

It was impossible to ride through Washington, D.C., and witness the monumental history of this nation without being reminded of the Pledge of Allegiance and all the lives that were lost in order for us to have the freedom we enjoy today.

"I pledge allegiance to the flag of the United States of America, and to the Republic for which it stands, one nation under God, indivisible, with liberty and justice for all."

One nation under God.

The phrase that has set us apart from other countries, it echoed in my mind as Luke and I rode away from the White House, each of us deep in thought.

The week seemed to have flown by and Luke would return home today. Wanting to share a ride through the capital before he left, we'd started this Saturday morning by driving from southern Maryland to Washington, D.C. The sky a vivid blue, the sun was warm, and the day glorious as we visited as many monuments as possible before he caught his flight.

After dropping Luke off at the airport, I decided to put in more miles around Washington. Without Luke at my back, I would be on my own so I found a safe riding path that took me along the Potomac River.

Seeing the image of the Lincoln Memorial reflected on the water, I checked all the signs to make sure I wouldn't break any rules by taking my bike up the steps of the monument.

No signs were posted so I lifted the bike and carried it up the stairs. A 19-foot marble statue of Lincoln sat in the center of the Memorial. Both the Gettysburg Address and the second inaugural address were inscribed on the walls.

Wanting a picture next to the statue, I asked a guard if he would mind snapping one.

"It's against the law to have a bike in a government building," he said.

"Oh, I'm sorry! I looked for a sign and didn't see one."

"There aren't any signs."

Before I got thrown off the site, I found someone who couldn't speak English but knew how to use a camera. Thanking him for the picture, I grabbed my bike and fled back to the path.

Living History

Hopping on the bike, I clipped my shoes into the pedals and wheeled along with other tourists, admiring the view.

The sights and sounds of each city are typical of its location, but Washington, D.C., has a feel all its own. With Redbuds and bright blossoms fragrant in the spring air, I felt as though I had ridden into a historical museum.

I had, I realized.

In the distance I glimpsed acres of white crosses, and pedaled on toward Arlington National Cemetery. Pulling up to the site, I felt a solemn sense of honor for all those fallen heroes. Their sacrifices helped forge this nation into a place where the sound of freedom and hope still rings.

Sun glinted off row after row of crosses standing erect as silent sentinels.

There was a different atmosphere at the cemetery than any other place I'd visited. Tourists mulled about, but they were subdued in the face of the ultimate price which had been paid so many times. Sun glinted off row after row of crosses standing erect as silent sentinels.

Passing the cemetery, I rode on along mile after spectacular mile toward Mount Vernon. The path toward George Washington's estate was easy until I reached half a mile from the grounds.

The road went straight up.

I pedaled to within 150 yards of the top. Then, for the first time on my journey, I climbed off the bike and walked it up the precipice. I could have ridden it, but I had nothing to prove and the fight wasn't in me to conquer it.

A Rich Heritage

Topping the hill, I saw Mount Vernon standing stately in the glow of the setting sun. A two-story white brick colonial, it sported 15 shuttered windows across the front. Curved arches linked the main house to the carriage house standing in the shade of a giant tree that had stories to tell if it could have spoken.

Truth be told, it all spoke to me. Mount Vernon, Arlington National Cemetery, the Lincoln Memorial, the Jefferson Memorial with its domed top, the Washington Monument, the U.S. Capitol, and the White House.

What a rich heritage.

If the U.S. was a melting pot, Washington, D.C., offered an international blend of design from classical Greek, to Roman, and ancient Egyptian. Without a doubt, the hungry and poor, the oppressed, and the dreamer had all left a mark on the city.

The bike path was only about 18 miles each way, but as I rode I didn't fret about the distance. Partly because I was hundreds of miles ahead of my schedule, also because in the 42 miles I'd ridden for the day, I'd traveled all the way back to the roots of our nation.

Back in Time

Marveling at the majestic reminders of those roots, I couldn't help comparing them to Haiti's. In some ways they're similar. Even historians agree about that. The American Revolution took place only a few decades before the Haitian slave revolution gave birth to the free republic of Haiti. And both were successful attempts to achieve permanent independence from a European colonial power.

Yet the United States became prosperous, wealthy, and the recognized world leader. And Haiti – once beautiful – became the poorest country in the Western Hemisphere.

Why the disparity?

I believe the answer lies in that one phrase.

One nation under God.

While witchcraft took deep root in Haiti, our Founding Fathers established this nation on Judeo-Christian values straight from the Bible. And we have lived to enjoy their fruit.

It was a long drive back from Washington, D.C., to the campgrounds in Maryland that night. The next morning, Sunday, was my Sabbath rest.

Booting up my laptop, I clicked on a link to join a live worship service at Oasis Church. Basking in the long-distance fellowship with my church family, I thanked God that we had the right to worship.

I thanked God that we had the right to assemble.

I thanked God for our Founding Fathers.

I thanked Him that we'd been founded as…*one nation under God.*

The White House, Washington, DC

CHAPTER 22
The Second Century

I wasn't taking any chances. After riding more than 1,000 miles without a single dog chase, I'd barely survived two in one day, so I decided I should share my safety lessons from the road.

"I want to rehearse what to do if a dog goes after me," I said to my new two-man support team, Ben Windle and Joel Collins. "If a dog goes after me, do whatever it takes to stay between the dog and me."

This week was supposed to have been just Joel and me. Ben had been scheduled for the following week. There is, however, a price to pay for success. With only 344 miles left to New York City, I could ride less than 60 miles a day and still make it to the Big Apple by Saturday. Rather than have Ben miss the trip altogether, we decided to double team for this last week of the ride. I could already tell it would be a much easier week with a team of two, even though it took awhile for everyone to settle into a routine.

We planned a pleasant 60-mile ride through quaint little towns with an ocean view.

The day dawned cool and cloudy and I rejoiced to be miles away from the bridge from hell and speeding logging trucks. The beachside roads offered great bike lanes that protected me from traffic. I set a comfortable pace with music in one ear.

This was the biker's dream.

Pedaling like a madman, I glanced back but all I could see was the sun glinting off the sharp fangs in the biggest, baddest dog I'd ever seen.

Lost in gorgeous views and in my own thoughts, I was jerked from my reverie by the sound of snarling and snapping. Adrenaline shot through my veins. Pedaling like a madman, I glanced back but all I could see was the sun glinting off the sharp fangs of the biggest, baddest dog I'd ever seen.

Legs pumping like pistons, I wondered if I could outrun the huge buff and brown German shepherd.

Behind me, Ben pounded the horn relentlessly and aimed the SAG wagon toward the dog, trying to get positioned between us.

Meal on Wheels

The German shepherd, unfazed by the perpetual horn blasts and Ben's automotive aggression, remained determined to sink his teeth into me. I couldn't imagine why. I'd lost so much weight that there was hardly any meat left on my body. Although I hadn't weighed since leaving home, I could tell just by looking at myself that I weighed less now than I did as a young man.

I don't know if the dog decided eating me wasn't worth getting run over by a car, or if he finally realized I was too skinny to make a meal. All I know is that Ben won.

The dog trotted off.

I was still shaking when we stopped awhile later.

"Ben, you saved my life! I owe you big time!"

"That dog was 120 pounds of pure muscle," Ben said. "You would never have outrun him."

So it wasn't really a rat terrier that looked big and terrifying to me!

Back on my bike, I pushed off and set a comfortable pace. With a tailwind at my back, the miles seemed to zip by without a lot of effort. The dog had attacked at the end of my first hour. The next few passed without incident. The cloud cover kept me cool and the wind felt like a gentle hand on my back pushing me closer to New York City.

Wind at My Back

Once my heart rate settled back down, I enjoyed the quaint towns, the scents and sounds from the ocean, and the joy that came from being alive and in the center of God's will. When my odometer clicked onto 60 miles, I motioned for Ben and Joel to pull over and talk. "I've had a tailwind all day," I said. "With this cloud cover and cool weather, I have energy to spare. I'd like to keep riding."

"Go for it," Joel encouraged.

I never would've imagined that 22 days into the ride, I would have so much energy at the end of the day, I wouldn't want to stop.

I couldn't think of a single day in Haiti when I hadn't seen at least one car wreck.

I'd been afraid fatigue would overwhelm me after 20 days on a bicycle seat. But the opposite had happened. Although my body was whip thin, my muscles were strong and my energy levels higher than they had ever been in my life.

Riding a bike path with Ben and Joel behind me, I felt as safe as a man in spandex could feel. My thoughts drifted to Haiti where there was little security and the roads weren't safe. I couldn't think of a single day I'd spent there when I hadn't seen at least one serious car wreck, if not more. Cars on the island are old and not well maintained. It's not uncommon for brakes to fail on the many mountainous roads.

Haiti has its share of crazy drivers and, unlike in the U.S., few of the roads have lines in the middle. Many unpaved roads have holes deep enough to lose the vehicle.

On my last trip, I'd crossed five rivers without a single bridge. Although I expected each time to make it across without a problem, I knew that the week before, another member of our church had run into trouble: His Jeep had overturned in a rushing river.

The Jeep had required a new engine, and its passengers were blessed to get out of the river alive.

Different Dangers

On my next trip, on the same road, our SUV had gotten stuck in the river too. It took several hours and a tractor for nearby villagers to pull us out and get us on our way. That's life in a third-world country.

Life is full of risks. But I would rather be in danger in Haiti in the middle of God's will than out of God's will and living anywhere else with a misplaced sense of security.

I knew that Joel Collins, who was riding behind me in the SAG wagon, would heartily agree. He'd had some hair-raising experiences in Haiti himself. But he wouldn't trade them for anything.

Recalling one particular trip, he said, "We were driving to Port-au-Prince, a two hour journey...It was market day and we happened to hit it right at the peak of business. I can only compare it to when everyone converges on the mall at home before Christmas. We were on a two-lane street with barely enough room on either side for people to walk. Cars were trying to zoom by right next to all the vendors.

"We were trying to get down the street in a huge SUV when our driver parked and said he was going to get food to take to the orphanage.

Ten minutes passed and we felt nervous about his absence. Finally, he returned with a bunch of burlap bags filled with rice, beans, cooking oil, and charcoal.

We reached the orphanage and when he gave them the bags, it wasn't the food that made them almost weep for joy. It was the charcoal. Without the charcoal, they couldn't have cooked the food. We take so much for granted!

With Haiti, rushing rivers, car wrecks, and charcoal on my mind, and a wind at my back, the miles flew by.

Room With a View

When the odometer clicked to 100 miles, I stopped. Dirty, sweaty, and stiff from eight hours on a bike, I looked up in shock as Joel and Ben shoved a camera in my face.

"How does it feel to have just finished your second 100 mile day in a week?"

Raw with emotion, I almost choked on my reply.

"What would you like to do next?"

"Go to Disney World."

Where had that come from?

The Disney World remark had popped out of my mouth. I suspected that I'd had enough reality to last me for awhile. I was ready for a little bit of fantasy.

We camped near Ocean City, Maryland, at a waterfront property called Frontier Town. Joel discovered the place and it was the best campground so far.

Sitting in the camper just 25 feet from the ocean, we had a million-dollar view.

After riding my second 100 miles day in a week, it was another gift from God.

CHAPTER 23
Love Doesn't Look Away

Waves lapped against the ferry in Delaware as Joel, Ben, and I looked out across the bay. The ferry chugged along toward the southern tip of the Jersey shore, cutting through the water at a steady pace.

Two months ago when I'd scouted this final leg of my journey, our destination—Cape May, New Jersey—had been nothing more than a name on a map. I'd never been through New Jersey except on I-95. Since I'd only seen the big cities, this had originally been the scariest part of the ride.

I'd expected to be so exhausted by now that I would barely be able to pedal the bike. I'd also assumed that the traffic across New Jersey and into Manhattan would be the worst. I was wrong, though. The truth turned out to be the polar opposite of my fearful fantasies.

How often I'd found that to be true.

Fear and dread worked overtime magnifying the unknown in my mind. If I had given in to them I would never have learned to live a radical life in Christ.

In April, on my exploration trip to this area, I'd rented a bike and made plans to ride up the coast for two days. The temperature was in the 40s and the beaches deserted. On my first day it rained, so I opted to drive up the coast and investigate the roads. The following day, I rented a bike and felt fear melt under the reality of scant traffic, ocean views, and little beach towns nestled next to the marshes.

Fear and dread had worked overtime magnifying the unknown in my mind.

While riding the rental bike, I'd had a flat tire—the only one I experienced in 1500 miles of training and another 1500 miles of the ride. The tire flopped like a deflated soufflé and I panicked. I'd been along the coast somewhere – I didn't know where. I had no idea where anything was located, nor did I know a single person to call.

Stopping a pedestrian, I asked for help and someone pointed me to a bicycle shop only half a mile away. The bike shop repaired my flat and I finished 40 miles that day. When I returned the bike, the rental shop knocked the price of the flat tire off my bill.

Cool people live on the Jersey shore.

Preparing for Summer

Now, instead of dreading this leg of the journey, I anticipated it with great joy. When the ferry docked at Cape May, I admired the beautiful little town. Driving past bed and breakfasts, I made a mental note to return sometime with Tonia.

I crossed more bridges that day than I'd crossed the entire trip. It seemed as though each village had a bridge going into town and a bridge to cross when you left. None of the bridges were very tall, but they were old and hardly passable in traffic. I imagined what it would have been like to cross those bridges after Memorial Day when people flocked to the coast.

Everywhere I looked people scurried around to finish painting, laying asphalt, and planting flowers.

For now, I had them pretty much to myself.

Most of the towns had their own distinct personalities and offered wooden boardwalks and lots of family-friendly activities. Everywhere I looked people scurried around to finish painting, laying asphalt, and planting flowers.

Partial to my beloved Florida coastline, I had to admit that very little compared to the beauty and variety of scenery in New Jersey. Back home where it was summer all year round, nothing much changed this time of year. Here, with each little town coming out of winter's hibernation and preparing for summer, there was a sense of excitement. It felt like preparations for a grand opening.

Bittersweet Victory

Instead of being exhausted, I was exhilarated. For the first time, I started tasting victory. It was bittersweet.

On one hand, I couldn't wait to see Tonia and the rest of my family. I looked forward to moving out of the camper and back into the comforts of home.

Chatting with Tonia each evening.

Home cooking.

My own bed.

Seeing my Oasis family.

Sharing these experiences from the road.

And yet…*it was almost over.* This radical ride…this moving from the mundane to the miraculous…this journey with Jesus.

I wanted to go home. But I didn't want to go back to the old me.

He had never felt so close. I'd learned to listen for His whispers and feel His touch in a whole new way.

I wanted to go home. But I didn't want to go *back to the old me*. I didn't want to live in the mundane. I didn't want this experience to become a dim memory overshadowed by fear, doubt, unbelief, or apathy.

I didn't want to live within the limits of my limitations. I wanted to mount up on wings like an eagle and soar with Him.

With every mile, I tasted the sweet sorrow and abounding joy that meant the end of my journey. I felt as though I was floating on air because I wanted to live this way for the rest of my life. I wanted to go home and go back to Haiti knowing I had conquered my fear.

Loving Lucy

As the day wore down, I saw the skyline of Atlantic City ahead. Just when I threatened to take myself too seriously, I burst into laughter.

Only two miles south of Atlantic City, in the town of Margate, New Jersey, I saw Lucy, the world's largest elephant.

Built in 1881, Lucy stands 65 feet tall. She is 60 feet long and 18 feet wide. The only elephant in the United States designated as a national historic landmark, she has earned the honor by defying for decades the winter winds that whip in from the Atlantic Ocean.

Storms have come and gone but no gale has been able to blow Lucy off her perch.

The thought kicked my mind back to Haiti. The monsoon rain and winds there had blown whole tent cities into the sea. At one of the orphanages, even the tarp they used to replace the tent had blown away. They had tried to put it back, lashing it above a picnic table. But to no avail.

Life had such a fragile hold in Haiti, especially since the earthquake. With smiles on their faces and backs straight with dignity, the people fought to claw a life out of the rubble.

The hard earth and the rubble fought back.

In spite of the problems, God commanded us to love.

Love doesn't look away.

Head down, I pedaled toward Atlantic City. I would reach my destination. I would finish my ride.

I wouldn't look away.

Atlantic City Boardwalk, New Jersey, Ben Windle

CHAPTER 24
The Longest Ride

Ben and Joel woke me at six this morning. When I climbed on my bike an hour later, I shivered in the chilly 59 degree air.

As the morning sun burned off the mist, I rode north along the Jersey shore through one incredible beach town after another. This promised to be an exceptional day. The coastline flouted its beauty with magnificent vistas, long stretches of pristine beaches; the ocean flirting with the shore like a siren of the sea.

God delighted in showing off His handiwork.

26 days.

The realization that I'd ridden a bike for that long almost boggled my mind. I had experienced every moment of the journey and I still found it hard to believe.

Pedaling into the little town of Manasquan, I detoured to the bike shop where a man had fixed my flat tire on my training ride in April. He'd explained that everyone rides south toward Florida, not north toward New York City. Leave it to me to ride against the tide.

Shocked to see me, the owner of the shop seemed surprised that I had done what I said I would do that cold, rainy, April day. After taking pictures of us together, he wished me well and I set my sights north out of town.

With the help of a cloud cover the temperature hovered at a delightful 68 degrees as I pedaled through towns like Sea Girt…Spring Lake…and

Asbury Park. Somewhere along the way I noticed a woman behind me snapping pictures. Curious, I pulled over and stopped.

"I spotted your Bike for Haiti sign!" she said, pointing to the SAG wagon. "I have friends who did a similar ride. You inspire me!"

Her encouragement felt like another blessing.

Divine Appointment

Awhile later we stopped for a break along the side of the road and some bikers who had passed us going south turned around and joined us. "We're from Canada," one of the men said offering a handshake. "We saw your Bike for Haiti sign and decided we had to stop and meet you. We're biking for Haiti as well!"

Sharing stories and Gatorade, I stood shivering in my long-sleeved jersey. Those young guys in their 20s must've felt like 68 degrees was a heat wave compared to Canada. One of them was shirtless.

"After the earthquake we just decided to do something for the Haitian people," they explained. "We decided to ride south from Canada to Mexico and then hop a plane to Haiti."

> **Somewhere along the road I realized I'd never experienced a day so perfect or ride so fun.**

Unlike me, they didn't have a support team or a SAG wagon. They didn't have a Bike for Haiti sign or a route mapped out. They had nothing but their bikes and a tent. They slept on sofas offered by strangers and on open beaches. They'd been fed by the people they met along the way.

How radical! I felt inspired by their generosity and honest desire to make a difference. As we waved goodbye, I realized this had been another God Sighting.

If I'd had a month to plan, I could never have orchestrated this meeting along the Jersey shore. Now, like the Bisiklet Boys, I was nearing the end of my ride and they had many miles to go.

Energized by the weather, the view, and the God Sightings, I rode smiling as the miles melted away. Somewhere along the road I realized I'd never experienced a day so perfect or a ride so fun.

A Slice of Heaven

Toward the end of the day, I still had energy to spare. Since I'd gotten an early start, this might well be another 100 mile day. Ben and Joel decided to make it more fun by taking turns riding alongside me on the extra bike my daughter-in-law, Jenni, had loaned me as a backup.

On this momentous day so close to my final destination, in addition to perfect riding conditions, I would have company on the road.

One providential change we'd made to the itinerary had been adding Sandy Hook recreational area to our route. Discovered by Sea Captain Henry Hudson in the early 1600s, Sandy Hook was a large extension of the barrier peninsula along the coast.

With miles of bay beaches and spectacular surf, the peninsula was separated from the mainland by the estuary of the Shrewsbury River. On the west side, enclosed by Sandy Hook Bay, it had long been a great place to anchor ships before sailing into upper New York Harbor.

The reality of my dream stood before me, its tall towers pointing toward heaven like the finger of God.

Alive with 300 species of migratory birds and other wildlife, Sandy Hook seemed more like a little slice of heaven than anything else. Fish jumped in the water, birds sang and insects hummed as we wheeled around one of the most beautiful rides of my journey.

Looking across the bay, I fell silent, choking on my own emotion. There against a backdrop of blue/grey sky stood New York City.

If not for the clouds I could have seen every building in Manhattan.

The reality of my dream stood before me, its tall towers pointing toward heaven like the finger of God.

God's Grace

I'd done it; my goal was almost close enough to touch.

Tomorrow I would ride into Manhattan and finish what I'd started.

I'd done it.

I was alive and well.

In one piece.

Sure, I'd suffered sore muscles, cramped shoulders, saddle burns, and blisters. I'd been sunburned and wind burned.

I'd been whipped by logging trucks and 18-wheelers.

I'd been chased by dogs.

I'd fallen.

But I hadn't been injured. I hadn't suffered a broken bone. I hadn't bled.

Just last evening, I'd met a woman biker who said she'd been hit by cars five different times.

I hadn't been hit once.

I hadn't been sick.

I hadn't run a fever.

I never once felt too tired to get up and ride another day. I had energy to spare each evening, usually staying up to post blogs and answer e-mails after others had gone to bed.

How was that possible?

Although I was narrow as a rail, I exuded health.

It was supernatural…surreal.

Thank You, God.

I wiped tears on my sleeve as Joel put a microphone on me. He and Ben, who'd ridden 20 miles each, wanted to video me as I finished the day.

98.

99.

100.

101.

I'd just finished the longest ride of my life. *101 miles*. If that weren't enough, I'd just finished my third 100-mile ride in eight days.

By now I knew my body well enough to know that I had enough energy left in the tank to ride another 25 miles. I chose to stop because we wanted to get back to the camper before dark.

Tomorrow I would ride into New York City.

But for now, I basked in today.

This had been the best ride of my life.

Bikers headed south from Canada. Jersey Shore, NJ

CHAPTER 25
The Big Apple

I felt nostalgic as I stepped out of the camper at the Tip Tam Campground in New Jersey. I'd just slept through my last night in the camper. Today was the last day of the ride.

Since February, I'd tried to find the safest way into New York City by bike, but I'd never figured it out. I'd finally decided that when I finished my next to last day, we would determine what route to take. So, after finishing 101 miles at Sandy Hook, Ben, Joel, and I spent the evening studying the map.

The bike route it recommended would have taken us onto three merging expressways and over two bridges that don't allow bikes. There was a definite problem with that plan.

First, it wasn't safe.

It also didn't happen to be legal.

The second option the map suggested involved circling west around New York City through New Jersey. Entering the Big Apple from the North, we could walk the bike across the George Washington Bridge before heading toward our final destination – the site of the former World Trade Center.

That would add on an extra 70 miles of horrendous city traffic to the route, making this my longest day of riding. Not a practical choice since we were expected at the memorial site by 2:00 p.m.

Our final plan was one I knew would work. We would cross the bridge into Staten Island, ride across the island, and then take a ferry which would put us one mile from our destination.

We all agreed this was our best choice. My only concern was surviving the traffic.

Beacon of Hope

Joel and Ben traded off riding through Staten Island with me. Scrambling up the stairs of the ferry with my bike in tow, we were among the last people to board. *Manhattan, here we come!*

On the ferry, I could see the New York City skyline and my emotions swelled like the incoming tide. Just when I thought I had them under control, we passed a couple hundred yards from the Statue of Liberty. In the shadow of that statue, I felt overwhelmed with gratitude to God that we – one nation under God – had been a beacon of hope to so many.

When we arrived in Manhattan, we grabbed a sandwich. We were right on schedule. Only a mile from Ground Zero, we had time to spare.

Ben and Joel were like deer in headlights as we merged into traffic. This was their first trip to New York City.

Although I'd been here many times, I'd never biked through the city streets. It's not for the faint of heart.

Joel wanted to get video of Ben and me riding the city street so he pulled ahead of us.

That's the last we saw of him.

One mile from our final destination – and we'd lost Joel. As time passed and we couldn't reconnect, all three of us felt stressed. Joel had gotten lost in a city teeming with millions of people. Ben and I worried about him and all the people waiting for us at the World Trade Center.

The quiet euphoria of riding in long sleeves along the Jersey shore yesterday was gone.

I didn't know if anyone from the media had shown up, but I knew that my wife, Tonia, my son, Corey, my granddaughter, Selah, and other friends and supporters were there waiting for us.

The Longest Mile

The quiet euphoria of riding in long sleeves along the Jersey shore yesterday was gone. A muggy 91-degree day, it felt like we'd ridden into a sauna. The traffic screeched and roared around us in the Financial District in Lower Manhattan, raising my blood pressure and setting my heart pounding in my chest like a jackhammer.

I'd ridden almost 1500 miles.

But I wasn't sure I would survive this last mile.

In retrospect, ending the ride at Ground Zero hadn't been the best idea.

There were no signs. No confetti. No Fox News or CNN. No family.

Knowing that I couldn't keep everyone waiting, I phoned Joel. "You're on your own," I said. "Find your way to Ground Zero and meet us there. We can't keep everyone waiting."

"Will do," Joel agreed.

Ben and I pulled up at Ground Zero right on time. We must have looked as puzzled as we felt. Gazing around, I saw only one familiar face. Anna Quinones Cardinale and her 2-year-old daughter, Emma Grace, had braved the heat and traffic to greet us. Grateful for her smile, I searched the crowd for a glimpse of Tonia, Corey, and Selah.

Where was our welcoming committee?

There were no signs. No confetti. No Fox News or CNN. No family. The disappointment tasted bitter on my tongue. I had looked so forward to this moment.

Corey, a professional photographer, had planned on taking some shots as we rode into the city. Worry and fear clawed at my throat, fighting to upstage my disappointment.

Where were they? Where was Joel?

Reunited

My cell phone rang. "We stopped for lunch and then got stuck in traffic," Tonia explained. I heard 2-year-old Selah fussing in the background.

Joel arrived, and I sighed with relief. Thank God he was safe!

When my family finally arrived, Anna, Emma, Ben, Joel, and I cheered *them*.

I shouted for joy when I saw my mother! Although she'd begged me not to make this trip, she had supported my decision and flown to New York City to welcome me home as a surprise.

What a blessing.

We were all relieved to be reunited, although no one was very happy. All the while, tweets, Facebook posts, and congratulatory messages flooded in from all around the country.

We spent 45 minutes taking pictures, downloading the day, and planning where we would meet to celebrate that evening. Selah was hot, fussy, and didn't want me to hold her. She'd run out of water so Tonia rushed to the corner store to buy cool bottles of water for everyone.

By the time Tonia returned, Corey was in panic mode. Selah wasn't just hot – *she was burning with fever!*

"I'm taking her to the hospital to be checked," Corey said. Sabrina, Corey's wife, had left the day before with her parents to tour Italy. Corey felt the weight of responsibility, and now Selah wanted her mommy.

I still needed to do some riding so Joel could film the video he'd missed. In addition, we had to go back to Staten Island to pick up the SAG wagon.

Tonia and I were staying with Corey, but I'd booked a hotel room for the guys so they could get a good night's rest before going home tomorrow.

More Bad News

Agreeing to meet my family for a celebration dinner, we parted ways. Awhile later Corey called. "Selah has pneumonia and they decided to keep her in the hospital," he said.

Nothing had prepared me for this day.

Five minutes later, Tonia called.

"As we were leaving Manhattan, your mother almost fainted," she explained. "The police called an ambulance and she was rushed to the emergency room. They're not sure if this is her heart or related to the heat. They've decided to keep her in the hospital to run some tests. She and Selah are in the same hospital just a few beds apart.

"You're almost an hour away so I don't think you should come back downtown. Ben and Joel have never been to New York City. Take them out to dinner and celebrate. Corey and I will stay at the hospital."

I hung up the phone and rubbed my hands over my face.

This stinks.

Nothing had prepared me for this day.

The guys and I went to dinner but it was hard to celebrate when two of the most important people in my life were in the hospital. It was almost midnight by the time I headed to the hotel to drop off Ben and Joel. Along the way I phoned Tonia in hopes of a little good news. Nothing had changed.

"Just go to bed," she said.

I hung up the phone and looked around. Where would I sleep? I had a bed at Corey's apartment, but no key to get inside. The room I had rented for Ben and Joel only had two beds – and guys don't sleep together.

A Different Ending

The hotel was hosting a softball tournament and was filled to capacity. I couldn't get another room. Grabbing a pillow, I dropped to the floor without sheet or blanket. I was exhausted and ready for this day to end.

Joel and Ben wouldn't let me finish riding 1500 miles by sleeping on the floor. I felt embarrassed, but they insisted that I take one of the beds.

I didn't really care at that point. I was worried about my mother and granddaughter and so tired I could sleep anywhere. Feeling guilty, I climbed onto one of the beds.

Listening to the nightlife in New York City, I closed my eyes and processed the day.

This wasn't the ending I had imagined.

However, I had ridden 1507 miles.

Thank You, God.

Unharmed.

Thank You, God.

Given a choice, I would've written the script with a different ending. My script would've ended with ABC, CNN, Fox News, and thousands of cheering crowds up and down Wall Street.

Unable to stop myself, I laughed into my pillow.

Get real, Guy, this isn't about you.

Finishing Well

Finishing well didn't mean cheering crowds and news reporters. Ending well meant that $130,000 would go to starving, desperate families in Haiti. To kids who didn't remember what it was like to sleep in a bed.

> ***Real success meant that today while I finished my ride, our first medical team of 15 doctors, nurses, and support staff had boarded a plane in Florida and flown to Haiti.***

With pillows.

With sheets.

With a roof over their heads.

Real success meant that today while I finished my ride, our first medical team of 15 doctors, nurses and support staff had boarded a plane in Florida and flown to Haiti. With thousands of dollars of medicine donated by Bike for Haiti, they would treat almost 500 children.

We would build orphanages and seminaries. We would feed the hungry and keep some children out of the hands of slave traders. We would make a difference in Haiti one child at a time.

I trusted that the same God who held back the storms and kept me safe on my ride would watch over my mother and granddaughter now. I felt my body relax into the deep, soft mattress.

I had stepped out of the limitations of my own mundane life.

I had traveled with God on an epic journey.

One last thought imprinted itself on my mind before I fell into a peaceful sleep.

I had no regrets.

That, I realized, was the life I wanted to live.

A life without regret.

Welcome to New York City. Ground Zero

CHAPTER 26
No Recession in God's Economy

One of the things I love about reading the Bible is seeing what happens when the power of God intersects with the lives of mortal men. Stories about God teaming up with people are always worth reading and the results are unforgettable.

The mistake most of us make is thinking that the men who walked on water, escaped the lions' den, and killed a giant with a rock were Super Saints.

That's not true.

With the exception of Jesus, every person whose name appears on the pages of the Bible was ordinary—somebody normal like you and me.

Imagine how ordinary David must have looked when he took on Goliath. He didn't compare (on the outside anyway) to the Philistine giant whose taunts had left the armies of Israel quaking in their sandals. In fact, when David challenged him, Goliath was insulted. The boy looked young and small. He wasn't even wearing any armor!

It was true. Frustrated with the bulkiness of breastplates, shields, and swords, young David had ripped them off and cast them aside. Picking up five smooth stones, he'd remembered how he protected his father's sheep from the lion and the bear.

David might have been young, but he wasn't stupid. He knew God had helped him win those victories. Convinced God would have his back, David charged the giant, felling him with a rock from his slingshot.

Another seemingly normal young man can be found in 2 Kings 2. It tells the story about the Prophet Elijah's young protégé, Elisha, who, knowing that his mentor was about to depart for heaven wouldn't let Elijah out of his sight.

"What can I do for you before I leave?" Elijah asked him.

"Let me inherit a double portion of your spirit."

What nerve! What arrogance! Asking for twice the power of Elijah just doesn't seem right! Wouldn't a humble man say, "May I please have a smidgen of your power?"

Elijah admitted that the young man had asked a hard thing. However, he replied that if Elisha saw him leave, God would grant his request.

The next thing you know *Poof!* Elijah disappeared in a chariot of fire.

Left alone, Elisha struck the river and the waters parted.

Rewriting History

In his lifetime, Elisha did twice as many miracles as Elijah.

He understood something that most of us with our modern, Western mindset don't grasp: God loves it when people want to partner with Him and move from the mundane to the miraculous. He enjoys showing off His power through the most unlikely of people.

The very best qualification for moving into the miraculous realm is being…*unqualified*.

Think about it.

God chose fishermen – not scholars – to change the world with the radical news of the gospel.

The Bible has been published, but God is still rewriting history. And He's doing it through ordinary people living mundane, ordinary lives.

When God decided to confront Pharaoh and bring the children of Israel out of Egypt, He didn't use a great political leader. He called a man who stuttered so much he could hardly talk.

God's ways are so contrary to the way we think, they're sometimes hard to grasp.

His strength shines best in our weakness.

As hard as it might be to believe, God called a 55-year-old pastor with a heart condition to make a radical 1500 mile ride. That proves God hasn't changed. The Bible has been published, but He is still rewriting history through ordinary people living mundane, ordinary lives.

People like me. People like you.

The Power of Helping Haiti

As I write this, the economy here in Florida remains dismal. Five years after the onset of the recession, we haven't recovered. While the national average unemployment rate is 9.1percent, here in Broward County it is 11.2percent. In Dade County it is a staggering 13.9percent. I suspect it will be years before the economic climate we enjoyed in 2007 is restored.

Churches are still shutting their doors. Ministries continue to collapse. Yet here at Oasis Church, we've experienced a strange phenomenon.

For the first time in five years we're in the black.

It doesn't make any sense! How could the economic climate of our church be so different than that in our county and state?

I believe the answer to this strange phenomenon is found in Proverbs 19:17. "He who is kind to the poor lends to the Lord, and he will reward him for what he has done."

When God called us to give out of our lack in order to help the people of Haiti, it was His way of helping them…*and us.* We didn't realize it then but God considered our gifts to them a loan to Him. And without a doubt, He has paid us back with interest!

"He who gives to the poor will lack nothing, but he who closes his eyes to them receives many curses" (Proverbs 28:27).

Helping people who are helpless and in need wherever they may be—in Haiti or anywhere else—always aligns us, as believers, with the heart of God. James 1:27 says, "Religion that our Father accepts as pure and faultless is this: to look after orphans and widows in their distress and to keep oneself from being polluted by the world."

In 1 John 3:17-18, we read, "If anyone has material possessions and sees his brother in need but has no pity on him, how can the love of God be in him? Dear children, let us not love with words or time but with actions and in truth."

In 1 Timothy 5:3 the churches were urged to, "Give proper recognition to those widows who are really in need."

Precious Promises

The Bible is filled with verses on the topic of giving. In fact, Jesus spoke more about the giving of our resources and treasure than He did on any other subject, including prayer.

For instance, "He who gives to the poor will lack nothing, but he who closes his eyes to them receives many curses" (Proverbs 28:27).

Jesus said, "For I was hungry and you gave me something to eat. I was thirsty and you gave me something to drink. I was a stranger and you invited me in" (Matthew 25:35).

"Cornelius stared at him in fear. 'What is that, Lord?' he asked. The angel answered, 'Your prayers and gifts to the poor have come up as a memorial offering before God'" (Acts 10:4).

"If you spend yourself in behalf of the hungry and satisfy the needs of the oppressed, then your light will rise in the darkness, and your night will become like the noonday" (Isaiah 58:10).

"If anyone is poor among your fellow Israelites in any of the towns of the land the Lord your God is giving you, do not be hardhearted or tightfisted toward them" (Deuteronomy 15:7).

The first thing God wanted to resuscitate after the effects of the recession was my faith.

"There will always be poor people in the land. Therefore I command you to be openhanded toward your fellow Israelites who are poor and needy in your land" (Deuteronomy 15:11).

These verses are just a sampling of what the Bible says about giving to the poor.

Helping Hands

I often think back to the day I took a deep breath and told God I would to try to raise $10,000. The memory makes me shake my head. I can see clearly now what I couldn't back then—that the first thing God wanted to resuscitate from the effects of the recession was my faith.

Obviously, it was a major undertaking. I, quite literally, had a long way to go.

Although I knew God had promised to bless those who give to the poor, when God told me to raise $50,000 for Haiti, I staggered in unbelief. Our church had been buffeted by bitter economic winds for so long that my heart sank like Peter did when he tried to walk on the water. Just as Peter took his eyes off of Jesus, I focused on what we'd lost rather than what God had promised.

My burden for Haiti, and the 3,000 miles I rode in training and making the actual journey, forced me to step out of that boatload of fear and unbelief. It launched me onto the deep waters of a growing faith where I found myself believing God would do what He promised.

Realizing I didn't need to be afraid of anything God asked me to do, I finally got it: He will always call me to do what I'm incapable of doing. His strength and grace are made perfect in my weakness.

I also learned a lot about God's character. God isn't boring. He's fun. And He will make the most tedious of times memorable.

Clearly, God's faith resuscitation plan worked.

I'm in awe of Him.

Through Bike for Haiti, Oasis Church, along with friends from Facebook and other networks raised $133,000 for Haitian children and their families. While that's not enough money to fix their broken nation, God has multiplied it among the families there like He did the fish and the loaves of bread.

He's enabled us to send medical teams to Haiti, along with thousands of dollars worth of lifesaving medication and medical supplies.

Because education is not free in Haiti as it is in the United States, we are providing scholarship funds to send children to school.

Imagine having a 70 or 80-year-old parent starving, homeless, and without medical attention.

Working with local churches, we are feeding the hungry.

One of our partners in ministry lives and works in a village where there has not been clean water for 50 years. As a result of the money raised for Bike for Haiti, those villagers now have clean drinking water.

Some of our partners have suffered through a cholera epidemic. Many lives were saved because we sent them the funds to buy the medication to rebalance electrolytes and prevent death.

In Haiti, there is no safety net for the elderly. Once they are unable to work, they have to fend for themselves. Many end up homeless and hungry. Imagine having a 70 or 80-year-old parent starving, homeless, and without medical attention.

Ephraim Lucien, a Haitian member of Oasis Church, felt the burden to change that. Working with his brothers, they started a home for the elderly in their hometown. We are partnering with Ephraim to build homes so that the elderly will be able to live out their lives in dignity.

One of the Haitian ministers we partner with took over the care and feeding of children when their orphanage was destroyed in the earthquake. For a while they lived in tents but those were destroyed. Through Bike for Haiti we're raising money to build them a permanent home.

Strength in Weakness

These are just a smattering of the things we've done with the money. Over the next 10 years, God has directed us to raise $1 million.

I am a changed man. This time when God gave me the orders, I didn't laugh or gasp. I've learned a powerful truth: *This isn't about me and what I can't do.*

It's about God.

He is well able to do abundantly more than we can ask, think, dream, or imagine.

I stepped out onto the deep waters of a growing faith that God would do what He promised.

When I set out to ride a bike from Miami to New York City, I did it to change the lives of children and their families in Haiti. I never imagined that the first life changed would be mine.

God knew; that was part of His plan.

Live a Credible Life

During my training, I often saw an 80-year-old man on a bike. That old man lapped me like I was a kid on a tricycle.

I want to become like him.

I am so changed that I expect to ride a bike until I'm too old and feeble to climb onto the saddle. Now, I *have* to get outside and ride several times a week. My body demands it. My soul needs it.

If I'm too busy to put in at least 20 miles, I feel keen disappointment.

Perhaps the biggest change I've noticed in my life is in the area of credibility. It's one thing to preach about moving out of the mundane and into the miraculous life in God.

It's another thing to do it.

Doing it earns a level of credibility that doesn't come any other way.

Drawing on that credibility, please hear what I'm about to tell you. If you haven't heard anything else, please get this.

God has a radical ride for you.

Yours may not be to help Haiti.

It may not be on a bicycle.

However, God wants to move you out of the mundane, boring Christian life.

You may never be called to a pulpit. But you are called to live a miraculous life in Christ.

Answer the call.

CHAPTER 27
A Fork in the Road

One of my favorite philosophers of all times was the former catcher for the New York Yankees, Yogi Berra. In his own, inimitable way, he made many points worth pondering. Among the best was this:

"When you come to a fork in the road, take it."

Yogi meant, of course, that we will all face life-changing choices at some point, and when we do we need to be prepared to make the right ones. Robert Frost agreed. In his poem, "The Road Not Taken," he penned these words:

"I shall be telling this with a sigh

Somewhere ages and ages hence;

Two roads diverged in a wood, and I –

I took the one less traveled by,

And that has made all the difference.[2]

I have no idea what road Robert Frost felt prepared – or pressured – to take. His family may have expected him to do the predictable and become a farmer. His peers may have pushed him to become a lawyer.

I'm so glad he took the road less traveled and became a poet.

Do you ever wonder how much has been lost because people, when faced with a choice, followed the trodden path?

What if Leonardo da Vinci had taken the road more traveled instead of becoming an artist?

What if Mozart had claimed music as a hobby instead of a passion?

On the road to Damascus, Saul was traveling a popular path. He'd joined a crowd that was determined to wipe Christianity off the face of the earth. But he came to a fork in the road and the choice he made changed everything.

It not only resulted in his name being changed to Paul, it changed him from the persecutor to the persecuted. It cost him the favor of the spiritual leaders in Israel. It put him on course to be beaten, whipped, stoned, left for dead, snakebit, and lost at sea.

It also launched him into the most profound experience known to man and propelled him into a partnership with God that rewrote the history of mankind.

One thing is very clear when reading what Paul wrote late in life. He had made the right choice. He had taken the right path.

He'd lived a life without regrets.

The human condition is fatal, but it isn't necessary to live a life of terminal boredom.

The rich young ruler, on the other hand, chose a different route. When he met Jesus at a fork in the road he wasn't prepared to give up everything and follow Him. He took the road most traveled and lost more than we'll ever know.

Proverbs 14:12 says, "There is a way that appears to be right, but in the end it leads to death."

Be careful when choosing your fork.

This book has brought you to a fork in the road.

Right here.

Right now.

The human condition is fatal, but it isn't necessary to live a life of terminal boredom.

God has created you and called you for something very specific.

You can continue on the road more traveled or you can live life without regrets.

You can do something bigger than yourself.

A Road Less Traveled

How do you do that?

You'll find the answer in Hebrews 12:1-2. It says, "Therefore, since we are surrounded by such a great cloud of witnesses, let us throw off everything that hinders and the sin that so easily entangles. And let us run with perseverance the race marked out for us, fixing our eyes on Jesus, the pioneer and perfecter of faith. For the joy set before him he endured the cross, scorning its shame, and sat down at the right hand of the throne of God."

According to those verses the first thing you must do to live a radical, regret-free life is throw off the things that hinder you. Throw off things like the economy, the balance in your checkbook, the color of your skin, your age, your education, or your health.

Second, you must understand this: *You have a race to run!* God has created you and called you for something very specific.

You haven't been called to run my race. The radical ride that God has called you to will be very different than mine, and that's good. I want you to break out of the pack.

If you don't know what radical thing God has called you to do – ask Him! He will tell you, guide you, and direct you.

Third: *Keep your eyes on Jesus!* That's the most important thing of all. It will get you started in the race, help you finish, and keep you going in the middle.

Fix Your Eyes

Once you know that God has called you to do something significant, and key people in your life confirm it, look to Jesus. Fix your gaze on Him and don't look away.

According to the Bible, the race doesn't go to the swiftest, the fastest, or in my case, the youngest. I'm grateful that's true. Many times during my training, a woman passed me like a sports car passing a semi on a steep mountain road. I was lapped twice on the same route by a 70-year-old!

Every time it happened I felt embarrassed and disheartened. But I always remembered what, Dave, a man at my local bike shop told me. "Guy," he said, "you don't have to ride fast. You don't have to beat anyone. All you have to do is pedal until you reach New York City."

That sums up the race God has called each of us to run.

Writing this book, I'm tucked away in a cottage in the Smoky Mountains. As I prepared for this second impossible call, my 9-year-old grandson, Gavyn, gave me his most sage advice.

"Poppy, just say, 'I rode some and then I rode some more. Then I rode some more. Then I rode some more. After that I rode some more until I finished.'"

No kidding, that's really great advice. It's how you fulfill the impossible call on your life. Keeping your eyes on Jesus, you start. Then you go and you go some more.

You don't have to be the smartest. You don't have to be the fastest. You don't have to be the best.

Just ride and then ride some more. After that, ride more. Keep riding until you finish.

Do It Scared

"Wait, Pastor Guy, I'm scared!"

Yeah, so was I. *Do it scared.*

God won't give you the grace for the journey until you need it. Like manna from heaven, He gives grace for each step of the way—as you take it.

Faith requires action.
The gospel demands a response.

Peter didn't have the grace to walk on water until he stepped out of the boat. The man with a withered hand didn't receive his miracle until he obeyed Jesus and stretched it out.

Faith requires action.

The gospel demands a response.

Nothing miraculous happens until we grab Jesus' robe like the woman with the issue of blood. Grab hold by faith and don't let go.

Jesus said, "Enter through the narrow gate. For wide is the gate and broad is the road that leads to destruction, and many enter through it."

Did you get that? *Only a few find it!*

The most important fork you'll ever face is the narrow way that leads to eternal life.

Choose life.

Choose Jesus.

Eternity depends on it.

Choose a Different Ending

When I think about how different my ride ended than the way I had imagined, it reminds me of the disciples. Can you imagine how they felt? They thought Jesus would usher in a new earthly kingdom. Instead, they watched Him be beaten and crucified.

Jesus, the Son of God, hung on a cross like a common criminal.

That wasn't the ending the disciples had planned. Jesus, however, knew what to expect. He knew that He, though sinless, would take the beating we deserved. He would bear the shame of our sins and failures.

Jesus did the most radical thing anyone could do. He loved us so much that He went to the cross for us.

He picked up our tab. Paid the price in full.

Jesus did the hard part. Here's your part:

1. Recognize that you have sinned. According to the Bible, we've all sinned (Romans 3:23).
2. Understand that He loves you and died for you (Romans 5:8, 12).
3. Believe in your heart and confess with your mouth that Jesus died a sinless death, bore your sins on the cross and rose again (Romans 10:10, 13).
4. Accept His gift and receive eternal life (Romans 6:23).

The Bible says that whoever comes to Jesus will not be turned away. He will give you a new life and a new reason to live. If you've never prayed this prayer, I urge you to do it now.

Heavenly Father, I confess to You that I'm a sinner and ask that You forgive me. I believe that Jesus is the Son of God. I believe with my heart and confess with my mouth that He lived a sinless life, and died on the cross to pay for my sins. He was buried and in three days rose to new life with You. I invite Jesus to be the Lord of my life. I desire to move from the mundane to the miraculous from now through eternity with You. I pray this in the name of Jesus. Amen.

When you pray that prayer you become a new person in Christ. Old things pass away and you face God and the world with a clean slate.

From the courtroom of heaven, God pounds the gavel and rules in your favor.

"Not guilty!"

Lessons From the Road

Lesson From the Road:
Finding Your Call

From Genesis all the way to the last chapter of Revelation, the Bible tells story after story of how God partners with mankind to accomplish His will on earth.

In the beginning, He created man and partnered with him in the Garden of Eden. He gave man dominion over the earth and its fullness, instructed him to tend the garden, and gave him the delightful task of naming every living creature (Genesis 1:28, 2:19).

After Adam's fall into sin, God partnered with mankind in the plan of redemption. Through patriarchs, prophets, and seemingly ordinary people like Mary and Joseph, He brought forth our Savior.

His pattern hasn't changed. Today, He wants to be in partnership with you.

It doesn't matter if you were last in your class at school. It doesn't matter if you were voted least likely to succeed. It doesn't matter if you're the CEO of a Fortune 500 company or work at minimum wage.

God has a plan for your life.

Your assignment, should you choose to accept it, is to find out what sealed orders God has woven into your spiritual DNA and fulfill that mission.

Dione Sanders, the Hall of Fame Dallas Cowboys receiver, said it this way. "If your dream isn't bigger than you, there's a problem with your dream."

1. Do you have a dream that's bigger than you are? If so, what is it?

_____
_____
_____
_____

2. What would you do if you knew you couldn't fail?

_____
_____
_____
_____

3. What things has God told you to do that you *haven't* done?

_____
_____
_____
_____

4. Small acts of disobedience can block the flow of God's plan for your life. Has that happened in your life? If so what will you do to get going again?

_____
_____
_____
_____

5. List the things that have stopped you from moving forward in fulfilling your dreams.

___

6. What desire has God placed in your heart that you have never acknowledged?

___

7. What are you going to do about it?

___

Father, please reveal the plan for my life that is impossible in my own strength. Show me each step I must take to fulfill the call. Please give me the grace to succeed. I ask this in Jesus' name. Amen.

Lesson From the Road:
Get a Team

When a business succeeds, a sports team wins a championship, or a nation breaks a monumental barrier, there is always a celebration. But we rarely remember all the people, planning, and behind-the-scenes work it took to achieve that success.

That's one thing I learned to do through Bike for Haiti. I learned to remember—and celebrate—my team. I may have been the only one who pedaled for 1500 miles, but I was acutely aware, from the first day of the trip to the last, that I could not have done it without them.

Don't get me wrong, I was determined to answer the call and fulfill my mission. I would've attempted the ride without a support team, without a SAG wagon, and without a camper. But without the team, I'm not sure I would've succeeded. I certainly wouldn't have managed to keep the same pace, the same level of protection, and raise the same amount of money.

There were so many details involved in planning and executing my radical adventure that I never could have handled them all myself. In addition to the support crew who traveled with me, there were people back home, filling the pulpit, handling my meetings, and counseling members.

Someone handled all the printed materials. Someone created the Bike for Haiti website. People wrote letters and tracked pledges. People worked behind the scenes dealing with the media.

While I was riding a bicycle, teams were putting their lives on hold to take a mission trip to Haiti.

Although the bike burden was mine, I couldn't accomplish my goal without an incredible support team.

Neither can you.

Whatever your epic journey, you will need other people to believe in you, support you, cheer for you, and pray for you.

Solomon, one of the wisest man who ever lived, said it best. "Two are better than one, because they have a good return for their labor: If either of them falls down, one can help the other up. But pity anyone who falls and has no one to help them up. Also, if two lie down together, they will keep warm. But how can one keep warm alone? Though one may be overpowered, two can defend themselves. A cord of three strands is not quickly broken (Ecclesiastes 4:9-12).

1. Make a list of everything that, as far as you know right now, must be accomplished to fulfill your mission.

_____   _____   _____
_____   _____   _____
_____   _____   _____
_____   _____   _____

2. Make a list of the people you would like to have on your team.

_____   _____   _____
_____   _____   _____
_____   _____   _____
_____   _____   _____

Father, I pray that You would call the people You have chosen to support me in fulfilling my mission. Please put the desire to help in each of their hearts. I ask that You set my team in place with the right people and the right motives. I ask this in Jesus' name. Amen.

Lesson From the Road:
Success Is in the Preparation

Preparation is boring. It's not exciting. It's not glamorous. It's not newsworthy. Yet most of the time, preparation will make or break the outcome of your mission.

Imagine an unprepared SWAT team trying to handle a crisis. Picture a president giving a speech without any preparation. Even writing this book required research, planning, time to write, and a getaway to the Smoky Mountains.

Preparation is the key to winning.

More than raw talent, it's what separates great athletes from Olympic gold medalists. And in our lives, it's part of what separates the mundane from the miraculous.

The Apostle Paul wrote, "Do you not know that in a race all the runners run, but only one gets the prize? Run in such a way as to get the prize. Everyone who competes in the games goes into strict training. They do it to get a crown that will not last, but we do it to get a crown that will last forever. Therefore I do not run like someone running aimlessly; I do not fight like a boxer beating the air. No, I strike a blow to my body and make it my slave so that after I have preached to others, I myself will not be disqualified for the prize" (1 Corinthians 9:24-27).

Notice that Paul says preparation takes *strict training*. Strict training is intensive! Without it, you will wilt in the heat, the wind, and the storms. So start training now for what is coming.

Wait on God for the radical call, but be prepared when it comes. And I don't mean just physically. Mentally prepare yourself by taking your thoughts captive and meditating on the promises of God that will give you strength to overcome.

If you're not in strict spiritual training now, you won't be ready for the intense warfare required to fulfill your assignment.

1. What kind of spiritual preparations can you start making now for your future?

   _____
   _____
   _____
   _____
   _____
   _____

2. What should you meditate on to prepare yourself mentally?

   _____
   _____
   _____
   _____
   _____
   _____

3. What kind of physical conditioning will you need?

   _____
   _____
   _____
   _____
   _____
   _____

4. How do you plan to begin your preparations?

_____
_____
_____
_____
_____
_____

Father, I thank You for being interested in every detail of the preparation for fulfilling this call. Please give me wisdom and direct all my steps. I ask this in Jesus' name. Amen.

Lessons From the Road:
Family Matters

My epic 1500 mile journey gave me plenty of time to ponder the things that are most important to me. It gave me an opportunity to reconfirm the priorities God has established; priorities that, kept in proper order, will bring balance to any life.

God first.

Family second.

That's how much family matters. You don't exalt your loved ones above God. Neither do you exalt yourself, your career, or your ministry above your family.

The members of my family were the first people I told about my radical idea. Theirs were the first opinions I asked to hear. The first prayers I requested.

Even though the counsel of friends was very important to me, there was no one whose opinions counted more to me than that of my family.

I know there are a lot of dysfunctional families; I grew up in one. I walked the streets at night to avoid an angry, abusive, alcoholic father. I should've been a statistic. That's probably why I have so much faith that what we're doing will change the lives of children in Haiti.

I'm a living example of that redemption.

My mom, essentially a single mother of four, lived 18 years with an alcoholic. Hers was an uphill battle from the start. Yet God has rewarded her faithfulness through many tough trials. Today she has been richly blessed with godly children, grandchildren, and great-grandchildren who love and honor her.

I didn't have a godly father as a role model. But I had grandfathers I admired. I had pastors who set a wonderful example in my life. Tonia's father was a children's pastor who left an imprint on my life. Often the families that matter most are not related, except by the blood of Jesus.

If you don't think your family is supportive enough, ask yourself this question: Am I as supportive and encouraging to them as I should be?

Sometimes it helps to look in the mirror.

I believe that anyone who is loving and supporting to others will receive the same back. It's all about sowing and reaping. Maybe it won't come back every time, but in the end it will return to you.

If you're like me and didn't grow up in a home like the one portrayed in the TV sitcom, *The Adventures of Ozzie and Harriet,* there is something you can do.

Rewrite your family history beginning with you.

As I typed these words, my son, Nathan, called to announce that we have another granddaughter on the way. What a blessing! What a legacy! All because I chose to rewrite my family history.

I chose not to repeat the sins of my father and inflict them on my children. Instead, I cried out to God to help me be the father to them that I never had.

All because...family matters.

1. Have you given your family the priority they deserve in your life?
   _____
   _____
   _____

2. In what ways have you been less than loving and supportive?
   _____
   _____
   _____

3. How do you plan to change that?

_____

_____

_____

4. When it comes to your epic journey, what will you share with and ask of your family?

_____

_____

_____

Father, thank You so much for my family. I ask You to teach me to be loving and supportive to them, and to help me reap back a rich harvest. I ask this in Jesus' name. Amen.

Lesson From the Road:
Sabbath or Sabotage

The idea of the Sabbath rest seems ancient. Actually, it is ancient. It was first recorded in Exodus as one of the 10 Commandments that God gave to the children of Israel. Every seventh day, they were told to take a day of rest.

The Jewish people still follow this practice.

We would be wise to do the same.

I believe "resting" is one of the most neglected disciplines of the Church today. Notice I called it a discipline. Although it may sound illogical, it truly does take *discipline* to set aside some time to rest each week, each season, and each year.

Personally, I have to work at it. I have to put it on the calendar. I have to practice taking my Sabbath rest.

I learned a long time ago that if I don't pull apart from my hectic pace, I eventually come apart. That's why I knew that I wouldn't succeed in my epic journey if I didn't take a Sabbath once a week. I needed that day to rest my body and pull aside to worship and renew my spiritual strength.

A real Sabbath rest involves resting not only the body, but the soul and spirit as well. Too often, Christians do the opposite. On the go all the time, even when we're off work most of us don't rest or worship. (If your eyes are glazing over from reading this, that's probably the reason.)

Taking time to rest and relax is one of the greatest keys to a balanced life. If we don't do it, we pay the price by sabotaging our health, our families, and our spiritual lives.

God Himself set the example. He took the seventh day of creation to rest.

Jesus pulled away for Sabbath rest too—and made sure for His disciples did the same. "Because so many people were coming and going that they didn't even have a chance to eat, [Jesus] said to them, 'come with Me by yourselves to a quiet place and get some rest…Man was not given to the Sabbath, but the Sabbath was given for man'" (Mark 6:31, 2:27).

Clearly, God gave us the Sabbath as a gift so that we could rest and be restored.

A number of years ago, the Oasis Council approved sabbatical leave for all full-time pastoral staff every five years. This is the second one I've had the privilege of taking, and I wouldn't have been able to make my radical ride or write this book without it.

If every church would do this for their full-time pastors, more of them would learn to live in the radical lane of life. Fewer of them would get burned out and leave the ministry.

Rick Warren, senior pastor of Saddleback Church and author of *The Purpose Driven Life,* said, "Balance is a key to stress management. I constantly remind my staff to – divert daily – take a mini-vacation every day to recharge."

I believe that much of the stress, nervous breakdowns, and immorality in the Church and among the clergy are because we have neglected one of God's most basic commandments.

Our lives would change and rebalance if we took a Sabbath rest one day a week. In addition, we each need to take an extended period of time off every year.

Sen. Joe Lieberman, a U.S. senator from Connecticut and a practicing Jew, wrote a book, *The Gift of Rest: Rediscovering the Beauty of the Sabbath.* He is a great example of living out his faith in and obedience to this commandment. He even turns off his BlackBerry during the Sabbath.

The bottom line is this: God created us to require our Sabbath rests. In truth, it is much more than a commandment.

It is a gift.

I don't believe you should attempt your epic journey without incorporating this rest and balance into your plan.

1. Do you observe the Sabbath rest once a week? _____
2. When you observe a Sabbath rest, do you pull apart to worship and actually rest? _____
3. Do you plan and take time away from your busy schedule to rest each year?_____
4. What should you change about your Sabbath rest?
_____

Father, I thank You for providing the Sabbath rest. Please help me to receive this gift and incorporate it into my life. I ask this in Jesus' name. Amen.

Lesson From the Road:
Life Is Short. Make It Count.

One of the greatest lessons I learned through my adventure is that regardless of age we can all do something significant. When I was young, I had all kinds of dreams and looked forward to the years ahead to accomplish them.

My philosophy has always been, life is a journey, not a sprint. Now that I'm approaching the fourth quarter of my game, most of that journey is behind me.

Life is short!

If you're young, I know that's hard to believe. Youth feels invincible. Life doesn't appear terminal. But the first time you lose a friend to a car accident or to cancer, you'll be shocked into a new reality.

As a pastor, I've preached my fair share of funerals. It's difficult to stand before grieving families wrestling with the brevity of life.

It just seems to flash by at the speed of light. One minute you're aching to start your race and before you know it you've crossed the finish line.

I like the way Jesus said it. "Now listen, you who say, 'Today or tomorrow we will go to this or that city, spend a year there, carry on business and make money.' Why, you do not even know what will happen tomorrow. What is your life? You are a mist that appears for a little while and then vanishes" (James 4:13-14).

Life is short! Make it count!

Solomon got to the heart of the matter in Ecclesiastes 12:1-8. *Remember your Creator in the days of your youth, before the days of trouble come and the years approach when you will say, "I find no pleasure in them"—before the sun and the light and the moon and the stars grow dark, and the clouds return after the rain; when the keepers of the house tremble and the strong men stoop when the grinders cease because they are few, and those looking through the windows grow dim; when the doors to the street are closed and the sound of grinding fades; when people rise up at the sound of birds, but all their songs grow faint; when people are afraid of heights and of dangers in the streets; when the almond tree blossoms and the grasshopper drags itself along and desire no longer is stirred. Then people go to their eternal home and mourners go about the streets.*

Remember him—before the silver cord is severed, and the golden bowl is broken; before the pitcher is shattered at the spring, and the wheel broken at the well, and the dust returns to the ground it came from, and the spirit returns to God who gave it.

"Meaningless! Meaningless!" says the Teacher.
"Everything is meaningless!"

Many of you reading this book are far younger, more talented, and much more gifted than I am. Others, like me, have most of your journey behind you.

None of that matters.

Don't waste your life on meaningless things.

It's wonderful to make money and find success in the world's eyes. But when you do something for God you are investing in His kingdom – and that brings eternal rewards.

Trust me: Life is short. But it doesn't have to be meaningless.

1. List the significant things you would like to accomplish in your life.

_____
_____
_____
_____

2. List the steps required to meet each goal.

_____
_____
_____
_____

3. What will you do to start now?

_____
_____
_____
_____

Father, please help me to make my life meaningful and accomplish Your plan for my days on earth. I ask this in Jesus' name. Amen.

Lesson From the Road:
It's Not a Cakewalk

The Christian walk isn't easy. Your epic adventure with God won't be a cakewalk. Just as a marathon challenges everything in a runner, life will challenge you as a disciple for Christ.

I'm telling you this because many people believe that becoming a Christian is like wearing a talisman to ward off disaster.

It isn't.

The Bible is very clear on the subject. The rain will fall on the just and the unjust. Bad things do happen to good people.

If you don't believe me, you should read the Bible for yourself.

Daniel was thrown into the lions' den.

Shadrach, Meshach and Abednego were thrown into a fiery furnace so hot that it killed the men who tossed them inside.

Paul was beaten, whipped, stoned, left for dead, shipwrecked, and snakebit.

The Bible isn't a rosy picture of a picnic in the park. The heroes of our faith faced intense spiritual warfare. Yet in the midst of their toughest times they said, "We are hard pressed on every side, but not crushed; perplexed, but not in despair; persecuted, but not abandoned; struck down, but not destroyed" (2 Corinthians 4:8-9).

I can guarantee you will face problems on your epic adventure. People will oppose you. Storms will threaten. The winds and waves of life will slap you.

I can also guarantee, if you won't quit, you'll win.

How can I say that?

Because Daniel survived the lions' den. Shadrach, Meshach, and Abednego walked out of the fire without the smell of smoke. David killed Goliath. Paul lived to a ripe old age and turned the world upside down with the gospel.

The Scriptures are filled with stories about people who faced impossible odds and won every single time: a young shepherd boy turned king who won every battle he ever fought; a nation that won every war God told them to fight; a man who prayed and the sun stood still.

How can you follow in their footsteps?

First, know what God has called you to do.

Get that settled in your heart.

Don't expect a cakewalk. Prepare for the wind, the heat, the storm.

Then keep your eyes on Jesus.

Don't quit.

Do these things and you will win your race.

1. How certain are you that God has called you to this epic adventure?

   _____
   _____
   _____
   _____
   _____
   _____

2. How can you become more settled?

   _____
   _____
   _____
   _____
   _____
   _____

3. How will you prepare for the wind, the heat, the storm?

_____
_____
_____
_____
_____
_____

Father, please help me understand that while the race You've called me to run won't be a cakewalk, through Your strength I will win if I refuse to quit. Help me prepare for the wind, the heat, and the storms. I pray this in Jesus' name. Amen.

Lesson From the Road:
Do It Scared!

I've been blatant in my honesty about the fear I battled to complete my journey. Fear was my constant companion; the enemy I had to defeat 1,000 times before I finished my ride.

Courage isn't the absence of fear.

True courage is refusing to let fear stop you.

Nike's slogan is, "Just do it!"

My slogan is, "Do it scared! Just do it!"

I was afraid of being run over by a truck, an accident resulting in death or disability.

In reality, it never happened.

I was afraid of the tall bridge near Charleston.

In reality, it was one of the highlights of my trip.

I was afraid my body would collapse – too weak to continue.

In reality, I grew stronger with each mile I rode.

Fear is a fact of life. Giving into fear is deadly.

Think about the spies that the children of Israel sent to check out the Promised Land. All 12 of them came back with reports of a land flowing with milk and honey. But 10 of them also said that the giants there were too big to conquer. Only Joshua and Caleb claimed that Israel could defeat the giants and live in the Promised Land.

Sadly, Israel agreed with the 10.

What the 10 spies said made perfect sense, but God called their negative report *evil!*

Did they report the accurate facts?

Yes.

So why was the report evil?

Because they weren't just saying that the giants were too big. They were saying that *God was too small*.

That's evil!

In Deuteronomy 20:1-4 we are told:
When you go to war against your enemy and see horses and chariots and soldiers far outnumbering you, do not recoil in fear of them; God, your God, who brought you up out of Egypt is with you. When the battle is about to begin, let the priest come forward and speak to the troops. He'll say, "Attention, Israel. In a few minutes you're going to do battle with your enemies. Don't waver in resolve. Don't fear. Don't hesitate. Don't panic. God, your God, is right there with you, fighting with you against your enemies, fighting to win" (The Message).

Jesus said, "Peace I leave with you; My peace I give to you; not as the world gives do I give to you. Do not let your heart be troubled, nor let it be fearful" (John 14:27, NASB).

The Bible admonishes us not to fear 365 times – once for every day of the year.

I'd like to let you in on a little secret.

On your epic adventure, you may need to defeat fear 365 times a day. I did.

Don't make the mistake of putting your epic adventure on hold until your fear is gone. It won't happen.

Do it scared! Just do it!

1. List the greatest fears you have about your own epic adventure.

   _____

   _____

   _____

   _____

2. How will you respond to those fears?

   _____

   _____

   _____

   _____

Father, both in life and in my epic adventure with You, help me to remember that while I may be too small to defeat the giants on my path, You are not. Grant me the strength to conquer my fear. I ask this in Jesus' name. Amen.

Lesson From the Road:
Don't Look Back

There were numerous times during my ride when for one reason or another the support team wasn't behind me. On occasion, my teammates had to leave in order to reposition the camper. Sometimes I sent them ahead for one reason or another.

Without anyone to watch my back, I found myself constantly looking into the mirror attached to my handlebar. More times than I can count, I was so concerned about what was happening behind me that I began to drift off course.

Eventually I got a revelation: *When you look back, you wander off the road!*

Focusing on the road ahead helped me stay in my lane, think, meditate, and pray.

It made an incredible difference.

Sometimes life becomes so chaotic that we need someone to watch our back so that we can stay focused on the mission. When no one is there, we must trust God and keep looking forward.

There are a lot of things that can tempt you to look back during your epic journey. Things like broken relationships and strife. Things like unforgiveness or fear for those you left behind.

Loose ends.

Tie them up and keep your eyes on the road ahead.

1. Ask God what loose ends you need to deal with so that you won't be looking back.

_____

_____

_____

Father, please reveal the things in my life that need to be dealt with so I can concentrate on Your call. Please give me grace to tie up each loose end so I can move on and fulfill Your purpose for my life. I ask this in Jesus name. Amen.

Lesson From the Road:
Be Ready for Giants

There will be giants on your path. I just thought I should warn you.

I can even tell you where to expect them. They show up as soon as you win a victory—when you're excited, relieved, and off guard.

That's when Satan is most dangerous. The enemy of our soul, he loves to attack when we least expect it.

In life and on your epic adventure, you'll be on the mountain one day, celebrating a great victory; and then things will change. You'll have a valley to cross.

The road down the mountain of success is not always easy. Nor is it easy to climb the next mountain. So you'd be wise to ask yourself these crucial questions.

Are you prepared for what follows victory?

How will you respond?

Will you become prideful or let down your guard?

Will you kick back and relax; stop pressing forward?

Never forget that you're most vulnerable at the point of your highest mountain peak.

In 1 Kings 18, Elijah celebrated one of the greatest victories a man could ever achieve. He won a power encounter against Baal, calling fire down from heaven. Then, while the idol worshipers wept in vain, he defeated 450 prophets of Baal.

But in the very next chapter, a woman named Jezebel struck such fear in him that Elijah ran for his life. When God finally got Elijah's attention He said, "Go back the way you came."

Elijah wasn't prepared for the enemy that came after him on the heels of his great victory.

I want you to be prepared.

Whether it's on your epic adventure or in business, you need to be ready for the giants and the Jezebels who will try to defeat you on your mountaintop.

God told Elijah, "Go back the way you came." At some point, most of us need to go back to what brought us success. It might have been hard work, good planning, strategic mapping, a good team...or humility.

Make sure you don't forget where you came from.

Even in victory, be ready for giants.

1. Knowing that the valleys follow mountaintops, how will you prepare for giants and Jezebels?

_____
_____
_____
_____
_____
_____

2. What brought you to the point of success? Where did you come from?

_____
_____
_____
_____
_____

3. How will you respond to success?

_____
_____
_____
_____
_____
_____

Father, I ask You to prepare me for success. Remind me to keep my guard up and not allow the giants and Jezebels to divert me from Your path. I ask this in Jesus' name. Amen.

Lesson From the Road:
Stop and Smell the Flowers

God isn't a diehard taskmaster. If you think He is, you need to get to know Him better.

In the beginning when God put Adam and Eve in the Garden of Eden, He didn't require them to toil and do hard labor. He walked and talked with them in the cool of the day. I don't think He met them with a list of Things to Do or a PowerPoint presentation, either. I suspect He had only two things in mind.

First and foremost, He loved talking to His children as much as I love talking to my sons, daughters-in-law, and grandchildren. God delighted in their companionship.

Second, because God loves beautiful things, I believe He enjoyed the beauty in the garden. Having created the heavens and the earth and pronounced them "good," I think He stopped to smell the flowers.

During my trip to New York City, my family and friends sent me texts and messages on Facebook saying, "Stop and smell the flowers." They thought I was too focused on the end of my mission to really enjoy the journey.

They were right.

Heeding their advice, I kept my eye on the prize while being sensitive to the sights and sounds around me. I enjoyed the marine base, the banners, the beaches, the old houses, and the history along the way.

I enjoyed the cornfields and the wheat fields. Once, I stopped and climbed off my bike and lay in the middle of a field of flowers. Thank God for the experience.

That's what God wants for us not only on our epic adventure, but in the journey called life.

He wants us to slow down and savor the moment.

Most of all, He wants to enjoy it with us.

1. What's your perception of God? Is He a hard taskmaster?
_____
_____

2. Do you make a habit of enjoying the moments of your life? Do you focus on the finish line and miss smelling the flowers?
_____
_____

3. What adjustments do you need to make?
_____
_____

Father, please help me to slow down and enjoy Your company. Help me to learn to smell the flowers and enjoy the incredible life You've given me. I ask this in Jesus' name. Amen.

Lesson From the Road:
Little Foxes

Pay attention to the little things.

I fell three times while riding 3,000 miles. In all three cases, it was little things that tripped me up.

A car never hit me.

A truck never ran me off the road.

I never hit a pothole and flew off my bike.

In life and during our epic rides, it's the minor oversights more than the major obstacles that cause us to stumble. Which is why Solomon wrote, "Catch for us the foxes, the little foxes that ruin the vineyards, our vineyards that are in bloom (Song of Solomon 2:15).

Any number of Bible characters can testify to how much trouble a little fox can create. For David, that fox was a glance from his balcony at Bathsheba. For Samson, it was his playful little games with Delilah. For Peter, it was the prideful boast that he would never deny Jesus.

None of those situations ended well.

For you, a little fox might be postponing Bible reading and prayer. It might start out as missing church or your small group.

Small omissions can lead to big problems. They can trip us up and send us sliding down the slippery slope into sin. Little foxes can distract us from the important things in life – our spouses, our kids, and most important – our walk with God.

Satan loves to take Christians down.

Pay attention to details.

1. What "little foxes" have tripped you up in the past?

   _____
   _____
   _____

2. What minor omissions or subtle distractions might cause you to stumble on your way to fulfilling your dream?

   _____
   _____
   _____

3. How will you pay attention to details?

   _____
   _____
   _____

Father, please help me pay attention to details. Open my eyes so that I can see the little foxes that could trip me up in my life, my career and my walk with You. I ask this in Jesus' name. Amen.

Lessons From the Road:
The Secret Weapon

In sports, a secret weapon is a surprise game-winning play. In World War II, the atomic bomb was a secret weapon.

Christians have a secret weapon. It ought not to be a secret, but too often we forget about it. We fail to use it on a daily basis.

What is the secret weapon?

Prayer.

Because of intercessory prayer, I encountered only 90 minutes of rain in 216 hours of riding—even though forecasters predicted a 30 to 70 percent chance of rain every day.

Because of intercessory prayer, I never had a single flat tire—even though I rode 1500 miles on roads that, at times, were hardly fit for cars much less a bike.

Because of intercessory prayer, I never suffered a ride-ending injury—even though I was chased by dogs, failed to unclip my shoes, and was almost sucked into the downdraft of numerous 18-wheelers.

In addition to all the things we pray about on a daily basis, the Bible admonishes us to pray for some things in specific.

1. <u>Pray for those in authority</u>. According to 1 Timothy 2:2 we are to pray, "for kings and all those in authority, that we may live peaceful and quiet lives in all godliness and holiness."

2. <u>Pray for pastors, missionaries, and ministries</u>. In Philippians 1:19 we read, "for I know that through your prayers and God's provision of the Spirit of Jesus Christ what has happened to me will turn out for my deliverance."

3. <u>Pray for friends and family</u>. Job 42:8b tells us, "My servant Job will pray for you, and I will accept his prayer and not deal with you according to your folly. You have not spoken the truth about me, as my servant Job has."

4. <u>Pray for the sick and suffering</u>. We are admonished in James 5:14, "Is anyone among you sick? Let them call the elders of the church to pray over them and anoint them with oil in the name of the Lord."

5. <u>Pray for your enemies and those who forsake you</u>. This may be the toughest one of all. In Matthew 5:44 we are told, "But I tell you, love your enemies and pray for those who persecute you."

Another tremendous passage on intercessory prayer is found in Daniel 9:1-19.

If you want to succeed at life and complete your calling in Christ, you've got to make prayer your top priority. You also need a team of intercessors praying for you.

From this day on, let the words of 1 Samuel 12:23 be the cry of your heart. "As for me, far be it from me that I should sin against the Lord by failing to pray for you."

1. At this time, what priority do you give prayer every day?

_____

_____

_____

_____

2. Do you make it a habit to pray for…

- Those in authority? _____
- Pastors, missionaries, and ministries? _____
- Friends and family? _____
- The sick and suffering? _____
- Your enemies? _____

3. Do you have people around you who are committed to praying for your success?

_____
_____
_____
_____

4. What adjustments should you make in your prayer life?

_____
_____
_____
_____

Father, please teach me to pray! And please call intercessors who will help me through prayer. I ask this in Jesus' name. Amen.

Lessons From the Road:
Live Life Without Regret

There's no joy in living a life filled with regret.

Having stood at the bedside of many people as they departed this world, I can tell you that when the end comes the saddest thing of all is the regret that comes from missed opportunities.

The last moments of life are not the time to think of all those things you should've done, could've done, and would've been if you had known then what you know now. Yet that's often when people realize how much they've missed. They see, only when it's too late, that they never moved out of the mundane and into the miraculous because they didn't think they could, or just never got around to it.

In the end, such excuses are meaningless.

Yet we often continue to cling to them because letting go means risking failure.

Our American culture discourages that. It's become so adverse to risk that most people try to avoid it at any cost. They want a bubble-wrapped ride to assure them they won't get bruised.

That attitude isn't anything new, of course. It's as old as the Bible.

Proverbs 22:13 tells us, "The loafer says, 'There's a lion on the loose! If I go out I'll be eaten alive!'" (The Message).

Ecclesiastes 11:4 warns, "Whoever watches the wind will not plant; whoever looks at the clouds will not reap."

Heed those wise words.

Don't let the risks distract you from your goal. Don't play it safe. If you do, you'll miss out not only on God's blessing, but on the most incredible adventure of your life.

Be daring. Put your faith in God. And take a risk!

Live your life without regret!

1. Looking back over your life, what regrets do you have so far?

   _____
   _____
   _____

2. As you look ahead to the end of your life, what regrets do you want to avoid?

   _____
   _____
   _____
   _____

3. How have you played it safe?

   _____
   _____
   _____
   _____

4. What are you going to do about it?

   _____
   _____
   _____
   _____

Father, please help me live my life without regrets! More than anything I want to hear You say, "Well done!" I ask this in Jesus' name. Amen.

Lesson From the Road:
Success Brings Challenges

If the fear of failure is the primary thing that keeps people from living a life without regret, the fear of success comes in second.

Success brings its own set of challenges and obstacles. While it brings excitement and euphoria – it also brings change.

In professional sports, when a team wins a championship, team members spend the entire off-season writing books, accepting awards, traveling the circuit, and negotiating new contracts. I believe that's why a winning season is often followed by a lackluster one.

Whether in business, sports, or life, most people are so busy trying to figure out how to achieve success that they aren't prepared to deal with it when it comes. They are so busy in the rat race scrambling for the top of the mountain that they don't have a plan once they get there.

How should you respond to success?

How do you follow a great victory?

Over the years, some of the biggest challenges I've encountered in leading Oasis Church have been how to follow up on success. It's challenging.

Surpassing every goal on my journey to New York City presented new challenges. Each success meant rerouting the rest of the ride, finding new places to camp, and restaging the camper. It even changed the schedule for the support crew.

Likewise, when facing your own epic adventure, don't just plan for problems. Plan for success!

1. Looking back over your life, what challenges has success brought?

   _____

   _____

   _____

2. When planning your future, what adjustments have you made for success?

   _____

   _____

   _____

3. What challenges would success likely bring?

   _____

   _____

   _____

4. How can you plan for those challenges?

   _____

   _____

   _____

Father, I pray You will not only help me through the challenges of obstacles along my path, but also give me the wisdom to know how to plan for the challenges of success. I ask this in Jesus' name. Amen.

Lesson From the Road:
Finish Well

One of my most heartfelt prayers has been that I would finish well. I wanted to finish my ride well. But even more important to me is the desire to finish this journey of life well.

I want to leave a legacy for my children and grandchildren. I don't want to be remembered as an old guy passing time until his life ended. I want to leave them a legacy of a life well lived.

A life without regrets.

I want to leave Oasis Church with a legacy of a pastor who not only started the church on September 15, 1991, but finished his course at the same church still serving Christ. That's my prayer.

In the many books and articles I've read over the years on the subject of finishing well, I've learned this: Nine out of every 10 men who enter the ministry drop out.

I don't want to become one of those statistics.

Nor do I want that for you. I want you to finish—and finish well.

To do that, however, you must first begin. If you don't begin – you will never finish.

That seems obvious, right?

Yet many people never take the first step out of the mundane and into an epic journey with Christ. They never finish their dream because they never begin.

There are a lot of reasons for that, I suppose. But the most common are fear and doubt about the ability to finish the dream.

I understand those things. I battle them every day of my life. But now, having won many such battles, I find it sad that so many people allow fear and unbelief to define them. I know from experience what they're missing. God has designed great adventures for them.

Some people start the journey and then stumble, fall, and give up. I suspect that too happens as a result of not beginning well. I suspect those people didn't launch with the tools they needed for a strong finish. No matter what the goal, there are some necessary preparations that must be made to succeed.

Lewis Carroll said it best in *Alice in Wonderland.* "Begin at the beginning and go on till you come to the end; then stop."

What a great quote.

Finishing well doesn't necessarily mean hats, horns, television and radio announcers, or bands playing. Finishing well means that you began at the beginning, kept going until you came to the end, and then you stopped.

Here's the last lesson I want to leave with you.

In order to finish well, you have to begin.

1. What will it take for you to get started? List the things you will need to do in order of priority.

   _____ _____ _____

   _____ _____ _____

2. What is your first step and when will you take it? Be specific.

   _____

   _____

   _____

   _____

Father, I pray for the person reading this book. I ask that You take them from the mundane to the miraculous in Christ. I ask that You help them not only to begin, but to finish well. I pray that they might live a life without regrets. I ask You to bless them in the name of our Lord Jesus. Amen

- Pastor Guy Melton -

Begin at the beginning and go until you come to the end; then stop.

Lewis Carroll, *Alice in Wonderland*

Guy Melton is the founder and senior pastor at Oasis Church of South Florida. A multiple campus church, Oasis is a diverse congregation with members from more than 80 nations. Pastor Guy earned a Bachelor of Science degree in Theology from Baptist University of America in Decatur, Georgia, and has done graduate work at Liberty University. He and his wife, Tonia, live in Hollywood, Florida.

Melanie Hemry, winner of the coveted *Guideposts* Writing Contest, is a writer and editor who loves to use her gift in helping bring to life the ongoing drama of God's interaction with mankind. She believes it's the most under reported story on earth. www.MelanieHemry.com

ENDNOTES

Endnotes Chapter 1:

1   "How to Buy a Child in 10 Hours." *Nightline.* ABC News. 8 July. 2008. Television.

Endnotes Chapter 27:

2   Frost, Robert. "The Road Not Taken." Poetry X. Ed. Jough Dempsey. 16 June 2003. '07 Aug. 2012. http://poetry.poetryX.com/poems/271/7.

The End

I want to be the first one to celebrate with you this step of faith you just made. And I pray that you connect with other believers and His Church to flourish in the abundant life Christ offers to those who believe in Him. I also pray that our Heavenly Father will give you a hunger to learn His Word and that His Holy Spirit will guide You as you walk and mature as His child. It is an honor to lead you to Your Savior.

> "For God so loved the world that he gave his one and only Son, that whoever believes in Him shall not perish but have eternal life." (John 3:16)

ARE YOU READY?

If you have turned to this very last page, I want to invite you to consider God's creation. He made it all good in His eyes, but as sin entered the world, brokenness also entered. However, God loved His creation so much that He sent His one and only Son to restore us back to that perfect relationship He created us for.

Maybe you have experienced the brokenness the Bible talks about: pain, heartache, loss, death, among other hardships humans experience on this side of heaven. And now you are ready to be restored and receive this wonderful relationship the Creator of the Universe desires for His children. He looks at your heart, and as you pray the following prayer, know that He sees you and hears you:

Father, I have come short of the life You want for me. You are holy. I am broken. I ask You to forgive my shortcomings, my sins, and restore me. I accept the new life and eternal purpose You offer to anyone who trusts in the gift Your Son Christ Jesus came to give: eternal life with You. I now surrender my life to YOU, the Living God. Help me and guide me to live a life according to Your parameters You have given us in Your Word of Life, the Bible. Thank You for accepting me into Your family as Your child. I love You.

If you are reading this, it means you made a generous donation to Bike for Haiti or someone on your behalf did. In any case, thank you for reading, for listening to my heart, my pain, and my whining at times. I hope it's been an inspiration to you and has spurred you on to move forward with your own journey and follow God's calling for your life. May it be as inspirational to you as this journey has been to me. May it make you sweat, cry, whine, squirm, worry, fear, and any other verb you can think of. You see, no call from God can be accepted without at least some of those things. If you have none, then you haven't yet taken the step of faith to follow God's calling in your life. If you can do something without needing God's help, then it's not of God; it's you.

Some of my staff, and lately my grandsons, have told me I still have another ride left in me. This time my two grandsons, who are now young adults, would ride it with me. They are calling it "Ride for Haiti, 80." HMMMM, not sure I'll even be alive at eighty, but we will see. There is another part of the U.S. I haven't ridden! The Northern Tier, 4,200 miles (6,759 kilometers).

To be continued . . .

It's not about a Bike. It's not about a Guy. It's about a People: Haiti.

FINAL THOUGHTS

I saved these last words until we were ready to publish the book. Many have said writing a book is like going through nine months of pregnancy and the pains of delivery. I wouldn't know; I've never been pregnant. Forgive me, ladies, for likening it to that. I didn't; others have. But I would not wish this journey on anyone.

This "pregnancy" has lasted almost seven years. For some reason, I could never complete it. I have been mere pages and paragraphs from finishing but couldn't. For some reason the thought of trying to sum this journey up has paralyzed me. I think the gravity of it still weighs on me. When I revisited the pictures, reviewed the notes I took along the way, and relived the experiences I had, for some time I was afraid to put it on paper—to reopen my heart and emotions. I'm sorry if you don't understand. Maybe someday you will.

I am now on the sabbatical our church gives to our pastors every five years and am finally penning the final words to hand off to my assistant, Katia. She will clean it up and then hand it off to others who will edit, proof, arrange, and finally put this book in your hands—you whom I have written it for.

Not because of a bike ride or a person, but because of you. You who have supported and continue to support our call to Haiti.

journey was something I couldn't get my arms around. Honestly, I still can't. As the reality of, "Okay, now starts the last month of my sabbatical. What will I do now?" set in, there was bound to be a letdown. The adrenaline I woke up to each morning for months before and during the ride was gone. Now what?

Well, first it was unloading the camper, cleaning it, and selling it. All that was daunting since for the last several months, all I had to worry about was getting on a bike and riding until I couldn't ride anymore, eating, sleeping, and getting up to ride again.

Before the chores, though, one of the most amazing things took place. Throughout the trip Corey had helped me keep things in perspective, and once again he came through. I will let my Instagram post sum up what took place in our little Hollywood home, which I called a cottage.

I posted a picture of a little wrapped three-dollar log you can put in a fireplace or fire pit. So, imagine one lonely log burning in the fire pit on our patio a few feet from our pool.

> The log had been bought in San Diego the week before the ride when we stocked up on supplies for the camper. It was to be the first of many nights of a fire at the end of a long day of riding. That's what you do in campgrounds! Well, we never used it or got to burn one fire. Late rides, late night check-ins and long days never made it possible. So tonight, while clearing the camper out, Corey hands me the log and says, "Tonight's the night." So, this fire officially ends our ride.

But for Bike for Haiti and the beautiful people of Haiti we get to serve, it's only the beginning of the next chapter. Schools built, orphanages funded, pastors supported, churches built, and roofs put on. Thousands of meals provided, lives saved physically and spiritually, and countless lives changed.

Days Ahead...
Home: Hollywood, Florida
Miles Pedaled: 0

ONE LAST LOG

Before I close this book, I want to wrap up a few more things. That day on Hollywood Beach was one I'll always remember. I had dipped my tires in the Pacific Ocean in San Diego, California, sixty-three days prior. Now I plunged into the Atlantic, riding uniform and all, and took the bike with me. I had seen guys who had ridden cross-country do that in South Carolina during my first ride, and that feeling was one I had dreamed about.

But then to look up from the water and see one of my beloved partners, Pastor Jephthe Lucien, and his brother, Ephraim, standing on the banks of the Atlantic waiting to welcome me home and to thank me on behalf of the Haitian people they minister to blew my mind. I don't know if I can ever get over that feeling.

After saying our goodbyes, we drove over the Hollywood Bridge to our home in Hollywood Lakes. The relief of being home after experiencing this

The picture taken of that embrace was special the day it was shot, but it is even more so now. A couple of months later later she would be diagnosed with pancreatic cancer and live only three more weeks. It still hurts to think of it, but that embrace sums up the kind of mom I had. She was my greatest cheerleader.

Then came Tonia's embrace—and my realizing she did not have to pray for my safety on the highways of the places she had never seen, not knowing the dangers I would face day to day. It had been a burden to me, knowing my mom and my wife worried about me. I had put them through so much. Their hugs that day were healing for me and for them, I believe. Even as I write this many months later, tears are flowing down my face. I can hardly see the screen to type as I remember that day and the love I felt from so many. And mostly, the love I felt for my Haitian friends.

our Oasis family has continued to support the cause and send down our resources. So many have given and continue to give to Bike for Haiti.

The faces, the posters, and the signs were a sea of jumbled love as I pedaled those last few strokes of Bike for Haiti, the Southern Tier of the United States. In my mind I can still see them today. The love I felt. The emotions. I wish I could share my feelings on paper, but they were too powerful. Even a picture can't express them. Unlike the arrival in NYC when there was no media or fanfare to meet me, this time our local TV station arrived to document the event and to share its purpose: Haiti.

As they say, you just had to be there. Yes, I have pictures on my social media. We still have our Bike for Haiti Facebook and Instagram. Even though they are pretty silent at the moment, the pictures of those days and the arrival home remind me of the tremendous feat God had done, not just through me and the many guys who drove the camper and took care of me and the bikes but also through the team of hundreds who continue to support the people of Haiti to this day.

I have to mention a few personal moments that took place as we reached Charnow Park pavilions and the historical paddleball courts I played on as a kid. Probably the most vivid memory is my mom standing there waiting to give me a hug, and my brother, Tracy, who was there on vacation with his daughter, Kari, and her family. I often look at the picture someone took of me embracing my mom, knowing how relieved she was to have me safely home. She never wanted me to do the first ride to New York and almost disowned me when I told her of this one. She feared for my life and could not understand how I could do such a stupid thing at my age—at any age. But she was there, more relieved than I was to have me safely home.

Day: Final

Hollywood Beach Broadwalk, Florida

Miles Pedaled: 0

HOME

I was home.

It seemed surreal coming around the corner of A1A and Garfield Street and seeing several hundred people lined up on both sides with banners, screaming and cheering and showing more love than I could have ever dreamed of—more than I ever deserved. While I was grateful they showed up, I am humbled when something like this takes place because I am not that good.

I don't deserve all God has blessed me with. It's very awkward, even embarrassing. The real heroes are our friends in Haiti loving one another, working to survive—our partners who tirelessly minister each day to hundreds who are hungry, hurting, and dying with little hope. I salute them. My Haitian friends, I can only say this homecoming was for you. I applaud you, and I love my beloved Haiti, which I've not been able to see now for several years. As I pen these words at the end of riots, unrest, a pandemic, and a president being assassinated, I declare that someday I will return. Thankfully, though our trips were canceled through those times,

still desire to (and, at times fear not being able to) finish well. I don't want to be that proverbial runner who leads the race and is tripped up in view of the finish line, never to complete the race. Until we breathe our last on this earth, we must strive to finish well—to enter heaven and hear our Master say, "Well done, my good and faithful servant."

I finished this riding journey. My journey. Now many months later as I write these final words, the same question persists: How will I finish my earthly journey? I get to decide the answer. So do you.

What's your journey? What race has God called you to? What have you begun and not finished? What is He calling you to do that fear is paralyzing you from starting, much less finishing? I would rather start what God has called me to do and stumble along the way than to never try, to never start. If you've started, finish well. If you haven't, start the work God is nudging you toward.

Quit waiting. This is your sign. Do it. Do it now, and someday you will look back and have a sense of gratification knowing you did what God called you to do.

become boring. But not this day. Today it was a ride of twisted emotions, thoughts, and expectations. Who would be there at Hollywood Beach?

Or would it be a disappointment like the NYC trip when I got to Manhattan and hardly anyone was there to meet me? This time I held my expectations in check and kept reminding myself I was doing this for the children and the beloved people of Haiti. It would have been easy to let the hype of a ride across the country, and all the social media comments, distract from the real reason I was doing this in the first place.

Those last 2 miles (3 kilometers) seemed like an eternity. Logistics kept stopping us—riders falling behind, riders getting stuck on bridges. So many things kept us pulled over to the side of the road. It seemed to me like hours but was probably more like thirty minutes.

Our church family had gathered at the pavilion on the beach. I had no idea at the time that this would be something etched in my mind until I breathe my last.

This was our final stretch after several million pedal strokes over ten states and 3,200 miles (5,150 kilometers).

TODAY'S REFLECTION:

2 TIMOTHY 4:7

I have fought the good fight, I have finished
the race, I have kept the faith.

Nothing is more fitting than to use this verse to end an amazing journey, a journey that began so many months prior when the seeds to do this germinated in my mind before I could ever speak them aloud.

One of the themes of my ministry is "finishing well." I want that. I'm in my fourth quarter, maybe in the final two minutes—only God knows. But I

Ten miles (16 kilometers) from home. As I approached the Pier Sixty-Six Hotel on 17th, which connects the mainland with the beach on the north end of Port Everglades, I began to get nervous, even giddy, knowing I would be able to see Hollywood Beach from the top of the bridge. On a normal day, the bridge looks tall and daunting. I don't even remember pedaling to the top this day. It was the most exciting bridge I had ever crossed even though I hate bridges, a fact I've shared with you many times.

For some of the group riding together, the bridge was the end. The Oasis shuttle that had brought many up to meet me began to pick them up as the miles went by and their legs gave out. That bridge had some interesting stories, but I won't share them here out of love for my friends who were beaten by her.

I could recount story after story of the landmarks from the bottom of the bridge on to the end we had passed during our first trip five years before, riding to NYC—the Starbucks where we stopped for our first break, the school where one of our family held signs cheering us on, the road some gave up on in their first hour even though they had planned to ride to West Palm Beach with us. (The names and details are in our first book, *Lessons from the Road.* I'll leave it there.) Then there was Dania Beach, where my father had a farmers' market that I helped in as a seven- and eight-year-old, and the condo my mom lived in for years at the Dania Jai Alai. We spent holidays there when my kids were small.

Finally, we rode the Dania Beach Bridge and onto A1A heading south. Only two miles (3 kilometers) left. I had ridden this stretch of the beach through John U. Lloyd Beach State Park, and along the intracoastal area to Port Everglades to prepare for both this and my NYC rides. It was a section I could ride with my eyes closed. I had traveled this route so much, it had with a few teens, would take their Saturday to ride with me down the busy, rainy roads of A1A to Hollywood was reason enough to get started. But add to that the excitement of seeing Tonia, other family members visiting Hollywood Beach, and my mom, and I had even more reason to get going. No, rain would not deter us.

Corey had the drone set up and took incredible pictures along the beach as we passed by a park I had visited with my mom and dad as a little kid. As an adult, I took my boys there and hosted youth retreats when I was a youth pastor. Hugh Taylor Birch State Park had lots of fond memories and one significantly bad one.

When I, a youth pastor in my twenties, took our high school seniors there to celebrate their graduation, I still did everything the teens did. I love football and played it in high school. Yes, I love football. Did I say I love football? Because I do. So, when the young guys got a pickup game going, I was in the middle of it. Partly, no doubt, to show them I still had the hands to catch a long pass and the speed to beat them to the goal line. Whatever the reason, I played.

In those days, I would always take off my wedding ring while playing sports since bad things happen to fingers with rings on them. I handed it to the most trustworthy senior I knew. You have already guessed where this is going. He lost it, and it was never found again. Needless to say, Tonia was not excited to see me that night. Thankfully, years later, she won a beautiful men's diamond ring. I still wear it today. We could have never afforded it when we bought that 79-gold band back in 1975.

So yes, this ride by Hugh Taylor Birch State Park brought back lots of memories. It's ironic that Corey took the footage without knowing how special that spot was.

Day 63

Red Reef Park Beach to Hollywood Beach, Florida

Miles Pedaled: 30

FINAL STROKES

As we mount for our final thirty miles, this is my view! We will ride today, rain, tropical storm, or hurricane! We WILL ride! God's cooling the air. Bring it on!

This was my social media post as we began the short but exciting last leg of our 3,200-mile (5,150-kilometer) trip from California. The view from our camper that morning was gloomy and dark. It was raining "cats and dogs," as they say in the South. Any other day I would have waited it out—it was that bad. It was the worst rain since the terrible day in Texas when everything went wrong. But this day, it was "ride or die." No way would anything keep me from finishing.

One reason I was so determined was that more than twenty of our Oasis family were staging their bikes about 5 miles (8 kilometers) south to ride with me for the last 20 to 25 miles (32 to 40 kilometers) of the trip. I had missed my Oasis family so much. To think these men and women, along like yesterday, traveling 55 miles (89 kilometers) after leaving Oasis Church. I was emotionally and physically drained and had not yet had my breakthrough. I was overcome with exhaustion. Johnny and José, the guys who had ridden with me all this day, were going to leave me, and reality had set in. I had 1,400+ miles (2,253+ kilometers) to ride by myself.

It was hard that first night in the camper—a lonely night in Jonathan Dickinson State Park. Very different from tonight, since I am ending, not beginning, my journey. I could have never planned it this way, but God always looks after the tiny details long before we ever know it.

This had been one of the shortest rides of the entire trip, but it left me 30 miles (48 kilometers) from home as we began our final and last day. Day 63.

Now off to a birthday party.

TODAY'S REFLECTION:

JEREMIAH 1:5

"Before I formed you in the womb I knew you."

God is always a step ahead of us on our journey. For me, it was the unforeseen child stopping us on the side of the road to give a donation to boost my spirits, the friends who arrived unexpectedly to encourage me, or the memories relived of my first ride as I ended my second. God is into details. He knows you. He knows your needs and desires. He loves you and wants to bless you. After all, isn't that what a father does?

He knew you before you were born. He knew the trials you would go through, and He knew how He would make a way out of them. He sees you. He loves you. And He is working out the details long before you are aware of it.

Trust Him.

Day 62

Jonathan Dickinson State Park to Island of Palm Beach, Florida

Miles Pedaled: 36.43

DAY 62

Like few others, day 62 began before sunrise. After staying the night at Jonathan Dickinson State Park—the same place we had stayed on the first night of our New York trip—in order to be able to spend the evening for my grandson's birthday, I made an early start, which is not easy for me. Thanks to Bruce and Corey for making it happen. They set the alarm for 5:30 a.m. and pried me out of bed. This would be one of the last two nights I would sleep in the camper that had brought me from the beaches of San Diego. I'd be so happy to sleep in my own bed in a few nights.

We had rain showers on and off all day—some heavy. It had rained more in the previous twenty-four hours of riding than it had my entire ride to NYC.

Day 62 was in the books. It was one of the most beautiful rides of the entire trip as I pedaled past storybook-looking mansions, some of the most expensive real estate in the USA. The highlight of the day was stopping at the northern end of the island of Palm Beach, the same place I had ended the first day of our trip to New York City. In certain ways, it seemed

What a journey it had been—as challenging and rewarding as anything I've ever done. Life is a journey, yet every day, each small step builds on another. Don't despise the small steps you take today. Don't underestimate the faith decision that scares you. It will be part of the foundation, the cornerstone, as Zechariah alluded to when they built the Temple.

Make each decision one of prayer, girded by faith, and trust in our God, who is able to do beyond anything you and I can ever imagine. That day north of the Jupiter Inlet, God gave me a big breakthrough. Looking back, it was only a small beginning of what He was doing in Haiti through Bike for Haiti, which as I write this has now raised over one million dollars.

Don't be afraid to step out to do what no one else has done and what no one thinks you should do. Trust God. When He gives you peace, it's the right decision. Yell at the top of your lungs, "I can do this; I can do this; I can do this . . ."

Even better, I should have yelled, "*We* can do this; *we* can do this; *we* can do this," because we, in reality, can't do anything without God. Amen.

or construction worker thought I was crazy or drunk, but I was so full of emotion, I could not keep it to myself.

Up until that point I had experienced so many questions, fears, and doubts. Yet I pushed through. I didn't see the breakthrough coming, but I could still feel the emotion even now, years later. I realized the enormous task I had undertaken was going to happen. It was possible! I'm so glad this revelation came so early and so unexpectedly.

Now here I was, almost 4,500 miles (7,242 kilometers) later after riding to NYC and close to completing my journey from San Diego, California. I was back where it had begun. Life is a journey of small steps that build on each other. If I had not received the peace and strength from God to get beyond the fears and doubts of the first day of riding to New York City, I would have never considered riding across the country five years later. To imagine God had brought me back to the same exact path was beyond words.

This would be my last full day of riding. The next day, I'd go spend the day with my grandson Gavyn, who would be turning fourteen, so I'd just ride a half day. Then, Lord willing, as I wrote on my social media post this day, I'd complete the full journey with another half-day ride to Hollywood Beach.

TODAY'S REFLECTION:

ZECHARIAH 4:8–10 (MSG)

> After that, the Word of God came to me: "Zerubbabel started rebuilding this Temple and he will complete it. That will be your confirmation that God-of-the-Angel-Armies sent me to you. Does anyone dare despise this day of small beginnings? They'll change their tune when they see Zerubbabel setting the last stone in place!"

Day 61

Sebastian Inlet to Jupiter Inlet, Florida

Miles Pedaled: 81.06

"I CAN DO THIS; I CAN DO THIS; I CAN DO THIS . . . "

I must admit that this day was full of emotions, nostalgia, and excitement all rolled up into a ball of nerves and anticipation. There was so much to think of and reminisce about, it's hard to put it into words without taking pages to do so. This riding segment was almost identical to my first Bike for Haiti trip riding to New York City, except five years before, I was in only my second day.

I'll never forget that first time here I was on Hutchinson Island, having just begun my ride from Jupiter Inlet. As I maneuvered through the morning beach traffic and construction, God gave me the peace to know He was there. At that moment, I finally realized I could do it. I could ride all 1,500 miles (2,414 kilometers) to New York City. Right then I began to shout as loud as I could, "I can do this; I can do this; I can do this!" I don't know how long or how many times I yelled it, but the excitement and joy were so powerful I just kept shouting it. I am sure more than one driver

There is *no* security in this life outside of God Himself. May we embrace Him and give our lives to Him until our "puff" is gone. May our pile be given to others while we live.

Open hands instead of clenched fists.

ridden from Florida to Maine and toured France and the United Kingdom on bikes. They are amazing. They were such a great help with supplies, support, and information for me on both my rides. I love them. What a blessing to have them drive from Miami to Melbourne to ride with me for a while. It was a great encouragement.

TODAY'S REFLECTION:

PSALM 39:5

You have made my days a mere handbreadth; the
span of my years is as nothing before you. Everyone
is but a breath, even those who seem secure.

David reminds us our lives are short, so we need to make them count. In Psalm 90:12 he said, "Teach us to number our days, Lord."

The Message paraphrase of Psalm 39:6 says this:

"Oh! We're all puffs of air. Oh! We're all shadows
in a campfire. Oh! We're just spit in the wind.
We make our pile, and then we leave it."

Wow! If this doesn't paint a perfect picture of twenty-first-century humans in the USA, I do not know what does. We accumulate so much stuff just to leave it to—as the Bible says in Matthew 6:19—rust, burn, and be stolen. The more we hold on to our stuff, the more we lose it. The more we give away, the more God gives us. That is the biblical way to live.

Make everyday count. *Carpe Diem,* as they say. Seize the day. At my age and stage of life, which I like to say is the fourth quarter, I have more passion than ever to make my life count—to make an eternal difference in the lives of those around me, those I serve at Oasis, and my friends in Haiti.

Day 60
Sebastian Inlet to Oak Hill, Florida
Miles Pedaled: 92.67

SPACE AND TREASURE COASTS' RIDE

I love the Space and Treasure Coasts of Florida. The locals have given each beach in the area their own names—ten in all. I've now ridden from the First Coast to the Gold Coast. Most do not know that Florida has over 1,200 miles (1,931 kilometers) of coastline, by far the most in the United States. It's an amazing state, and I've ridden all the eastern coastlines from Pensacola to Jacksonville to Miami to Key West.

On this day I didn't make a century. I didn't need the miles to finish my ride in a few days. The humidity was typical Florida—nearly 100 percent, the weather guys said—92°F (33°C), and felt like 100°F (38°C).

While in the Melbourne Beach area, I had another surprise—the highlight of the day. One of my good pastor friends, Russell Johnson, who pastors Global Church, a bilingual church in North Dade County, was waiting for me on the side of the road. He had coordinated with my son and our team to join me for a few hours of riding. Russell and his wife, Bev, have

countries do not have drinking water. There are still one *billion*—yes, billion with a *B*—people around the world who do not have clean water to drink. Remember that when you shower tonight and use the 150 gallons (568 liters) that go down the drain. How convicting is that?

When we fast from food, we can better understand what Jesus is saying. I fasted a week while writing the beginning of this book, and I can vouch for that. Nothing makes me hunger for righteousness more than when I am fasting. There is something about giving up the physical food my body craves that causes me to crave more of God, His food, His Word, His Spirit.

May we all thirst and hunger for righteousness.

the exact way I had done on the first trip going to NYC. Every day was different in almost every way, but this is one of the easier changes—just reversing our direction.

The first day of our Reunion Ride was just 45 miles (72 kilometers), but it put me in the perfect position to make it to Hollywood Beach by the weekend, hopefully by Saturday afternoon if all went well.

TODAY'S REFLECTION:

MATTHEW 5:6

"Blessed are those who hunger and thirst for righteousness, for they will be filled."

Three times this past year, I have visited the mountainside where Jesus brought the Sermon on the Mount. This sermon takes on a more personal experience when you sit in the place where it was given and imagine Jesus speaking these words on the hillside, which has not changed in the last two millennia. If you have not gone to Israel and experienced the Holy Land, you must. It will be life-changing. You will never read your Bible the same again.

Many believe the Sermon on the Mount is the greatest sermon of all time. Within His words delivered on the hillside on the northern shores of the Sea of Galilee are what we know as the Beatitudes. None are more important than this verse.

The people of that day could relate to hunger and thirst. They did not have supermarkets or bank accounts as we do today. For many, every day was a fight for survival, much as it is for many in Haiti. They do well to get a piece of bread or maybe some rice. If they are extremely fortunate, they get some type of meat once a week. Many in Haiti and other third-world

Day 59

Ormond Beach to Oak Hill, Florida
Miles Pedaled: 45.47

REUNION RIDE

On day 59 we began our eighth and final week of Bike for Haiti. I called it the "Reunion Ride" since it's the exact route I had taken five years before as I rode north from Hollywood, Florida, to New York City. On that occasion, it was the start of a long journey, new to me with lots of unknowns. This time, I enjoyed the ride much more, knowing I'd almost made it home, accomplishing a goal I never imagined—riding coast to coast, 3,200 miles (5,150 kilometers) on a bicycle at the age of sixty. Only God.

Today would be a short ride. We got a late start after visiting our teens at camp, but then we made our way down the beautiful coastal beach cities of central Florida.

After I finished the day's ride, we drove a while longer for our stop that night to stay at our son Nathan's home at Indian Harbour Beach, just south of Cocoa Beach. It was worth the extra drive to see him and his family. I began my ride south and then went north on this one segment,

A side note: Tonia and I were both at the same camp the year we surrendered to full-time ministry. We did not know each other at the time. She came with her church from Jacksonville, and I was with my church from South Florida. We did not even know we had attended the same camp that year until long afterward. Only God.

TODAY'S REFLECTION:

GALATIANS 6:7–9

> Do not be deceived: God cannot be mocked. A man reaps what he sows. Whoever sows to please their flesh, from the flesh will reap destruction; whoever sows to please the Spirit, from the Spirit will reap eternal life. Let us not become weary in doing good, for at the proper time we will reap a harvest if we do not give up.

For a person who lives off the land, this principle means everything. We do not eat what we do not plant. We do not eat what we do not raise. It's that simple.

As Christians, we do not produce what we do not possess. If we feed the Spirit of God in us, we will reap spiritual rewards. If we live for our fleshly desires to please ourselves, that is what we will receive. If we know Jesus, we know love. If we know love, we will give love. If we live in the Spirit, the fruit of the Spirit will be evident in our lives. Whatever we sow into our lives is what we will reap.

The Christian life is not easy. It's not easy to live for God when everything else points the opposite direction, but the apostle Paul reminds us if we do not give up, we will reap a harvest in God's timing.

Don't give up living for God even when you don't see the result. Trust Him.

Day 58
Pensacola, Florida
Miles Pedaled: 0

WEEK 8 BEGINS AT CAMP

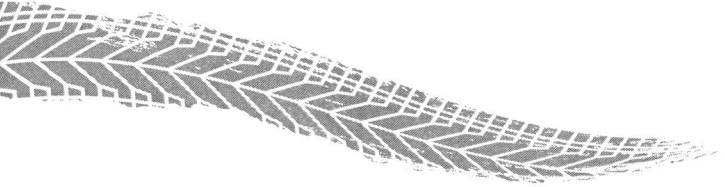

Week 8 began with a trip to camp to be with our teens for a few hours. Then we headed out for a late start to begin our final sprint to the end of Bike for Haiti Part 2. As Tonia and I closed out this incredible birthday/anniversary weekend, I left her in Pensacola with her parents and returned to the east coast.

Summer camp is the most important part of a young person's spiritual journey as far as I am concerned. Tonia and I both surrendered our lives and were called to full-time vocational ministry while we were junior high schoolers at camp. Camp has always been a major part of my ministry because of what it meant in my life. I've seen hundreds of lives changed, and I look forward each summer to spending a few days with our youth at camp.

Being on the ride this year, I did not think I would get to see them, but it worked out perfectly since my ride route was not far from camp in the north central part of the state. Even though I would spend only a few hours with the kids, I wanted them to know I was thinking about them.

Neither of us would recommend marrying so young, but it was the right thing for us. I remember when our oldest son, Jim, turned nineteen, Tonia called her mom and said, "What were you thinking letting me get married so young?" I'll never forget her mom's response: "Oh, you and Guy were old even at nineteen."

We have had a lot to learn, but we had a calling on both our lives to follow Jesus and to be in full-time vocational ministry, so why not? So far, so good. It's not been easy pedaling this two-seater bicycle, but I would not choose anyone else to ride with me. It's definitely been a cross-country ride, but she has been with me every pedal of the way. A true life "built for two."

I love you, Babe. Happy anniversary! From the sunset in Santorini to the sunset tonight over Mobile Bay, it's been an incredible ride.

TODAY'S REFLECTION:

ACTS 20:24

> However, I consider my life worth nothing to me;
> my only aim is to finish the race and complete
> the task the Lord Jesus has given me—the task of
> testifying to the good news of God's grace.

In our marriage, this is our prayer. Our life has been incredible. We could have never dreamed forty-seven years ago (as of the publishing of this book) that God would do so much in us and allow us to see Him work in so many ways.

As Paul says, we do not count our lives to be nearly as important as the race God has called us to. We are determined to finish the race well, as Paul did.

Day 57

Magnolia Springs, Alabama
Miles Pedaled: 0

A BICYCLE BUILT FOR TWO

As we celebrated our anniversary, Tonia gave me a card. I wish I could show you the picture. It was a bicycle built for two, and the words said, "Life Built for Two." That it is. What a perfect thought.

One thing Tonia had made clear to me since I began to ride for Bike for Haiti was that she would not ride with me. She will ride her beach cruiser with the little girly basket to Hollywood Beach, but none of those crazy rides. I have even offered the two-seater and to do the pedaling. *Nope!* Simple as that. I have pretty much given up that she will ever come with me on any long ride.

However, one thing that is 100 percent true is that she has been pedaling with me every step of the way for forty-one years since we said "I do" on that platform in our home church in West Hollywood, Florida, when we were married on her nineteenth birthday. *Wow!* Just kids.

Seeing the uncertainties about this ride when we went on our scouting trip ramped up her anxiety. Bicyclists are hit and killed in South Florida almost weekly. Biking can be dangerous in this day of drugs, cell phones, and texting. I could understand why it worried her for me to take this ride, but as she always tells people when they ask about my crazy ideas, "I just try to stay out of his way!"

Happy birthday and happy anniversary, Babe. Forty-one years, no regrets. I would do it again today. I love you, Babe.

TODAY'S REFLECTION:

ACTS 16:14

> One of those listening was a woman from the city of Thyatira named Lydia, a dealer in purple cloth. She was a worshiper of God. The Lord opened her heart to respond to Paul's message.

God does it again. Yes, this verse was in line for the next devotional before I knew what I was writing for today's update. Lydia was one of the most respected women in the New Testament early church. Not only was she an entrepreneur in business, but she and her husband also started a church in their home. She was not just a worshiper but also a faithful wife. After receiving Paul's message, she invited him and his team into her home. She must have been an amazing woman.

This could have easily been my wife. Lydia's name could have been Tonia. She is a faithful servant, wife, mom, and "Tata" to our grandkids. My ministry is her ministry. I am in front, but she is a rock star to all who know her. When our legacy is written, she is the one who will be credited with so much that God has done through our lives. She is truly a Proverbs 31 woman.

Day 56
Point Clear, Alabama
Miles Pedaled: 0

HAPPY BIRTHDAY— HAPPY ANNIVERSARY

On this day, Tonia and I celebrated our forty-first anniversary, and I celebrated her birthday. Yes, we were married on her birthday. She had always dreamt of doing it that way. Every year I get hit with a double whammy of two special days. And double the presents. No . . . just because we celebrate two occasions on the same day doesn't mean there is one present. Try doing that to your spouse. You may not make it to your next anniversary!

Many years after we were married, I committed to Tonia never to shortchange her special days. I have tried to hold to it and think I've done pretty well to this point. Hence, forty-one years of marriage. Yes, we were married as just kids!

This anniversary was a little more special than most. To be away from her for two months while on the road in a camper with guys had been tough. I hate leaving her even for a few days, although she likes an occasional break from me. I don't know why though.

TODAY'S REFLECTION:

LUKE 9:23–24

> Then he [Jesus] said to them all: "Whoever wants to be my disciple must deny themselves and take up their cross daily and follow me. For whoever wants to save their life will lose it, but whoever loses their life for me will save it."

When I planned today's update on Mike Riddering's martyrdom, I had no idea this passage was next on the list of daily verses that Nathan sent me. I promise. Don't tell me God doesn't order and plan every step and event in our lives. These verses are perfect for Mike's life and his willingness to give up his earthly life for eternity, where he is now celebrated as one of the great martyrs of faith.

Enough said. Let these verses and Mike's story sink in today.

schools for single women—the list goes on and on. Truly, I have never seen so much done in such a short length of time.

Mike's life was cut short months before this ride. Not long after his death, Amy, with their two adopted Burkinabè children, returned to Africa to continue their mission. I was concerned her monetary support would run out and their many projects would stop. I felt God telling me to give a portion of the donations of this ride to Amy and the ministry in Burkina Faso, so we announced to our Oasis church family that 10 percent of all the monies raised from Bike for Haiti would be tithed to Mike and Amy's mission in order for it to continue. We even included his picture in the Bike for Haiti graphics we put on the camper.

I remember one day in the Arizona desert when the ride had been hot and long—I think the temps were over 100°F (38°C). We came upon a small town and stopped to have lunch. As I mounted the bike on the back of the camper, I saw Mike's picture. Emotion overcame me. I dropped to the ground next to his image and wept. The thought that this man gave his life for the calling to follow Jesus humbled me so much. All I was doing was sweating and riding a bike. He gave his life. I still get emotional from remembering that day. Only Corey saw the moment as he walked up to help me with the bike. He thought I was having a nervous breakdown. He had seldom, if ever, seen me sob so deeply I could hardly breathe.

I am glad to report that we continue to support Amy in West Africa and have given to a special project to build a preschool building for one hundred Burkinabè children out of our tithes from Bike for Haiti.

Day 55

Magnolia Springs, Alabama

Miles Pedaled: 0

REMEMBERING MIKE

While taking a few days off with Tonia over the weekend, I had time to reflect on the previous two months since I had left San Diego's Ocean Beach. One of the most poignant memories I had was a component of the ride many may have forgotten.

In January 2016, one of our missionaries to Burkina Faso, West Africa, was martyred by Islamist extremists while having coffee with a local pastor. Mike was one of the most amazing persons and missionaries I've ever known. He and his wife, Amy, had been in Africa for only four years. They had sold everything, left their two young adult girls in college, and moved to this poverty-stricken country few have even heard about.

Mike and Amy oversaw an orphanage and a school of over four hundred students and began a host of initiatives, from digging wells in villages to doing hydroponic gardening, setting up medical clinics, starting sewing on the bottom of my clip-on shoes, and for driving. You are the man! Chris, thanks for being his assistant and getting my bike ready every day, along with the other things that go with it. You were a blessing to us.

TODAY'S REFLECTION:

JOHN 10:18

> "No one takes it from me, but I lay it down of my own accord. I have authority to lay it down and authority to take it up again. This command I received from my Father."

Jesus had one focus when He came to this earth: to lay down His life for His sheep. Earlier in John 10, He calls Himself the Good Shepherd and shares His love for His sheep. I'm so glad He chose to come and lay down His life for me. I don't deserve His love. I don't know why He did it, but I'm so thankful.

As we approach the end of our journey across the United States, my heart breaks for those who do not know the Good Shepherd. I do not want to be guilty of not sharing God's love with my friends in Haiti or not making sure you who are reading about my cross-country journey hear of the one I will take someday when I leave this earth.

The Bible tells us in John 3:16 that God loved the world so much that He sent His only Son to die for our sins so those who believe would have everlasting life. That is you, and that is me. I hope you know Him. If you don't, at the end of this trip I will share how you can. You can turn to the *last page* now and accept Jesus, our Good Shepherd, who laid down His life for us.

Day 54
Ormond Beach, Florida
Miles Pedaled: 0

MAP 7 COMPLETE; WEEK 7 IN THE BOOKS

On day 54, I began a long weekend off to celebrate Tonia's birthday and our anniversary. I drove back from the east coast of Florida to Pensacola, where she was with her parents. Then I would spend a few days with her in Magnolia Springs, Alabama, just over the line. This was a long way from where I finished my seventh week of Bike for Haiti, but well worth it to spend some time with my babe and celebrate *our* special day and *her* special day. As I headed her way, I knew my body would appreciate some rest. I couldn't wait to sit on a swing in a bed-and-breakfast in this quaint little town on the Alabama coast. It was a long way from sleeping in my camper in the middle of nowhere or in a Walmart parking lot.

This had been a short week of riding. I want to thank my support team of Kevin, Chris, and Corey for all you did to allow me to ride and to reach this point so I could take some days off. I was glad Chris could ride with me on one of the days. Kevin rode about one tenth of a mile (0.16 kilometers), but hey, it's a start. Thanks for fixing all the flats and the cleats

of Bike for Haiti—not just to feed children or educate them but also to let them know that someday they can live in a mansion and worship the One who created them—a place of awe and wonder for all those who love Him and accept Him as Lord and Savior.

Holy, holy, holy, Lord God Almighty.

from our first ride. I loved the unspoiled beach and the little old town with the village feel. It's one of those places you want to return to and spend the day. Not this day, though.

Two months before, as I dipped my pedals in the Pacific and rode out of San Diego, I could not imagine reaching the east coast of Florida. It was a dream, and a scary one at that.

I had survived and couldn't wait to get home. It was all downhill after this, baby.

TODAY'S REFLECTION:

> REVELATION 4:2–3, 8
>
> At once I was in the Spirit, and there before me was a throne in heaven with someone sitting on it. And the one who sat there had the appearance of jasper and ruby. A rainbow that shone like an emerald encircled the throne. . . . Each of the four living creatures had six wings and was covered with eyes all around, even under its wings. Day and night they never stop saying: "'Holy, holy, holy is the Lord God Almighty,' who was, and is, and is to come."

From the very first Bike for Haiti, every mile, every map, every minuscule or monumental achievement, and every pedal stroke were fueled by the thought of bringing the hope of Christ to our beloved Haiti. Yes, I can't help but think of our Haitian friends who live in such poverty on this earth but believe wholeheartedly that those who receive the Living Water through our mission will someday live with me in heaven. What a day that will be! This passage gives us a beautiful picture of what we have to look forward to.

The many persecuted, enslaved, and hurting people throughout the world have this same great hope that is promised to each of us. This is the purpose

Day 53

St. Augustine to Ormond Beach, Florida

Miles Pedaled: 48.9

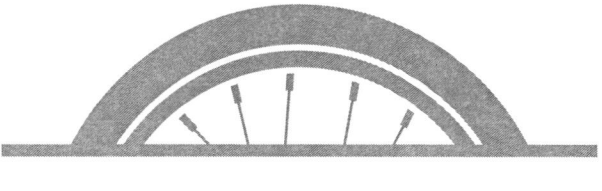

SOUTHERN TIER COMPLETE

This day saw a monumental achievement. I completed Map 7 of 7 of the Southern Tier Bicycle Route across America. San Diego to St. Augustine—3,000 miles (4,828 kilometers). I had probably pedaled only 2,800 miles (4,506 kilometers), since I made several detours and mapped our own route a number of times to avoid mountains and major construction and to ride on the beaches of the Gulf Coast from Mississippi to Florida.

Most cyclists who complete this route stop in St. Augustine. There are no maps for the next 300+ miles (483+ kilometers) down the east coast of Florida, but having ridden this five years before, I pretty much had it down by heart.

The ride on this day was a shorter one as I began to prepare for the last sprint. I stopped in Ormond Beach, which is one of the quainter beach towns along Florida's east coast, not far north of Daytona Beach. I remembered it

Creator and Savior. Verse 28 reminds us we are His offspring. He is involved in everything we do.

May we all be *one* and live in *unity* with Him and with one another. I want my life to be more about Him and less about me. Amen.

me. I was so excited about accomplishing this goal, but God wanted me to keep the focus on the children of Haiti, not my selfish motives.

It would have been a special memory. Not many can say they've ridden a double century. I can't either. I wish I could say I had peace about stopping, but I didn't and don't think I ever will. But I still would rather have done it this way than to look back always questioning my motives.

As it got dark, we reached the I-95 sign outside St. Augustine. I asked Corey to get a picture of me in front of the sign that said, "Miami, South." For the first time I realized I was almost home. Yes, I cried. I still feel emotional when I look at the picture—almost as if it just happened.

TODAY'S REFLECTION:

ACTS 17:26–27

> From one man he made all the nations, that they should inhabit the whole earth; and he marked out their appointed times in history and the boundaries of their lands. God did this so that they would seek him and perhaps reach out for him and find him, though he is not far from any one of us.

God did a beautiful thing when He created man and scattered us all over His creation. The church I am honored and very humbled to have served for the last three decades began with only eleven adults and five children, all born and raised in the USA. It is now a church of ninety countries who gather together at the foot of the cross each week. There is no way to describe the beautiful worship lifted up by those coming from all over the world.

His love for us is amazing. It's beautiful that He would make us so different and plant us in so many places, yet bring us together as *one* around our

Day 52
Lake City to St. Augustine, Florida
Miles Pedaled: 90:53

SOME DAYS JUST DON'T GO AS PLANNED

After everything went so smoothly for the century ride the previous day, this day began with both bikes getting flats in the first 25 miles (40 kilometers). I hadn't had a bike flat since before Phoenix, Arizona. On this day both were down at once.

Plans are important, but delays happen pretty much every day.

It was a bittersweet day. After riding over 100 miles (161 kilometers) the previous day, I had the chance to do a double century—that is, back-to-back hundred-mile days. I had never done that before and would not have the chance to do it ever again.

As we approached St. Augustine, it was getting dark. I had plenty in the tank to get the hundred but had just finished reading the book *Not a Fan* by Kyle Idleman. In the book, he speaks about pure Christianity. The Holy Spirit convicted me: If I went for the double century, it would be all about churches, which is still being used around the world. I am beyond proud of him and consider him a special friend. Thanks so much, Kevin, for the dinner.

TODAY'S REFLECTION:

AMOS 9:11–13

"In that day 'I will restore David's fallen shelter—I will repair its broken walls and restore its ruins—and will rebuild it as it used to be, so that they may possess the remnant of Edom and all the nations that bear my name,' declares the LORD, who will do these things. 'The days are coming,' declares the LORD, 'when the reaper will be overtaken by the plowman and the planter by the one treading grapes. New wine will drip from the mountains and flow from all the hills.'"

Restoring the ruins of Israel sounds very much like a time of pressing, grueling, and constant work but on a much grander scale than a 3,200-mile (5,150-kilometer) bike ride. God gave Amos the prophecy that He would restore the ruins of Israel. They had brought much of the distress and pain on themselves, but they also were persecuted and attacked by many countries, kings, and enemies. But just as God did other times in the past, He forgave His people and restored them and their land. We see the same happening in modern-day Israel.

We can take comfort in knowing God is a God of forgiveness and love. He will forgive our failures and our sins. No matter how broken your life is right now, no matter how dark it seems, please do not turn away from Him. Turn *to* Him. He wants to rebuild the walls of your life, which may take pressing, grueling work. Let Him do it.

Day 51

Apalachicola to Lake City, Florida
Miles Pedaled: 102.11

THIRD CENTURY IN THREE WEEKS

On this day we welcomed our new crew. As we took off from what I call "the armpit of the state," where the panhandle meets the rest of Florida, we moved through the boring parts: pine trees, cypress swamps, farmland—and once in a while, a person.

It was a brutal ride. We had the wind to our faces the entire day. But even with a new crew, and after six weeks of pressing, grueling, and constant pedaling, we accomplished a hundred-mile day for the third week in a row; 102 miles (164 kilometers) and almost 9,000 calories later, we ended our day in Lake City. Combining our two Bike for Haiti trips, we had now ridden six centuries. That is something I would have never dreamt possible—especially at sixty years old. God is good and merciful.

We met Kevin McCord and his son, Mason, who treated us to dinner, where we did a lot of catching up. At one time, Kevin was our administrative pastor. While he worked at Oasis, he created a computer program for

Oh, this is convicting! Would I be so bold under persecution? Would I give my life for Christ? I want to say yes, but the reality is we live easy lives here in the USA. I'm not sure we truly understand this verse about suffering for the kingdom of God.

The next two days I would be closing in on the east coast of Florida, hopefully. It would be challenging. We had about 200 miles (322 kilometers) yet to go through pine forests and rural roads, but I was ready.

TODAY'S REFLECTION:

ACTS 14:21–22

> They preached the gospel in that city and won a large number of disciples. Then they returned to Lystra, Iconium and Antioch, strengthening the disciples and encouraging them to remain true to the faith. "We must go through many hardships to enter the kingdom of God," they said.

For centuries since these words were penned, we have continued to see people discipling people. Just like Kevin, countless brothers and sisters continue to take others under their wings. We are His disciples, making disciples of Christ. We are to mentor each other to be true to the faith through the hardships and the daily toils life brings, just as Paul and Barnabas did. They did not have it easy. Paul had just been stoned and left for dead in Lystra, yet he and his cohorts did not back down or quit preaching the good news that Jesus had come to save us from our sins through His death, burial, and resurrection.

(Lystra, Iconium, and Antioch are in modern-day Syria and Turkey. In Syria, ISIS and other Islamic extremists are still persecuting and killing Christians today. Sadly, it's not much different there today than it was two thousand years ago.)

Each of us needs Paul's and Barnabas's tenacity. We can't let hardships, bullying, and obstacles keep us from sharing the good news of what God has done in our lives. They acknowledged they must endure afflictions and became martyrs for the truth.

Day 50

Apalachicola, Florida

Miles Pedaled: 0

ANOTHER WEEK, ANOTHER WALMART

This was a day to just chill as I awaited our next team. Corey would be back. Kevin, our facilities director, would also return, and he would bring Christopher, a very special fifteen-year-old, with him. Kevin is great at mentoring young people, so this would be a good opportunity for both.

This day was all about drop-offs, pickups, restocking, cleaning, and repositioning—things we had a lot of while traveling along the coast.

That week we not only biked through the most beautiful 400+ miles (644+ kilometers) since San Diego, but we also experienced another Walmart parking lot. I was learning a lot about being a Walmart camper. Thanks, Walmart, for opening your property to weary travelers and also providing your twenty-four-hour security.

This had been a very emotional week as I entered my home state. I was back in my own time zone, which made me know I was home. Being welcomed back to Florida by my son and grandsons was just precious. Life is good.

positions of leadership, whether at work, at home, at church, or at another organization. We should not let imperfect people keep us from leading with a heart of integrity and skillful hands. Amen.

A note about Mexico Beach: As I began writing the record of this cross-country ride, Hurricane Michael, a category five storm, made landfall near Mexico Beach and destroyed it. Sad is not a strong enough word. Michael wiped the entire town from the map. It is taking years to rebuild, but the people of the Gulf Coast are resilient. They will be better than ever. We in South Florida have had our own share of hurricanes, so they have been and will remain in my prayers.

TODAY'S REFLECTION:

PSALM 78:40

How often they rebelled against him in the wilderness and grieved him in the wasteland!

PSALM 78:72

And David shepherded them with integrity of heart; with skillful hands he led them.

How often I feel like Israel and act like them too. It's easy to judge their constant disobedience, yet too often I find myself disappointing God. When we run after our own plans and desires, our human lives can resemble a town wrecked by a hurricane as Mexico Beach was. Brokenness everywhere. As Paul said, the things I know I should do, I don't do, and the things I know I should not do, I do. It's part of the sinful nature we are born with, and it's still there even after our salvation. Before I judge others for their failures, I must remember I have my share as well.

It's interesting—after all the talk about the nation's failings, this psalm records that God took David from the sheep pen and made him the leader of these sinful and disobedient people. Psalm 78:72 sends a clear message though: David led the Israelites with "integrity of heart" and "skillful hands." What a great lesson for those of us whom God has placed in

Day 49

Springfield Beach to Apalachicola, Florida
Miles Pedaled: 70.02

This was another beautiful day of Florida beaches. Mexico Beach is a little town I did not know about, but it was so quaint and inviting. I loved the large (and when I say large, I mean LARGE) Adirondack chair they had on the beach to welcome visitors to their little town. I sat in it and took pictures. I literally lay down in it crossways, and it was still wide enough for me, so you can imagine. It was at least six feet wide and probably twelve feet high. Mexico Beach was one of those towns that mark you.

Most drive a car through a place like this and never blink once. This is what I love about being on the bike. You smell every smell (not that they are all pleasant) and enjoy the salty beach air, the town feel, and every noise and critter along the road. There is nothing like seeing my country at 15 miles per hour (24 kilometers per hour) on a bike. The only way to understand what I'm saying is to do it. These memories will be with me for the rest of my life.

a frustrating and tiring day on the road when there was no gentleness to spare. Many times, the guys would get up earlier and stay up later than I would to prepare for the day ahead.

To bear with one another means to not be a bear! No grumbling and growling at those on our team. The ones we love most tend to be the ones we have the least patience with. But Paul says to be a Christian is to show humility, patience, and perseverance. That is love. That is Jesus.

I encourage you to read the passage in Ephesians 4:1–6, which speaks on the unity and oneness of the church of Christ. Priceless.

On that trip, God called on me to raise one million dollars over the next ten years for our Haitian neighbors. With the pledges of this ride, we were at about $750,000 and well on our way as people continued to give. One man's invitation ten years before had translated into another man's call for one million dollars to be given to the people of Haiti. Michael set us up with a local NBC station for an interview about our cross-country ride and what we were doing in Haiti. After the interview, Mike's sweet wife fixed us an incredible lunch at their home. Home-cooked meals were few and far between on this trip. Thanks to Sue for some great food.

How we did all this and got 82 miles (132 kilometers) of riding in, I'll never know. Even more surprising, I burned 7,700 calories this day. That's a lot of room for some good home cooking.

TODAY'S REFLECTION:

EPHESIANS 4:2

Be completely humble and gentle; be patient,
bearing with one another in love.

This may be one of the greatest challenges for each of us in the body of Christ. Humility alone is a hard one for most of us when our egos begin to scream from within. Our lack of humility can result in harshness toward others who are different from us. That makes gentleness a challenge.

And patience. Oh, do I even have to even mention patience? This ride had tested every one of Paul's commands to his brothers and sisters in the Church of Ephesus. In a small camper cramped with up to four men at a time, each being a leader in his own right, and each holding his own beliefs of how the day should go, patience had been a challenge for all of us. I must say every guy who came with us showed an amazing amount of humility in almost every case. They demonstrated gentleness to one another even after

Day 48
Miramar Beach to Springfield Beach, Florida
Miles Pedaled: 82.22

ONE MILLION DOLLAR STOP

On Day 48 we rode through some of the most beautiful beaches in the USA—cities like Panama Beach, Grayton Beach, Rosemary Beach, and Laguna Beach. God's handiwork is on full display here on the Gulf Coast of Florida.

During the ride this day, we connected with a very special person, Pastor Michael Perry. He was the first to take me to Haiti when he was the director of missions for our local group of churches in Broward County. After learning of God's calling in my life to serve the people of Haiti, Michael cordially invited me to stay at his seminary's guest house. In Haiti I met one of our primary partners, Pastor Jean Moise, whom we help support even now through Bike for Haiti. The schools we've built, the seminary we underwrite, the teachers whose salaries we pay, and the churches we support are all part of the Bike for Haiti call I received while in Haiti with Michael.

No doubt this was the most beautiful ride yet—and my favorite. It would be hard to beat this day. I was sad when we had to say goodbye to the kids and go back to the local campground on Miramar Beach. The Geronimo Campground owners were so moved by our purpose that they donated $50 to Bike for Haiti. God is good.

TODAY'S REFLECTION:

COLOSSIANS 4:4–5

> Pray that I may proclaim it clearly, as I should.
> Be wise in the way you act toward outsiders;
> make the most of every opportunity.

That was the day I got to taste this passage. The owners of Geronimo RV Park donated to our friends in Haiti. To some, $50 may not be much, and, in light of our over $500,000 pledges, it sounds like little. But the amount is not the most important thing—it's the heart and spirit in which it's given. Here, a couple in the hospitality business just trying to make a buck gave a gift to people they had never met and probably never would. This is a good example of what Paul told the church at Colossae: proclaim the good news clearly. The best way to do that is to act in a wise and hospitable way to those you do not know. That's making the most of our opportunities.

When was the last time you blessed someone you did not know? When was the last time you shared how God has changed your life? I hope it will be today. I know this couple lived out Colossians 4:4–5 on that day and challenged me to do the same.

Day 47

Pensacola Beach to Miramar Beach, Florida

Miles Pedaled: 61.18

WIND AT OUR BACKS

I was still numb from the previous day's emotional entry into Florida. What a great evening we spent with the grandsons, Nathan, and the in-laws. I got to sleep in another normal bed at the Gilmores' home, the one reserved for Tonia when she would visit. She wasn't with us this time, which was a bummer, but I'd see her soon.

Gavyn and Caleb trailed me in the camper on this day as I rode on some of the most beautiful beaches in the USA. If you have never been to the Gulf Coast beaches of Florida, they must be on your bucket list. You will not be disappointed.

There are so many little beach towns on the Gulf Coast of Florida. We rode through Pensacola Beach, Navarre, Fort Walton, Destin, and Miramar Beach. It was perfect weather, and the wind remained at our backs the entire time. I'd been waiting for this westerly wind for over 2,000 miles (3,219 kilometers). It picked a good day to visit.

This was a Cheerwine, Slim Jim day for sure.

God is good.

TODAY'S REFLECTION:

LUKE 24:32

They asked each other, "Were not our hearts
burning within us while he talked with us on the
road and opened the Scriptures to us?"

After His resurrection, Jesus was seen by over five hundred witnesses. On this particular occasion, a couple of disciples were walking down the road to Emmaus, which was not far from Jerusalem. Just as my grandsons shocked me that day on the road to Florida, Jesus shocked these men who initially had no idea whom they had encountered. I'm pretty sure their amazement went far beyond mine.

To have so many witnesses encounter the Savior after His resurrection should strengthen us. To have one person witness a historical event is good; two is better. But more than five hundred is more than enough for me. I still can't understand how people can reject Jesus as the ONE, the Savior, God in flesh, when there is so much proof. I believe people choose whether to believe or not. Those who reject Jesus not only as deity but also as a historical figure do so because they want to. Whatever their reasons, they have convinced themselves Jesus is not who He said He was. But that's not new. Even some who saw Him, heard Him, and witnessed His miracles rejected Him. I believe! Do you?

of the Throwed Rolls. It's hard to describe, but it's got the most fried food you've ever seen. They bring it by your tables in pots and throw it—yes, literally throw it—on the table in front of you. When you need one of their gigantic rolls, about the size of a small duck, they throw it across the room. It's a circus from the time you walk in till you leave. If you like Deep South cooking, this is the place for you. Since I'd been burning between 30,000 and 40,000 calories, I figure it would be okay this time. The in-laws, who lived about 45 miles (72 kilometers) away in Pensacola, drove over and met us. It was a good time. By the time we were done, the rain had passed.

Time to ride and get to my beloved Florida! Beginning at Fort Morgan, we followed the beautiful beach and rode through Gulf Shores and Orange Beach for about an hour or so until we finally saw the SIGN: the State of Florida—that beautiful blue sign that always welcomes people to the "Sunshine State." The Lord knew we needed some sunshine.

Nothing had prepared me for what happened next. As I rode up to the sign, all I could think was, "I'm home"—well, at least in my home state. All I could do was drop off my bike. Yes, I fell off my bike in front of the sign and rolled on the sand beneath it.

As I lay in the dirt, savoring the moment, I looked up. Standing over me were my two Florida grandsons. Nathan had driven them eight hours from Indian Harbour Beach to welcome me to Florida. It was the greatest Father's Day present I had ever received. I wept and hugged them until I practically broke their ribs. What an incredible feeling!

Having Gavyn, Caleb, and Nathan there to welcome me home was the highlight of the trip. Yes, even more than crossing the state line. This moment still brings tears to my eyes as I look at the pictures and recount that moment.

Day 46

Dauphin Island, Alabama to Pensacola, Florida

Miles Pedaled: 42

BEST DAY OF THE TRIP

I thought the best moment of my cross-country trip would be when I hit the Florida state line. I had dreamt of it and looked forward to it since the day we pedaled off the San Diego beach. It should have been the best moment, but it wasn't!

Day 46 started off with a plan to take the 20-mile (32-kilometer) ferry trip from Dauphin Island, Alabama, across Mobile Bay to Fort Morgan, Alabama. When we woke up, we could tell by the sky it wouldn't be a nice day. The ferry closed due to storms on the bay, so we had to decide whether to wait another day sitting at the campground a few hours from Florida or to take the two-hour trip around the bay in the camper and pick it back up at Fort Morgan. Not even a moment's hesitation in my mind. Take the two-hour detour. We had become accustomed to detours.

The rain came down in sheets the entire trip around the bay. No riding until that stopped, so what would you do when that happens? You go to lunch at one of your all-time favorite restaurants, a place we used to visit while going to Missouri to see Tonia's parents. Lambert's Café, the Home

kilometers). I was incredibly proud of him.

As we crossed into Alabama and headed across a stretch of pine forest and little rural fishing towns, I could almost taste the next day. Not far from where we camped that night was the place where we would ride into Florida. First we celebrated our century with Cheerwine and Slim Jims. I'm so glad my friend Luann got these for me. They are so good. Don't judge; it had been a long day.

The next morning, we would begin by taking a ferry from Dauphin Island Campground to Fort Morgan across Mobile Bay. I was excited!

TODAY'S REFLECTION:

PHILIPPIANS 4:13 (NKJV)

I can do all things through Christ who strengthens me.

This has been my life's verse since I was a thirteen-year-old in the seventh grade. No other verse is more appropriate than this one today. Who would have ever thought at the age of sixty I would be riding across the United States on a bicycle? Not me! Never! But when God calls you to something, He gives you what you need to do it.

People tell me all the time, "I could never ride a bike that far." Most of them are in their teens, twenties, and thirties. I chuckle and remind them they could if they wanted to. God will give you supernatural strength in ways you will never know until you trust Him and step out of your comfort zone.

What has God been prompting you to do for Him? If it's not bigger than you, I'm not sure it's Him talking to you. God normally calls us to greater works than we can do on our own. I hope you will prove Philippians 4:13 by facing your fears and letting God do something supernatural in and through you.

Day 45

Bay St. Louis, Mississippi to Dauphin Island, Alabama

Miles Pedaled: 101.88

WHITE SAND BEACHES AND ANOTHER CENTURY

Oh, it would be tough to beat this day! One hundred one miles (163 kilometers)—and most of them were along the most beautiful Gulf beaches of Mississippi. In years past, I had driven through Mississippi only to get to somewhere else. I had always heard how poor and backwoods it was. Riding through it on other trips pretty much made me believe that. But I had never been to their beaches; I never even realized they had beaches. They are breathtaking and provide the setting for some of the most beautiful old southern homes with large oak trees. This was not Forrest Gump's Mississippi Gulf Coast, even though I saw plenty of his shrimp boats along the way. I wish I could have drawn you a picture in words, but that wasn't possible.

Centuries are not easy to come by, but this 101-mile (163-kilometer) ride was a joy. My heart still beats a little faster as I write this, and my face still flashes a smile at the thought of that ride. To add to the special moment, Pastor Ricky rode almost the whole way with me—88 miles (142

in their waters through the years at Oasis Church. We would hopefully (without major setbacks, that is) see the Gulf by the end of the day and arrive at the Florida state line sometime on Wednesday. My heart was beginning to pound in anticipation.

TODAY'S REFLECTION:

ACTS 10:34–35

Then Peter began to speak: "I now realize how true it is that God does not show favoritism but accepts from every nation the one who fears him and does what is right."

ACTS 10:44–45

While Peter was still speaking these words, the Holy Spirit came on all who heard the message. The circumcised believers who had come with Peter were astonished that the gift of the Holy Spirit had been poured out even on Gentiles.

ACTS 10:47–48

"Surely no one can stand in the way of their being baptized with water. They have received the Holy Spirit just as we have." So he ordered that they be baptized in the name of Jesus Christ.

I love the book of Acts. It's so powerful and organic. In today's passage, Peter began to teach the gospel to the Gentiles—people like you and me. It was no longer just for the Jews. After the Gentiles started to come to Christ, Peter made sure no Jewish believer could stop them from being baptized.

In the New Testament everyone who converted to Christ got baptized right away. If you are a believer and have not been baptized, you need to do it the first Sunday you are back in church. It is a public declaration of your faith in Christ. Do not put it off.

Day 44

New Orleans, Louisiana to Bay St. Louis, Mississippi

Miles Pedaled: 58.12

HELLO, DIXIE

I was excited to welcome back my team from the first week, Ricky and Jordan. When they arrived in New Orleans at noon, it was storming. I made sure they got some good Cajun food for lunch, and, of course, we had to have beignets. Neither had ever had them. So, New Orleans po' boy sandwiches, jambalaya, and beignets. It's just what you want to eat before you ride all afternoon. I couldn't help myself; I had to do it. It was still raining lightly as we pedaled out of New Orleans with our goal of getting across the border of Mississippi before dark.

We were now biking through our sixth state. I could hardly believe there were just two states to travel through after Mississippi. As we entered the state, I had my traditional state line sign picture taken. Mississippians say their state was the "birthplace of American music." I'll take their word for it.

I couldn't wait to see the Gulf of Mexico and its beautiful beaches. My thoughts turned to my favorite Florida beaches. It wasn't just their beauty that came to mind but also the memories of many who were baptized

This morning as I was worshiping, I clicked the map available on our online site and noticed this tiny dot about halfway between South Florida and California. It was me. Such a little insignificant dot! It gives you a reality check when you see something like this—to see how small of a speck we are in this enormous universe. Yet I am also reminded I am more than a dot. I am a "drop," one who can be refreshing to someone in need of God's love.

You can be that "drop" too, an oasis to a weary traveler—just as my church was to me as we worshiped together.

TODAY'S REFLECTION:

ACTS 8:30–31

> Then Philip ran up to the chariot and heard the man reading Isaiah the prophet. "Do you understand what you are reading?" Philip asked. "How can I," he said, "unless someone explains it to me?" So he invited Philip to come up and sit with him.

Do you see a pattern here? Yesterday, we saw Stephen preaching and sharing the story of Jesus. We have seen Peter preaching the Word at Pentecost; now we see Philip.

Philip saw the rich and powerful assistant to the queen of Ethiopia and offered to help him understand the Scriptures. Jesus told His followers that we are to *go* and *tell*. His followers took that seriously—so seriously many of them were persecuted and martyred for their witness. I am rebuked when I hear and see these stories, knowing the extreme pressure these early Christians faced. Yet they were not afraid to share the life-changing message of Jesus Christ.

Sometimes we feel inadequate or think someone else is better qualified. That isn't true. Most of the early Christians had no education and were not professionally trained. They were ordinary people who had been radically changed by meeting Jesus. May we all learn to follow their lead.

Day 43

New Orleans, Louisiana

Miles Pedaled: 0

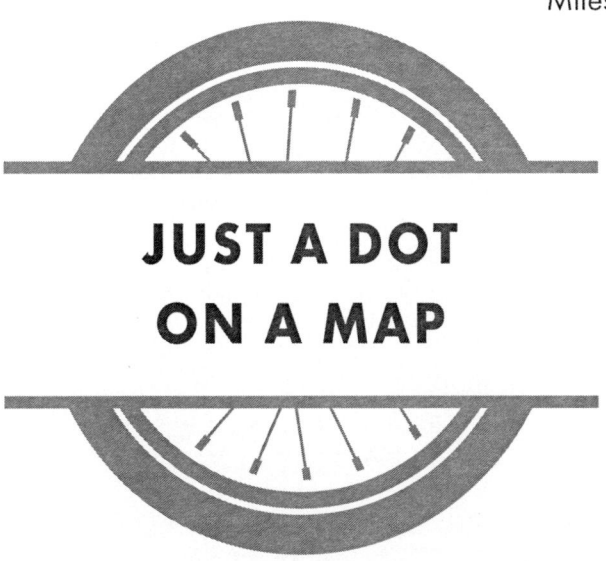

JUST A DOT ON A MAP

This was a real rest day. Since I had an extra day off that weekend, I had finished my chores the day before. Other than trying to get the door of the camper fixed, I decided to hang out at the camper all day. Camper doors aren't anything like the typical house door. It takes a special person to fix them, and we had called a locksmith since we didn't have that person out on the road with us. I grew eager for the locksmith to finish. I was tired of blocking the door every night with anything we could find to try to keep the boogeyman out.

I began the morning worshiping online with my church family in South Florida. I was more than thankful to have this connection available to keep in touch with Oasis. It was wonderful but made me so miss my church. Every face I saw made me homesick, but I had a calling to do on this trip. I was so grateful for an incredible team at home that allows me to be able to do things like this. They are amazing, and I am so grateful to each and every one of them.

books I want to read. Tuning into various radio stations, both secular and Christian, also broke up the monotony. I don't get to hear a lot of preachers and teachers during my regular schedule, so this time allowed for that too.

My fondest moments were spent listening to worship music and singing. Now, I can't sing, but when you are out on the road in the middle of nowhere, who cares? Who is going to hear? The cows and horses and an occasional alligator in Louisiana? Sometimes I lifted my hands—yes, both hands—while riding in worship. I also experienced moments when I was so overcome with emotion that I wept.

And then there were times I dreamed—just thought and meditated. So, in reality it wasn't as boring as many would think. I didn't even finish all the audio books and things I thought I'd blow through during the trip. I was blessed to have this time to grow as I pedaled.

TODAY'S REFLECTION:

ACTS 7:55

Stephen, full of the Holy Spirit, looked up to heaven and saw
the glory of God, and Jesus standing at the right hand of God.

I want to return to Stephen today. This verse was tucked into the story of his martyrdom. Can you imagine being so in tune with God that in the midst of having your life taken, you can see God in heaven and Jesus standing at His right hand? That is beyond comprehension.

I don't know anywhere else in Scripture where someone experienced that. God honored him by letting him get a glimpse of heaven. It must have been amazing! If we could get a glimpse of heaven, I imagine we would not want to stay here and deal with this nasty earth. Maybe Stephen reacted with such forgiveness because he got a taste of where he was going to spend eternity. *Wow!*

Day 42
New Orleans, Louisiana
Miles Pedaled: 0

RIDING AND WORSHIPING

The evening before, I said goodbye to my previous week's support team, Pastor Jonathan and Barry, as they headed home. I was grateful to them. They worked tirelessly to take care of me and support this ride. They saved me from barking dogs, cleaned out sewer tanks, prepared and fixed my bike, cooked dinners, and so much more. This ride would not be possible without guys like them.

Over the years I have been asked, "What do you do all day when you are riding for so long?" Many days I was on the bike from five to seven hours straight. Most of the time I rode by myself. It could get boring, monotonous . . . and boring. I was thankful several guys rode some of it with me. That helped, but it was only for a small portion of the time.

Hours on that little slim seat with hundreds of thousands of pedal strokes can get to you. I found great strength in listening to praise and worship music in my earbuds, my constant companions. I also listened to a number of audio books, which was good since I never find time to get to all the

There are so many lessons we can take from Stephen's faithful life and death, but I think the easiest one to understand is the need to forgive those who have hurt us. Is there any offense we could experience worse than being stoned to death? I think not. God made it clear in His Word that we are to forgive one another. Let us begin today. Those who cannot forgive cannot be truly happy.

together. Another big lift to our spirits as we continued this trek across America.

That night I began our weekend off for rest and recuperation. I couldn't wait to eat some beignets, which have been declared the official Louisiana doughnuts. I had been dreaming of eating some since crossing over into the state of Louisiana.

TODAY'S REFLECTION:

ACTS 7:59–60

> While they were stoning him, Stephen prayed, "Lord Jesus, receive my spirit." Then he fell on his knees and cried out, "Lord, do not hold this sin against them." When he had said this, he fell asleep.

Days or possibly hours earlier, Stephen had been chosen as one of the first deacons in the early church. Chapter 6 says he was a man full of faith and of the Holy Spirit. Scripture shows us many disciples of Christ like Stephen, who after being born again in the Spirit lived faithfully for Christ. This is true even today. You may find them in your church. For us, the Coopers remind us of the list of faithful believers who are giving their whole lives for our Lord.

Stephen's life was cut too short. He was martyred because of his faith and his willingness to preach it to the Jews. What a brutal death! Only a person filled with the Holy Spirit can be so bold and so willing to be put to death in such a manner. Stephen was that person. What really strikes me is that even as he was being stoned, just seconds from death, he asked God not to hold these men responsible. He forgave those who took his life. He sounded very much like his Lord and His final words on the cross.

Day 41

Baton Rouge to New Orleans, Louisiana

Miles Pedaled: 78.8

Week 5 of our Bike for Haiti 2 ended this day as we also finished off our fifth of seven Southern Tier Bicycle Route maps. Approximately 400 miles (644 kilometers) closer to home, we ended the day in New Orleans.

The previous night in Baton Rouge, we enjoyed a special dinner with two friends I have known since my high school days. Dave and Cindy Cooper took our team out after our long day on the bike. The Coopers had attended the church where I grew up in Hollywood, Florida. Cindy was Tonia's physical education coach during our senior year at Hollywood Christian School, and Dave was the TV and communications director. They were good friends with the Gilmores (Tonia's parents). Dave reminded me that night that he had built the pillars and all the decorations for the stage at our wedding. He had been on televangelist Jimmy Swaggart's team for many years, producing his international TV ministry. He also owns his own television company that features national sports telecasts. He's done it all, and he and Cindy were a great inspiration to us during this time because I did not want to take any chances. As we constantly said to each other, safety first. I was secretly hiding behind safety first.

If you know Jonathan, you know he can be very persuasive. He relentlessly tried to talk me into riding it. I agreed when he said he would ride it with me. I figured, if I died here, at least someone would go with me. But we did it, and I have Jonathan to thank for that. The views were incredible from 150 feet (46 meters) above the mighty river, but I was too scared to stop and take a picture, so you will have to take my word for it. But I faced my fear of high bridges and survived.

TODAY'S REFLECTION:

JOHN 8:36

"So if the Son sets you free, you will be free indeed."

Jesus told the Jews He was the Son of God—the Messiah they had been waiting for. He told them they were slaves to sin but reminded them that truth came only from God, and the truth would set them free. As the Son of God, the Truth, He could set them free.

Maybe someone reading this today needs to be set free from sin. Just as I had to make a choice to be set free from the fear of bridges, each of us must decide to follow Jesus or to continue in our sinful ways. It's our choice.

Let Jesus set you free from whatever sin—or fear—is keeping you in slavery.

Day 40
Innis to Baton Rouge, Louisiana
Miles Pedaled: 52.03

FACING MY FEARS

On day 40, we crossed the mighty Mississippi River. We were officially in the eastern United States. I'm not sure if you have ever been over one of the bridges that go over this massive river, but they are long, high, and many times very old. I often crossed them in a car when my in-laws lived in Missouri. Even in a car, they scare me.

My fear of large bridges dates to when I was a little Guy, about five years old, when my dad would take us over the Sunshine Skyway Bridge outside St. Petersburg, Florida. I was petrified of that bridge and would hide on the floorboard of our old 1955 Oldsmobile station wagon until we were safely over it. My parents always said it wouldn't fall. Well, it did on May 9, 1980. Thirty-five people died in the waters below, including those riding in a Greyhound bus. So, my fears were reinforced.

The bridge I was now facing was high and long—about 3 miles (5 kilometers). The winds were strong, and the traffic was crazy. Once, the steep climb on the bike would have kept me from crossing, but after the mountains out west, that wasn't an issue. I had decided not to ride it

One caution to anyone who may want to do a cross-country cycling tour. Don't rely on Google Maps. They are horrible for bicycling. We gave up on the digital mapping today and went back to taping an old-school bike map on my handlebars to make sure we did not end up on some dirt road or dead-end street. Google, I know you have a very limited budget, but you can do better than this.

TODAY'S REFLECTION:

ACTS 5:40–42

> They called the apostles in and had them flogged. Then they ordered them not to speak in the name of Jesus, and let them go. The apostles left the Sanhedrin, rejoicing because they had been counted worthy of suffering disgrace for the Name. Day after day, in the temple courts and from house to house, they never stopped teaching and proclaiming the good news that Jesus is the Messiah.

The early Christians were faced with persecution. Sometimes they were beaten and other times they were killed for their faith. Every time I read the book of Acts, I am convicted about how much they suffered and yet never shut up. Their lives had been so changed by Jesus that they had to talk about it. I often wonder if I would be willing to be so bold under persecution.

We are blessed to live in a country where there is religious freedom, but I fear we have become spiritually weak. We have total freedom to speak about our faith, and yet we miss so many opportunities. May we follow the lead of these early brothers and sisters and be willing to speak up for what we believe and not fear the consequences. Peter said, "I fear God more than man." Can we say that today?

Day 39

Mamou to Innis, Louisiana
Miles Pedaled: 72.94

THANKFUL FOR AIR HORNS

We experienced a beautiful ride in rural Louisiana on day 39. Great weather and gently rolling hills were the highlights of the day. We found a beautiful park to ride in, and Jonathan joined me for about 10 miles (16 kilometers). But the mosquitos were the size of pigeons and practically knocked us off our bikes. As Jonathan followed me through the Chicot State Park, he could see the mosquitos keeping up with my every pedal stroke. These Cajuns are so creative, they should figure out how to mix the mosquitos with the crayfish and make some type of new jambalaya! It was a beautiful 6,400-acre park with cabins, a lake, and all kinds of recreation. It would be a fun place to camp, but bring some strong mosquito repellent!

I was so thankful for the air horns. I did not use them in training, but they came in handy on this ride. We pretty much emptied them all on more dogs today. I'm not sure what was worse, the man-eating mosquitos or the mad dogs.

Have you ever struggled with God? Maybe it was something He was prompting you to do? Maybe it was something He wanted you to give? Maybe you have struggled with Him over your troubles in life. I think we all wrestle with God sometimes.

This story of Jacob struggling with what was most certainly an angel of God shows that God does not judge us for our struggle—He does not always punish us when we wrestle with Him or His will for us. Sometimes, though, we may come out of it with a limp like Jacob did. I believe it was given to him as a reminder of the day he wrestled with an angel of God. Don't begrudge the limp. It may be what keeps you tethered to God.

The voice issues I have had from a damaged vocal cord for almost twenty years now continue to this day. But they remind me how dependent on God I am. Every day I remember it's by the grace of God that I still have a voice and can continue to preach and serve Oasis Church. It's *my* limp!

the road waiting for a biker in a spandex uniform to ride by. Jonathan and Barry protected me from nine dogs that chased me relentlessly until the RV threatened to make them roadkill. Thanks, guys, for saving my life again from a record number of dogs. I think every house and trailer in the state had a dog sitting on the porch just waiting on me.

For the hard work the guys put in, I treated them to some authentic Cajun food in Mamou, which included sampling their gourmet crayfish. At least, Louisianans think they are gourmet. They eat them from a bucket that rests on the table. Everyone sits around the bucket, takes a crayfish out, sucks the brains out of the head, and proceeds to eat the entire thing, shell and all. Yuk! But when in Cajun country, you eat like a Cajun. We stood out in this rural Deep South area like a flashing neon Krispy Kreme "hot and now" sign: an old white guy in spandex biker shorts, a black guy, and a Hispanic from Ecuador. Oh, yeah. You should have seen the looks. They could definitely tell we were not Cajuns.

On another note, a little girl pulled up with her mom to stop the camper in Oberlin, Louisiana, to give us a five-dollar donation in one-dollar bills. Mom said her little girl saw we were raising money for Haiti and wanted to help. It was so moving. That donation was as important as any of the over $500,000 that had been pledged already. It matched the only donation we received from our last ride to NYC, when a man stopped us and gave us a five-dollar donation out in the pine forest of Georgia.

TODAY'S REFLECTION:

GENESIS 32:28

Then the man said, "Your name will no longer be Jacob, but Israel, because you have struggled with God and with humans and have overcome."

Day 38

DeRidder to Mamou, Louisiana

Miles Pedaled: 65.95

BAYOUS, CRAYFISH PONDS, AND RICE FIELDS

Bayous as far as the eye can see and crayfish ponds for miles! Riding through rural Louisiana on this day gave me a real education. The ponds where they farm crayfish and the rice fields full of water were confusing until I got a true Louisianan to explain the difference to me. Rice fields and crayfish farms can work well with each other. Rice is an aquatic plant while crayfish can grow when rice production slows down. Not only that, but they both grow in alternating seasons. They are symbiotic in nature, with great benefits to Louisianans. Even some of the homes raise crayfish in their yards. Crazy but interesting.

The contrast between Texas and Louisiana couldn't be greater. Flat instead of up and down hills, 95 percent humidity, and an absolutely beautiful day with clear blue skies for the first time in over two weeks.

I wondered if we would ever view civilization again after miles of rural farmland. One thing we did see was a lot of dogs sitting on porches along

May we not get so busy and focused on ourselves that we can't hear and see God in His handiwork every day.

morning, we had to drop off the rental car our newest team member had arrived in. When we got to the airport, it was closed, with police cars all over the parking lot. They had a bomb scare and shut down the terminal. Then when it reopened a few hours later, our rental car desk decided to take a break. All we could do was sit and wait. This little tiny airport probably has never had so much excitement.

No matter how we plan, it never seems to work out quite right. Anyone identify with that? I am reminded today of Proverbs 16:9: "In their hearts humans plan their course, but the Lord establishes their steps." Or as my wife, Tonia, says, "Man plans; God laughs!" Yep!

Welcome, Barry, to our team. Thanks for coming out to support me.

TODAY'S REFLECTION:

PSALM 19:1–2

The heavens declare the glory of God; the skies proclaim the work of his hands. Day after day they pour forth speech; night after night they reveal knowledge.

These are such beautiful verses. The artistry of God declares His glory. This trip so far had certainly reminded me of the vastness of God's creations. From the tops of the highest mountains through the desert dunes and into the most beautiful valleys and meadows, God has shown off His splendor. The heavens declare His glory. Certainly, the western sunsets have reminded me of an amazing God. Anyone who could ever doubt that a supreme being made all of this must be deaf to reality. God's creation shouts His greatness. There is something about being on a bike by yourself for hours that allows you to take in the incredible creation our God has provided for us. If nothing else, this trip was worth it to experience the beautiful earth and sky He has gifted me with.

Day 37

Beaumont, Texas to DeRidder, Louisiana

Miles Pedaled: 54:54

HELLO, LOUISIANA . . . GOOD RIDDANCE, TEXAS

Four states down, and four to go! I had never been happier to leave a state than I was to leave Texas. I knew it would be a long 1,000 miles (1,609 kilometers) across Texas, but I had no idea it would take so long and we would encounter so many obstacles. If I never pedal another foot in Texas, it would suit me just fine. Nothing personal to all my friends there, but you can have it. Next time, you can visit me in paradise: South Florida.

Today was the first day since beginning the journey that we did not encounter a hill or mountain. That alone was enough to pull out the Cheerwine and Slim Jims! Even better, we didn't wait until the end of the day. I pulled them out at the state line. I was so excited to see that sign saying, "Welcome to Louisiana/*Bienvenue en Louisiane*." Yep, in French. I had to celebrate with my two guilty pleasures.

Oh, and why the short miles this day when we had perfect weather and flat roads? You can't make this up, but before leaving Beaumont, Texas, that

Your idol may be something else. It's time to fast from it—to cut it out of your life temporarily to remind you who should be the one-and-only love of your life above all others.

It was a day of few challenges and great weather but brought stiff winds and some of the last hills of Texas. Oh, and three dogs chased me—one mongrel got within 15 feet (5 meters) of taking a chunk out of my thigh. Thankfully, Jonathan saw him first and scared him off with the RV. We had a certain procedure for when a dog came at me, but I'll keep that as classified information between my team and me. (Because Jonathan saved my life this day, I forgave him for driving off and leaving my bike in a parking lot.)

Because of a mix-up with a rental car for our arriving new team member, we had some extra time waiting at the airport in Beaumont and decided to finish the last 14 miles (23 kilometers) there. Jonathan rode that last bit with me to celebrate the hundred mark together. It was an epic day. We were almost to the Louisiana border; I couldn't wait to see Texas in our rearview mirror. I hoped it would happen the next day. I could smell the bayous of Louisiana!

TODAY'S REFLECTION:

ISAIAH 46:9

> Remember the former things, those of long ago; I am God, and there is no other; I am God, and there is none like me.

Just as God had to remind His people in Old Testament times that He is the only true God, He still reminds us of that today. We may not chase the gods of the Babylonians, but so many things in our lives can become idols. Money, fame, pride, spouses, children, food, and so many other things can become false gods. For me, I must fast from food from time to time to break the addiction I have to it. Fasting for a prolonged time is a constant reminder of who is and should be the most important Person in my life.

Day 36
Conroe/Willis to Beaumont, Texas
Miles Pedaled: 101.33

A CENTURY, CHEERWINE, AND SLIM JIM

We did it! We finally hit the 100-mile (161-kilometer) mark in one day. A century! This is a big deal for a person my age. I did it three times on our ride to New York City, but I didn't think it would happen on this ride since the terrain was so much more difficult. The weather, roads, and various detours made a major impact on how far and how long I could ride each day.

This called for a celebration! Cheerwine soda and Slim Jims: Two of my favorites. I don't drink soda anymore and do not eat Slim Jims. They are filled with the worst ingredients ever put into food, but oh so good. (Warning: if you are going to eat a Slim Jim, *do not* read the ingredients first.) Cheerwine soda is a native North Carolina drink that until recently you could get only in North Carolina. For years, it would be the highlight of my vacations. Now it became the reward for biking a hundred miles. We stocked up with Cheerwine and Slim Jims to celebrate days like this one. I knew this might be the only century on this ride, so I savored the moment.

This was a Saturday, but because of a shift in our support team, we were taking this day as our rest day. In the evening I worshiped with our Oasis family online from my computer, which was perched on top of a washer. I worshiped and washed all at one time. Lots of firsts on this trip.

TODAY'S REFLECTION:

ACTS 2:28

You have made known to me the paths of life;
you will fill me with joy in your presence.

This passage is one of the most unusual ones in the New Testament, and it's so easy to miss. Peter, in his great sermon at Pentecost, where three thousand decided to follow Christ, quoted King David from Psalm 16:8–11 while speaking about Christ coming, rising from the dead, and bringing David to heaven with Him. What a powerful portion of Scripture linking the Old and New Testament prophesies. I encourage you to read both portions in their entirety.

Heaven is not spoken about much in this sense in the Old Testament, but here Peter connects the Old Testament Jewish eternal destiny with the New Testament Jewish heritage of eternal life through Jesus Christ. Yet many did not accept Him. It was no different from today.

We can't make people accept Christ, but we can do as Peter did and share the wonderful story of our risen Savior and how He has made a difference in our lives.

Day 35

Conroe to Willis, Texas
Miles Pedaled: 0

WORSHIP AND WASH

Texas had been flooding for several weeks. Sadly, the day before, six soldiers at Fort Hood, Texas, had drowned in the deluge. Everywhere we looked, water was rising. The previous night after dark, Jonathan had pulled into our campground on a beautiful lake. What I did not realize until I woke up that morning was that he had parked the camper so close to the lake that the back bedroom where I slept hung over the water. Really, Jonathan?

Two nights before, without realizing it in the dark, we had parked in a campground 50 feet (15 meters) from the Colorado River. That night the town had a severe flood warning, and the Colorado River overflowed its banks. I didn't even know the Colorado River ran through Texas. God is good; He continues to watch over us even in our ignorance. But I determined that from then on, I would check where Jonathan had us parked before I went to bed.

You've heard me say this ride was so much harder than the first one to New York City. However, one of the blessings I experienced much more on this ride was seeing a number of old friends along the way. That lifted my spirit and reminded me of the many blessings of a long-term ministry. You get to see God do so much in so many lives. Thanks, Sheryl and Randy, for dropping by.

TODAY'S REFLECTION:

HOSEA 6:3

"Let us acknowledge the Lord; let us press on to acknowledge him. As surely as the sun rises, he will appear; he will come to us like the winter rains, like the spring rains that water the earth."

What a perfect verse for today. The spring rains were watering the earth there in Texas. I love what the writer reminds the people of—a reminder that is good for all of us: God is taking care of us every day and in every season.

Whether we acknowledge Him or not, He tends the earth, giving us all we need. It is far better for us to recognize His goodness and love than to live like a "Christian atheist," as Craig Groeschel coins those who don't acknowledge Him in his book of the same title.[1]

May we live each day with gratitude to our Creator, the One who sustains, supplies, and provides our eternal salvation. We have so much to be thankful for.

---

[1] Craig Groeschel, *The Christian Atheist: Believing in God but Living as if He Doesn't Exist* (Grand Rapids, MI: Zondervan, 2011).

Day 34

Navasota to Conroe, Texas

Miles Pedaled: 43.34

IT'S A NEW DAY

It was a new day, and we were beginning a new bike map for our route. After my worst day of riding ever, I had a fresh start.

The great new day didn't last long. Just 7 miles (11 kilometers) and we got hit with heavy rains and had to pull over to the side of the road. A three-hour delay. When you can't see out of the camper windshield because of the rain, it's probably best not to ride your bike.

Despite the rain delay, it was a good day with some beautiful scenery as the Hill Country slowly faded from view. We were looking forward to leaving Texas and moving into Louisiana in the next few days. Couldn't wait.

Our ride was relatively short in mileage—just 43 miles (69 kilometers), but we had a surprise visit from one of the girls who grew up in our youth ministry in Hollywood, Florida. Sheryl Hancey-Strain and her husband, Randy, came up from Houston to hang out for a few hours. That was a blessing. Sheryl had been one of the sweetest girls in our youth group. God has used her and her husband in tremendous ways for many years.

for taking care of all these things so I could stay focused on riding! I could have never made it through today without them! Tomorrow's a new day.

TODAY'S REFLECTION:

PHILIPPIANS 4:12

> I know what it is to be in need, and I know what it is to have plenty. I have learned the secret of being content in any and every situation, whether well fed or hungry, whether living in plenty or in want.

Please allow me to take the liberty of using a scripture Nathan did not send me for the morning devotion. This verse fits too well not to use it. Thank you.

Paul had seen it all. He wrote much of the New Testament while either in jail or being beaten, chased out of town, stoned almost to death, shipwrecked, and on and on. You get the picture. Paul knew what a bad day was. I have never had any day remotely as bad as what he faced. And I have never had to deal with the challenges of living in a country like Haiti.

Haiti has so much natural beauty and potential. It breaks my heart to witness how our Haitian brothers and sisters endure poverty and unimaginable suffering. They are our neighbors! Do you realize when we fly from South Florida to Haiti, we travel the same distance as we would if we flew to Atlanta, maybe a little less?

How can we, who live in the most prosperous and blessed country in history, not be content? Oh, and we have the freedom to live as we please, worship as we please, and speak as we please. Please join me today in thanking God for all we have been given and in recommitting ourselves to Paul's attitude: to be content no matter what our circumstances.

- Miles of detours because a bridge was too low for camper.
- Seventy-five miles of detours, and no warnings from Texas till you get there.
- Chain broke on my spare bike several times when the gears jammed.
- Main new bike seat screws broke and made it unrideable!
- Both bikes were down at once.
- Two-hour detour to Home Depot for a screw for the seat.
- No campground after riding till after dark and no shower after riding all day! The water tank somehow drained and was empty so no portable water for showers. Thankful for Lysol Wipes! Yuk!
- Camper lock broke, won't lock!
- With all the delays, had to ride till after dark for the first time!
- Ate dinner at Sonic at 10:00 p.m. It was the only thing open in the entire city.

That's our day in a nutshell!

During one of our detours when I was just sitting killing time, whining and griping, I saw a picture on Instagram from Haiti with rain, mud, packed motorcycles, and people walking in terrible conditions. The Lord reminded me how good I have it and that all the problems I encountered today were just inconveniences! First-world problems! Many Haitians live under much worse conditions every day of their lives!

Soooooo, God is good and He is faithful and in the end I'm grateful for His many blessings! Especially thankful that I'm only 150 miles (241 kilometers) from the Texas-Louisiana border, woohoo! Thanks so much to Jonathan Jimenez and Corey

Day 33

Long Point to Navasota, Texas
Miles Pedaled: 64.91

WORST DAY EVER

If you don't mind, in order not to write a whole chapter giving you the raw emotions of this day, I will share my longest Instagram post ever.

> Worst day I've ever experienced on a ride . . . ! But let me share the good first!
>
> 1. God stopped the rain that was predicted at 100 percent today! Never rained.
> 2. We met our goal—we got to Navasota, Texas, and completed Map 4 of 7 for the Southern Tier Bicycle Route!
> 3. We're all safe!
>
> Now our day would take pages for me to describe, but I'll list a few things in a nutshell! I've told you the good; now let me share the bad and the ugly. No exaggeration either.
>
> • Washed-out roads and detours, no warning signs till the last minute.

"Feed my sheep." Jesus once again shows His willingness to use even broken vessels—those who have messed up.

Peter went on to be a major preacher of the early church and the one the Holy Spirit used on the day of Pentecost. Three thousand people came to Christ and were baptized that day.

God wants to use us no matter what our past is or how broken we are. If He can use a thrice-denier, He can use you. Forgive yourself; Jesus has already done so.

"Follow Me."

That's what He is saying to you and to me today.

TODAY'S REFLECTION:

JOHN 21:15–22

When they had finished eating, Jesus said to Simon Peter, "Simon son of John, do you love me more than these?"

"Yes, Lord," he said, "you know that I love you."

Jesus said, "Feed my lambs."

Again Jesus said, "Simon son of John, do you love me?"

He answered, "Yes, Lord, you know that I love you."

Jesus said, "Take care of my sheep."

The third time he said to him, "Simon son of John, do you love me?"

Peter was hurt because Jesus asked him the third time, "Do you love me?" He said, "Lord, you know all things; you know that I love you."

Jesus said, "Feed my sheep. Very truly I tell you, when you were younger you dressed yourself and went where you wanted; but when you are old you will stretch out your hands, and someone else will dress you and lead you where you do not want to go." Jesus said this to indicate the kind of death by which Peter would glorify God. Then he said to him, "Follow me!"

Peter turned and saw that the disciple whom Jesus loved was following them. (This was the one who had leaned back against Jesus at the supper and had said, "Lord, who is going to betray you?") When Peter saw him, he asked, "Lord, what about him?"

Jesus answered, "If I want him to remain alive until I return, what is that to you? You must follow me."

I gave up on my constantly failing bike seat, but God doesn't give up on us. In this passage, Jesus reinstated Peter. Peter had denied Him three times after He had been arrested. Now He finds Peter and the other disciples on the beach of the Sea of Galilee and gives him an important command:

Day 32
Winchester to Long Point, Texas
Miles Pedaled: 42.5

THANK GOD FOR BACKUPS

Today the weather forecaster predicted a 100 percent chance of rain, but thankfully that dropped to 15–45 percent during our ride. Humidity was 95 percent—the highest I'd felt since leaving South Florida. The West has dry heat and low humidity. I'll take the high humidity over rain any day when I'm on a bike.

The seat on the new bike I had bought for this trip had been a continual issue. On this day, we had to fix it yet again. To avoid losing too much time, we pulled out our backup—the old Jamison bike I rode to New York City. Thank you, Lord, for a good backup! It had 20,000 miles (32,187 kilometers) on it, but I think it rode better than my new bike, which cost me twice as much. I love my Jamison bike.

The rains had been torrential since before we left for Memorial Day. The last night in Austin, there were tornado warnings all night, which is not a good thing when you are in a camper. We were hearing rumors of flooding and major issues toward the east, where we would continue to ride.

TODAY'S REFLECTION:

2 KINGS 5:10–11

> Elisha sent a messenger to say to him, "Go, wash yourself seven times in the Jordan, and your flesh will be restored and you will be cleansed." But Naaman went away angry and said, "I thought that he would surely come out to me and stand and call on the name of the Lord his God, wave his hand over the spot and cure me of my leprosy."

I needed these verses that day. Nothing in the several days of riding the previous week had worked out the way I had planned. So many distractions and "wasted time" kept me from getting in all the miles I had scheduled. But in the end, God knows what is best. Just because it doesn't happen the way I want it to doesn't mean it's not in His plan.

Naaman was angry because God did not heal him the way he thought He should. He wanted this clean-cut miracle—he had it mapped out. But God had other plans. He would restore him, but Naaman would have to get messy first. God wants our obedience, not our plans. He isn't our genie. We don't rub His lamp, and POOF! Out He comes to say, "Your wish is my command." I am trying to learn to come on His terms and not mine because when I come on my terms, it usually doesn't work out so well.

Day 31
Austin to Winchester, Texas
Miles Pedaled: 70.94

We were back in Texas. After not riding for five days, it felt good to be "back in the saddle," as they say in the biking world. We made some good progress. Storms surrounded us, but they held off until we finished riding. The hills began to get smaller as we moved east. I knew I wouldn't miss the hills and mountains one bit.

This section of our bike map seemed as if it would never end. We'd been in Texas two and a half weeks, but it felt like two years—the worst two years of my life at that.

We were in the middle of nowhere again in the little town of Winchester. The map didn't even record their population. They did have an Old West type of saloon restaurant where we had a good meal before returning to our home for the last month of our journey: the camper.

beautiful DIL Sabrina, and our incredible granddaughter Selah! Now we will begin our second half of our Bike for Haiti journey back in Texas on Tuesday!

Enough said! I still get tears in my eyes while reading this and picturing her standing on the platform as my train pulled away. It forever marked me. I hope I never lose this feeling.

TODAY'S REFLECTION:

PSALM 121

I wonder if Nathan had any idea this chapter is my favorite in the Bible. I know he didn't realize how much I would need it that day. I'll let the psalmist speak by giving you the entire chapter; you don't need any additional comment from me.

> I lift up my eyes to the mountains—where does my help come from? My help comes from the Lord, the Maker of heaven and earth.
>
> He will not let your foot slip—he who watches over you will not slumber; indeed, he who watches over Israel will neither slumber nor sleep.
>
> The Lord watches over you—the Lord is your shade at your right hand; the sun will not harm you by day, nor the moon by night.
>
> The Lord will keep you from all harm—he will watch over your life; the Lord will watch over your coming and going both now and forevermore.

Day 30

New York City to Austin, Texas

Miles Pedaled: 0

MEMORIAL DAY: THE *R* TRAIN

Memorial Day in America. The day our nation mourns and remembers those who have given their lives so we can be free and live the way we choose. I salute those families who have made the ultimate sacrifice—those who have lost their loved ones in the service of our country.

This day I traveled back to Texas to begin the second half of our journey to South Florida with Bike for Haiti 2. If you will indulge me, I would like to share an Instagram post I made as I left Tonia for the airport. I wish I had the picture. It was the most gut-wrenching image of our trip.

> Seeing your love across the subway tracks as I take the *R* Subway Train one way to Brooklyn and you are taking the *R* train the opposite way toward the airport rips my heart out! As our train pulled away and I saw her waiting for her train, I asked myself how I could love someone so much it hurts this much to say goodbye for just one more month. I can't explain it, but I just experienced it! It was a great three days off with Tonia, our

others with the comfort she found in Jesus. She is an amazing picture of this passage of Scripture.

and spend time with me, while Sabrina was able to hang out with Selah. This was a good weekend, and I was blessed to be able to be with them.

I must mention how grateful I am for Tonia and for her sacrifice so Corey could come out and be with me. I also want to thank Sabrina for being so supportive of my ride and of Corey coming out with me for almost two months. You are two incredible women, and I love you more than words.

TODAY'S REFLECTION:

> 2 CORINTHIANS 1:3–5
>
> Praise be to the God and Father of our Lord Jesus Christ, the Father of compassion and the God of all comfort, who comforts us in all our troubles, so that we can comfort those in any trouble with the comfort we ourselves receive from God. For just as we share abundantly in the sufferings of Christ, so also our comfort abounds through Christ.

I love when I see someone God has brought through a painful experience now comforting someone who is going through a difficult time. There is no better person to help than one who has been helped. Someone once said, "Don't waste your pain; use it to help another."

People are amazed to watch Tonia serve those who are going through life-threatening events and terminal illness. My wife lost her little brother, Jimmy, when he was eleven years old from a heart issue he had from birth. As a thirteen-year-old, she was marked by that loss. Even today, though Jimmy would be sixty years old, the scars of losing someone she loved so dearly are still present. She uses what she has learned through that life-changing experience to help others. I have seen her sit with dying people for days. She sleeps in chairs next to them and even moves in with them to give their weary families breaks. Today some of her dearest friends are those with whom she has walked through crisis moments. She comforts

Day 29
New York City
Miles Pedaled: 0

TIME TO RECONNECT

This weekend was very special. After almost a month on the road in a camper with a support team consisting of just men every day, all day and night, it was good to be back with the love of my life. Tonia had come to New York the day after I left for California to begin my ride. Since Corey came with me to document this ride with pictures and video—something we regretted we had not done on the first ride—he left our wonderful daughter-in-law to keep their daughter, Selah.

This doesn't sound like much, but when you know Sabrina, you know her life is packed. She not only teaches dance at a high school in Brooklyn, but she also dances with a dance troupe. At the end of the year, they have daily, nightly, and even weekend practices on top of the ordinary year-round activities. She goes nonstop, and Corey's absence left a big hole. Tonia gladly went up to hang out and take care of Selah during this time. It had been a busy month for her too. On this weekend, she got a few days to rest

Thanks, Pastor Ricky, Jordan, Pastor Jeremy, Kevin, Bruce, and last but not least, my son Corey. You guys made that first month special. I will never forget all you did.

TODAY'S REFLECTION:

PSALM 34:18

The Lord is close to the brokenhearted and
saves those who are crushed in spirit.

This verse is so powerful and comforting. I have told several people this ride was far different from the first. Even though the last day arriving in NYC was disappointing, most of the first ride was filled with joy and excitement. It went pretty much as we had planned, and we had few obstacles and problems. We had no flat tires in 1,500 miles (2,414 kilometers). It rained only once for about an hour. The weather was near perfect the entire time.

This ride had been far different. You've heard me talk of the many plans that went awry and things that happened along the way, but those weren't the hardest for me.

From the first day of my ride, there were personal issues going on among some of my family members. Some had been hurt deeply by others, and others had broken hearts over family they love. This was especially hard when I was on the road. I couldn't do anything about it. I wish I could have reached out and hugged them and helped them, but I couldn't. This verse was a comfort to me on this day in New York. I know in our brokenness and hurt, God cares. He will heal and remain close to us.

Our extended and immediate family are no different from yours. We have the same hurts and broken spirits you experience. If you are brokenhearted, or a loved one is, don't give up hope. Reach out to God. The God who saves and heals is always near.

Day 28
New York City
Miles Pedaled: 0

MY CRAZY FRIEND

Since I was resting from riding that weekend, I want to take some time to thank a very special person who gave up a week of his vacation to fly out to Texas and be my support team for the week. My crazy friend Bruce Willix. Bruce has one of the biggest servant hearts of anyone I know. He acts crazy and loves to have fun, but when there is a serious job to be done, Bruce is there.

Bruce remained when nothing seemed to stay on plan, when we had distractions, detours. He stayed on the days when everything seemed to take the place of my riding. The previous week, I had ridden the least number of miles of any of the first four weeks. But Bruce just rolled with it and did anything he could to make my week a success. As I told him the last day, "We might not have gotten many miles in, but it was a success because I'm still alive."

I thought about the phenomenal support team I had enjoyed up to this point, and I was so grateful for all the men who gave up family, jobs, and ministries in order to serve me.

light would be gone from my life just a few short months after I completed this second ride.

There are bright lights in your life. Love them while they are still here. Tell them you appreciate them, and show them you care.

share the whole story in my book *Lessons from the Road: Moving from the Mundane to the Miraculous*. It is still a painful memory.)

That finish was so disappointing. I remember envisioning how great it would be to arrive in NYC and see family and friends. Instead, half my family was in the emergency room. It certainly didn't end the way I had planned, but isn't that true about a lot of things in life?

Five years later, this Memorial Day weekend would be different. Far better.

TODAY'S REFLECTION:

JOHN 12:35

> Then Jesus told them, "You are going to have the light just a little while longer. Walk while you have the light, before darkness overtakes you. Whoever walks in the dark does not know where they are going."

Jesus was trying to tell His disciples He was about to die and return to heaven. But they did not understand and did not realize what was happening. Isn't this like us? Often God tries to tell us something, but we are so consumed with the moment and our concerns that we miss it.

He has shown us the light and told us to walk in it. I choose darkness many times because of my flesh. When I do walk in the light, though, I don't struggle nearly as much.

I don't think the following thought hit me when my son sent this verse for my daily devotional, but it did as I am writing today: This verse could also hold true for our loved ones—they will not always be with us. We need to love them while we can. My mom was with me for the ending of both of my Bike for Haiti rides. While I am thankful for that, I did not realize her

Day 27
New York City
Miles Pedaled: 0

THREE INCREDIBLE WOMEN

I spent the next couple of days with three incredible women—three of the best in my life. My wife, Tonia, my daughter-in-law Sabrina, and my granddaughter Selah. Corey had some videography work to do out west, so he was not able to be here with us.

Five years before on Memorial Day weekend, I had ridden into New York City, finishing my first Bike for Haiti ride. Sabrina was in Italy at the time, and Tonia was in New York City helping to care for Selah, who was just a year old. My mom was also there. I had three incredible women on that day too. It had been a very different weekend though.

The day I arrived in New York City, Selah got so sick she had to be taken to the hospital directly from where they met me at the World Trade Center site. My mom got so dehydrated while waiting in the unusual 90°F (32°C) heat, she was rushed to the emergency room. So, my granddaughter and mom were admitted to the same ER a few cubicles from each other. (I

with her husband, Kevin, in our early years, arranged to keep it for us. I'm so thankful for people like Kevin and Lin who pioneered the new little church in a trailer, the church we now call Oasis Church of South Florida. Humble beginnings with some good people.

TODAY'S REFLECTION:

JOSHUA 2:23–24

> Then the two men started back. They went down out of the hills, forded the river and came to Joshua son of Nun and told him everything that had happened to them. They said to Joshua, "The LORD has surely given the whole land into our hands; all the people are melting in fear because of us."

God had promised His people the place they would come to call the "Promised Land." Joshua was now in command. Out of the twelve spies, only he and Caleb believed they could take what God had promised. The other ten let fear rule their lives. Now forty years later, some new spies had gone for one last survey before Joshua would lead them in to conquer it. Their report was, "We've got this!"

In a much smaller way, when I went up into the Hill Country, fear had gripped me. It wasn't pleasant pedaling, but I could see God had led me here to help fund the many ministries in Haiti. He had given us this land, and knowing that kept me going.

What has God laid on your heart? What challenge before you grips you with fear? What doubts paralyze you? Are you willing to go for it even if failure is possible? Anytime we step out in faith, failure is always a possibility. Otherwise, it would not be called faith.

Day 26
Austin, Texas
Miles Pedaled: 0

YEARS AGO

On the previous evening someone reminded me that five years ago yesterday I rode into New York City to complete 1,500 miles (2,414 kilometers) from Pembroke Pines, Florida. It was an emotional day, and one I will never forget. My mom flew up to surprise me. Selah, Corey, and Tonia were there for me as I completed my last mile at the World Trade Center. On that ride, Bike for Haiti and our partners were just a vision. Today, five years later, it's a reality. I am amazed at what God has done.

It rained hard on this day. It would have been a short ride day anyway, since my support team member Bruce Willix would be heading back to South Florida. I had to take him to Dallas/Ft. Worth International Airport about two and a half hours north of us. I would then leave for a long Memorial Day weekend to see Tonia, Selah, and Sabrina. It would be a good weekend of rest, and would also allow me to avoid the crowded highway with people on the roads for vacation.

Before leaving Austin, we left our camper at a local church for the weekend. One of our former Oasisers, Lin Monroe, who had attended our church

TODAY'S REFLECTION:

ISAIAH 58:6–7

> "Is not this the kind of fasting I have chosen: to loose the chains of injustice and untie the cords of the yoke, to set the oppressed free and break every yoke? Is it not to share your food with the hungry and to provide the poor wanderer with shelter—when you see the naked, to clothe them, and not to turn away from your own flesh and blood?"

Nathan must have picked these verses out knowing we were at Gabi and Don's home. Of course, he knows how she can cook because she used to cook for him all the time when they both worked on staff at Oasis Church.

Fasting was definitely not in order throughout those last couple of days, even though I do fast and believe strongly in it. (I am fasting this week as I begin the rough draft of this book.)

What got my attention was the reminder to feed the hungry, clothe the naked, and give shelter to those who need it. This is what Bike for Haiti was all about. This kept me pedaling each day even when I was tired, bored, and ready to see my wife and family. When loneliness crept into the camper and on the road when I was by myself, I was reminded that God had called me to be a small drop for the hungry, homeless, and naked in Haiti. Thanks, God, for this reminder today.

Day 25

Fredericksburg to Austin, Texas

Miles Pedaled: 41.09

SOAKING IN THE SCENERY

We said goodbye to Don and Gabi. As we left, they loaded us up with more great food to store in the camper and eat along the way. So much food and so much love! They gave us a special gift of love and a little break from the road—and we were so grateful.

We didn't get a lot of miles in this day, but we did try to take it slow and steady and soak in our last day in the beautiful Hill Country. I had not enjoyed the prior days of riding with so many other things going on around us. With plans being changed constantly, it was hard to breathe in the beautiful surroundings, but on this day I did. It was a beautiful ride from Fredericksburg to Austin.

Hopefully, 30 miles (48 kilometers) tomorrow, and we will be ready to leave Austin and begin a new week.

TODAY'S REFLECTION:

NUMBERS 13:30

Then Caleb silenced the people before Moses and said, "We should go up and take possession of the land, for we can certainly do it."

In the previous verses, the Bible mentions the various people groups who lived in the land God promised to Moses. Twelve spies had gone to check it out. Verse 17 mentions "hill country." That's where the Hittites, Jebusites, and Amorites all lived.

I could identify with that verse about the hill country. The slopes in so much of Texas seemed like the enemy when I was trying to take them on a bicycle. I owe many thanks to Bruce and Corey. They were my Joshua and Caleb through this challenging area, constantly telling me, "You've got this! You can do it!"

When God calls us to do something, no matter how big it is or how many giants we see in the way, He will give us the victory. Don't let the giants scare you. God is bigger than anything you and I may encounter. You can do this!

Day 24
Kerrville to Fredericksburg, Texas
Miles Pedaled: 26

TELEVISION IN AUSTIN

Austin, Texas, is not far from where we would be staying that night, so we drove there to be interviewed by the local CBS affiliate about our Bike for Haiti ride. It was an awesome chance to share our burden for Haiti and the needs there. Thanks to Corey, who, through his various contacts in New York, hooked us up with the people there.

I must admit while I was glad we could tell our story, all the driving to get there and doing the shoot pretty much busted our day of riding. We got only a few hours in. That was frustrating for me. I had this trip planned out, and this detour was not in the schedule.

On the flip side, we were staying with the Murrays again that night. We would have a great meal. Until the previous night at their home, I had not slept in a real bed for almost a month, so this was a real blessing! And Gabi is one of the best cooks I've ever met. She used to cook for our staff when she was a member at Oasis, and it was always a highlight when she prepared us lunch. Preparing food is her love language, and Don was a great support and had a gigantic servant's heart.

Since my ride, Don Murray has gone to be with the Lord. I will never forget his and Gabi's generous and wonderful hospitality in support of our Bike for Haiti ride. The love he showed remains in my heart and the hearts of those he served.

was not over either. That night we would eat with Don and Gabi and stay over at their home. I had been looking forward to that.

Oh! I almost forgot to tell you. If you are ever in Texas, stop in Kerrville. It's the coolest little town. We had found it years before when we did an overnight stop on our way out west with our boys. I never forgot it.

TODAY'S REFLECTION:

JOHN 13:7, 35

> Jesus replied, "You do not realize now what I am doing, but later you will understand. . . . By this everyone will know that you are my disciples, if you love one another."

We don't always understand what God is doing. In this passage, Jesus is washing the disciples' feet. He is showing servanthood and love toward them, yet they don't understand. Peter even protests, "No, Lord, I will not let you wash my feet." He didn't realize Jesus was trying to prepare them for the time when He would not be there physically.

Many times we won't understand what Jesus is doing in our lives, but remember it's for our best. He loves you; He proved that on the cross.

In verse 35, He makes sure His disciples know the most important thing is for others to see how they love one another. Oh, our society and Christian community need a healthy dose of love for one another! It's heartbreaking to see so much division and fighting, even among believers.

I experienced a healthy dose of love that day from Gabi and Don. They exemplified how we should not only *say* we love one another but also *show* it. They displayed it through their hospitality. How do you love others around you?

Day 23

Helotes to Kerrville, Texas
Miles Pedaled: 42.21

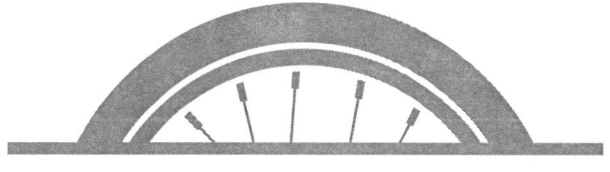

PEACHES, JAMBALAYA, AND BARBEQUE

Another beautiful yet painful ride in the Hill Country. Up and down, up and down—that was my day there. However, lest you think everything was gloom and doom at this point, it wasn't.

Gabi and Don Murray, two former Oasisers who had retired to Fredericksburg, Texas, a few years before, had sent ahead some of Gabi's famous home cooking. At every break, I got to jump into the camper and sink my teeth into some of the sweetest, juiciest peaches I'd ever eaten. Shrimp jambalaya, barbeque, and Gabi's homemade potato salad are about enough to wreck the day's progress. Who should be eating such incredible food while trying to ride cross-country? It seemed ungodly, but I was enjoying it. No, it is not the food recommended for riding up hills all day, but I was relishing the break from the mundane restaurant and fast food we were picking up on the run each day. The wonderful food was a highlight on our trek through Texas, making it a little more bearable. The blessing

TODAY'S REFLECTION:

JOHN 12:24–26

> "Very truly I tell you, unless a kernel of wheat falls to the ground and dies, it remains only a single seed. But if it dies, it produces many seeds. Anyone who loves their life will lose it, while anyone who hates their life in this world will keep it for eternal life. Whoever serves me must follow me; and where I am, my servant also will be. My Father will honor the one who serves me."

I must admit this passage is so appropriate for this journey since hardly an hour went by when I did not realize the dangers of the roads I was pedaling on. As beautiful as the Hill Country with the rolling hills and amazing farms was, it also had narrow, winding streets with no shoulders or bike lanes much of the time. Safety was a constant concern. However, as I said to those who worried about my safety and the dangers of riding a bike on public roads, I was willing to take the chance and risk death or injury in order to support my friends in Haiti.

There comes a time when we must all be willing to die for Christ. For most of us, it will never come to that, but a seed that never dies will remain a single seed. A seed that dies in the ground produces much more in abundance. We must decide: are we willing to die for the cause of Christ and for the One who died for us? Until we are able to say yes, we will never realize our full potential in Him.

Day 22
Hondo to Helotes, Texas
Miles Pedaled: 42

TEXAS HILL COUNTRY

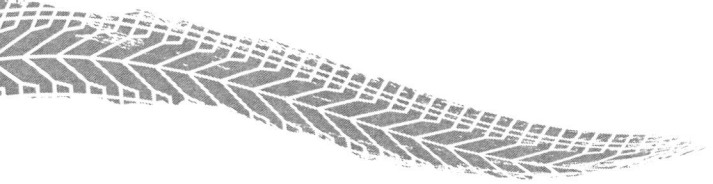

On day 22, we entered what I believe is the only area of Texas worth visiting. Others may disagree, but the Texas Hill Country is my favorite place in the state. It's a beautiful hilly area outside Austin, though I believe Austin would be considered Hill Country. If I ever return to Texas, it's the only place I hope to visit.

Now when they say *hill country*, that is not necessarily true, depending on where you are from and what kind of vehicle you are in. If you are in a car, it's hill country. If you are pedaling a bike, it's more like small mountains. They never stop coming. I think it was harder riding there than the 4,000- to 6,000-foot (1,219- to 1,829-meter) mountains out west. My thighs and calves have never hurt so much. You would think after approximately 1,500 miles (2,414 kilometers) of riding, I should have been okay with these hills.

This was the one area in Texas I had looked forward to visiting on this trip, but now I was having second thoughts. The next couple of days were going to stretch me, and I couldn't wait until they were behind me.

Psalm 139 is a familiar passage to many since it speaks of God creating each of us uniquely, knitting us in our mother's womb and fashioning us in His image. But today's verses are set prior to that familiar passage.

The psalmist reminds us that no matter where we go or what happens, God is there. He is always ready to pick us up, to love us, and to guide us. Do not be gripped with fear when faced with challenges. Sometimes it's dark; sometimes it's lonely. But the psalmist reminds us that God will watch over us. Remember this truth the next time you feel lonely and the darkness surrounds you.

I tried to explain I had ridden 1,500 miles (2,414 kilometers) to New York City and another 1,500 miles from California. I had seen hundreds of troopers and sheriffs, and no one had ever stopped me or said I could not ride on a road. Well, as only a person from the Lone Star State can understand, his response was, "This is Texas."

I will never forget those three words. Yep, it was Texas, and I couldn't wait to get out of that state! So, we lost 20 miles (32 kilometers) of riding. As soon as we crossed over the county line from Kinney, we got back on our bikes and never looked back.

When we got to the city of Hondo, where we would camp, I still wanted my 100 miles (161 kilometers), so I found another road that was perfect and not busy and began to ride, only to run into a dead end with no warning. Just a fence across the road. Oh, well, that was my day. It still wasn't bad at 92 miles (149 kilometers).

But I'll *never* go back to Kinney County, Texas. Never!

TODAY'S REFLECTION:

PSALM 139:5–12

> You hem me in behind and before, and you lay your hand upon me. Such knowledge is too wonderful for me, too lofty for me to attain. Where can I go from your Spirit? Where can I flee from your presence? If I go up to the heavens, you are there; if I make my bed in the depths, you are there. If I rise on the wings of the dawn, if I settle on the far side of the sea, even there your hand will guide me, your right hand will hold me fast. If I say, "Surely the darkness will hide me and the light become night around me," even the darkness will not be dark to you; the night will shine like the day, for darkness is as light to you.

Day 21

Del Rio to Hondo, Texas
Miles Pedaled: 92.45

WELL, THIS IS TEXAS

This was going to be the perfect day to do my first century. I was prepared to smash through it. And then . . .

Because we were headed into days of the Texas Hill Country, as they call it, we decided to improvise. Instead of leaving U.S. 90 and traveling on a back road as the bike map suggested, we stayed on the busier but better road.

Not long into our day, the roads were straight, hilly, and busy off and on. As we came over a steep hill, we passed a sheriff's car going the opposite way. That was a normal occurrence, except this time he turned around. In a matter of a minute, I was pulled over and lectured about how dangerous this road was and how trucks come over the hill at 90 miles per hour (145 kilometers per hour).

"You are to get off the road right now," he asserted. "Right now, you hear that?"

TODAY'S REFLECTION:

HABAKKUK 3:17–18

> Though the fig tree does not bud and there are no grapes on the vines, though the olive crop fails and the fields produce no food, though there are no sheep in the pen and no cattle in the stalls, yet I will rejoice in the Lord, I will be joyful in God my Savior.

The prophet Habakkuk had been wrestling and complaining to God about the trials and pains of his people, Israel. In chapter 3 he quit complaining and began to pray. In these verses, he sets a good example for all of us.

There will be times of pain and spiritual drought in our lives, illustrated by the desert and the dry landscape I encountered on portions of this bike ride, but despite the tough times, we can find *joy* in knowing our Savior. I need to be constantly reminded that I do not deserve all I have or all our culture offers here in the U.S. I did not earn it, and I am not entitled to it.

God can speak to me far more and far clearer when I am desperate and hurting than when everything is going well.

Day 20
Del Rio, Texas
Miles Pedaled: 0

BEING A KID AGAIN

I took the day to rest and began the morning worshiping online. I loved the opportunity online worship gave us to stay in touch with our Heavenly Father and my church family—Oasis Church.

I found myself reliving the laundry days I used to have in college. On this day, after finding a coin laundromat, I discovered a Sonic fast-food drive-in restaurant next door. Yeah! I felt like a kid again, sipping on a coconut cream milkshake. I never get to have things like this anymore—too many calories and too much fat. I would feel guilty, but after knocking down 411 more miles (661 kilometers) this week and burning 33,896 calories, I convinced myself it was okay!

We would start week 4 the next day, and then I would get to take a break and go see Tonia, my wife, for the Memorial Day weekend. There would be too much holiday traffic to stay on the road—a good excuse to go see my babe.

throughout the desert and mountains out west. From time to time when I was riding in a desolate place and seeing nothing for miles, I'd spot some border patrols on horseback or four-wheelers. I hadn't seen any coyotes or drug smugglers yet and hoped I never would.

TODAY'S REFLECTION:

JOHN 10:3–5

> "The gatekeeper opens the gate for him, and the sheep listen to his voice. He calls his own sheep by name and leads them out. When he has brought out all his own, he goes on ahead of them, and his sheep follow him because they know his voice. But they will never follow a stranger; in fact, they will run away from him because they do not recognize a stranger's voice."

One of the funniest moments in my cross-country ride was a day out in West Texas where it's nothing but cattle and horse farms for miles. While I was just riding and minding my own business, I spotted a large group of cattle grazing close to the road. Several calves got spooked and ran away from the fence. When they did, others started running toward me. For about a quarter mile (402 meters), they ran alongside me as if they knew me. I laughed so hard I could hardly focus on the road. Then I started mooing at them. The more I did, the more they ran after me. It was as if I was their shepherd—if cows had a shepherd. I still smile every time I think about it.

Jesus said His sheep will know Him, and they will follow Him. If a person knows the Shepherd, he will follow. This is a very distinct mark of a disciple. We will follow Him even if it means going to an unfamiliar pasture or ministering in a land not our own. He may call some to be missionaries, to return to their home country, or to join in a ministry they don't feel equipped to participate in. Let me encourage you, follow HIM! He's the Good Shepherd.

Day 19

Dryden to Del Rio, Texas

Miles Pedaled: 70.33

Week 3 was in the books. We stopped just shy of Del Rio, our goal for this third week of what I had been calling "the brutal weeks."

We had several firsts this day. I got to ride with my son Corey, who had been videotaping the entire trip, recording it for a future date. That was special. I'm proud of him and his tenacity to get everything on film, along with breathless drone footage every day. He had been my greatest encourager on my hardest days.

Another first was when Kevin had to fix two more flat tires on the camper. The roads out there were brutal on the camper, as well as on my bike and me.

After a day of rest, we would begin the next week by saying goodbye to the Mexican border we had constantly hugged over the previous 400 miles (644 kilometers). Several times I had to go through a Border Patrol checkpoint on my bike! That was awkward. These checkpoints are randomly placed

TODAY'S REFLECTION:

JOHN 9:2–4

> His disciples asked him, "Rabbi, who sinned, this man or his parents, that he was born blind?"
>
> "Neither this man nor his parents sinned," said Jesus, "but this happened so that the works of God might be displayed in him. As long as it is day, we must do the works of him who sent me. Night is coming, when no one can work."

Jesus had a sense of urgency I sometimes lack. He knew He had limited time to accomplish what He had been sent to do. I must ask myself this question regularly: do I sense the urgency of the mission God has called me to?

I stay amazingly focused when I have a long ride or need to get in a certain number of miles. On those days, it's all business. I can't afford not to make this city or reach that goal in order to finish the Bike for Haiti ride in the time I have planned. I wish every day was that way.

Jesus did not just have a sense of urgency—He was also living in order to display God's life-changing power. Do we live life with an urgency, not to make a lot of money, retire, or get a bigger house, but to live for God so others will see Him and want Him in their lives? Let's do it!

Day 18

Marathon to Dryden, Texas
Miles Pedaled: 81.67

BORING

Day 18 was one of those days. We racked up some good miles but rode out in the middle of nowhere. The bike map on the way out of Marathon said no services for 55 miles (89 kilometers). It was correct. That's a long way on a bike without seeing any civilization.

Half the ride was great with the wind at our backs, and half was tough, riding into the wind and uphill. Yes, the wind again. Other than an occasional glimpse of the border with Mexico and a Customs and Border Patrol station, that was basically it. Even the campground was somewhere between the little town of Dryden and nowhere. We were thankful for a self-contained camper.

This is the kind of day you listen to worship music or an audiobook and try to stay focused on the goal. Del Rio, Texas, would end another week of Bike for Haiti's cross-country ride. One more day to Del Rio.

Nast Magazine. WOW! We hit the jackpot that night. They had a beautiful fireplace burning, and we savored every moment.

TODAY'S REFLECTION:

PSALM 106:12–13

Then they believed his promises and sang his praise. But they soon forgot what he had done and did not wait for his plan to unfold.

The people of Israel saw God do miracles and observed His hand as no other people had ever done. He had saved them from slavery in Egypt. He had parted the Red Sea. He had fed them as they wandered in the wilderness. They sang His praises as we do so many times on Sunday morning. But on Monday, when the temptations come or the trials hit, we, like the Israelites, seem to forget all He has done.

The hardest thing to do is to wait on Him. I encourage each of us today to remember all He has done and wait for His plans to unfold. We will not be sorry.

I always regret it when I run ahead of God and kick doors in or move on to plan B when His plan A is far better. May you embrace the plan A God has for you today.

Day 17

Fort Davis to Marathon, Texas

Miles Pedaled: 63.34

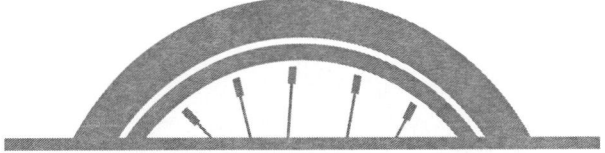

THE 12 GAGE

It was another cold morning, but I wasn't complaining. By the time we were to leave Texas, it would probably be 100°F (38°C) or more.

It seemed we'd had wind out of the east for most of the ride so far. It was a hard day of riding into the wind, but other than that, non-eventful. Well, the *ride* was pretty uneventful, which was good. But as we closed out the day about 40 miles (64 kilometers) outside the Big Bend National Park, we stopped in a little town of just four hundred people: Marathon. They had rolled up the streets before we got there, but we found one restaurant open. After a long day we decided to take a chance and give it a try. We had no other choice!

That was eventful. In this little tiny town in the middle of West Texas, 50 miles (80 kilometers) from any other town, was the 12 Gage Restaurant. If you don't know what that means, look it up. We learned that this restaurant had been voted the #1 restaurant in Texas and #17 in the USA by *Condé*

6,500 feet (1,981 meters). By the way, the high this day reached only 62°F (17°C).

Another eventful day. I guess the highlight was that we crossed over into Central Standard Time Zone! That was exciting—except the next time zone, Eastern Standard Time, was still 1,500 miles (2,414 kilometers) away. We wouldn't reach it until we got just west of Tallahassee, Florida. Onward!

TODAY'S REFLECTION:

JOHN 6:66–67

> From this time many of his disciples turned back and no longer followed him. "You do not want to leave too, do you?" Jesus asked the Twelve.

To me, this is one of the saddest passages in the Bible. Jesus had walked on water, fed the five thousand, and done one miracle after another. Yet most of those who experienced these wonders turned around and left Him. Jesus had to double-check with His own called disciples to make sure they were not going to walk away too. Can you imagine?

There are times in our lives when we consider walking away. We might not say it, but in times of spiritual drought, discouragement, and loneliness, it's easy to feel He has abandoned us. I assure you, He hasn't. He won't. Just hang in there. Keep trusting . . . keep following . . . and keep moving forward even when it seems as though you have a 1,000-pound (454-kilogram) weight attached to you. He is there. He promised He would not leave us or turn His back on us. Even if everyone else in your life has done that, He won't forget you.

Lean on Him. Trust Him even when you can't see Him.

Day 16
Van Horn to Fort Davis, Texas
Miles Pedaled: 54.76

ONLY IN TEXAS

BRRR! 49°F (9°C) that morning in Texas. We had just packed away our cold weather gear two days before, and now we had to dig it back out. Forty-nine degrees for this South Floridian riding a bike into the wind on a mountain at 6,000 feet (1,829 meters) elevation is COLDDD! BRRR!

The campground where we were staying had what they called a motel . . . I'm not sure I would call it that. But it did pay off. That morning they let us eat breakfast inside. They had a waffle maker like you see in so many hotels across the U.S.—except, wouldn't you know it, this one made waffles in the shape of the state of Texas. Only in the Lone Star State. They think they are so special. I wanted to get one in the shape of Florida. Wouldn't that be cool?

With me dressed like an Inuk in cold-weather biker gear, we headed out. But first we had to buy a few new tires in case we had more blowouts and nowhere to get replacements. This took us on a 100-mile (161-kilometer) detour, which gave us a late start to climbing our biggest mountain yet:

TODAY'S REFLECTION:

PSALM 34:17

> The righteous cry out, and the Lord hears them;
> he delivers them from all their troubles.

No better verse for today than this. We definitely started with trouble: a flat in the desert, no cell service, and stranded off the road in a place roadside service didn't know where to find us. We did pray, and I would even say cried out to the Lord. He heard us, and help arrived two hours later.

Has there ever been a time when you were in a crisis situation and cried out to the Lord, and He surprised you with an immediate answer? I love those times. It doesn't always happen, but when it does, I cherish it.

Psalm 34:8 says, "Taste and see that the Lord is good; blessed is the one who takes refuge in him."

Kevin and I tasted of the Lord's goodness that day. I cherish all the times I felt His presence and His hand in our ride and all that has come after. We have been able to support hundreds in schools, orphanages, and churches throughout Haiti. All because He has provided, and we have tasted His goodness.

Day 15

El Paso to Van Horn, Texas
Miles Pedaled: 84.01

On day 15, we rode 16 miles (26 kilometers) out of El Paso and into nowhere. Within the hour, our camper had a flat. I was so thankful we had road service, but when you are out in the desert, it takes a while for help to arrive. We did get service after a couple of hours and were off to tackle the West Texas Mountains. This day and the next would be two of our steepest climbs yet—with the next day's mountains at 6,500 feet (1,981 meters). I was thankful to get in 84 miles (135 kilometers) despite the flat tire.

We may have been flat, but we were not out—thanks to our new support team member Kevin Parrot, our facilities director at Oasis Church. There is almost nothing he can't or won't do. He got the tire fixed, and we were on our way. I could not have had better support with the rugged terrain we had ahead. He is one of a kind, and I was grateful to have him with me that week.

I remembered years before taking the boys on a trip. We stopped in El Paso and walked across the border into Juarez. It was heart-wrenching to see such poverty a few feet from our first-world affluence. We watched people board inner tubes and rafts to come across the river right in front of the customs border crossing like a constant stream. Who could blame them? It was a sad sight to see.

TODAY'S REFLECTION:

EPHESIANS 2:10

> For we are God's handiwork, created in Christ Jesus to do good works, which God prepared in advance for us to do.

We are created to do good works—to help others. We are not only created but also prepared for them. God has crafted us to do good.

When I stood across the border and looked through the fences and walls separating the USA and Mexico and saw the hurting and suffering people, my heart went out to them. I wished I could help them all, but I couldn't. You can't either. But we can help someone. Just begin with one.

That is why I'm doing this ride across the USA. To help as many Haitians as Oasis Church, my friends, and I can. Even if we help one person, it would be worth it. As I rode, I pictured the faces of the orphans, the cardboard huts, and people bathing in sewage-and-garbage-filled rivers in Haiti. This kept me focused on the goal—to be the "drop," even if it's for just one.

Who will be the *one* you show love to today? I invite you to join me and the hundreds of others who have given to help our neighbors in Haiti. You've begun by purchasing this book. Thank you. Let this be your first step of many.

Day 14

El Paso, Texas

Miles Pedaled: 0

TRANSITIONS

Day 14 was a day of transition. That fits better than calling it a rest day. Washing four loads of clothes, cleaning the camper, and taking care of lots of other details preparing for a new week of riding is not rest. I did get a deep tissue massage, which was so needed for this old body that had now ridden over 1,000 miles (1,609 kilometers) through deserts, over mountains, and in escapes from rabid dogs. Getting a massage was something I would have never thought of before my first Bike for Haiti ride. Other experienced bikers said they are important to keep your body loose and advised me to have one every week while on the road. I did pretty well on the first ride along the East Coast, but it had not been so easy out west. Every muscle I had was feeling my age—as if someone had twisted them like rubber bands in a knot. On this day, though, I would get this old body tuned back up.

El Paso, Texas, is on the border of Juarez, Mexico. I could literally see into the Mexican city. It saddened me when I looked over the border the previous night and saw very little light in the city of almost a half million people, while El Paso was lit up like Las Vegas. The poverty was evident as we rode along the places where the border had see-through or no fences.

> "Very truly I tell you, no one can enter the kingdom of God unless they are born of water and the Spirit. Flesh gives birth to flesh, but the Spirit gives birth to spirit. You should not be surprised at my saying, 'You must be born again.'" (John 3:5–7)

Jesus reminds us the only way we can have the Spirit of God in our lives—the only way to have eternal life—is to accept Him as Lord and Savior. When we have Him, He sends us the Holy Spirit, the wind that will direct us. We do not know where He is going, but He will get us there.

And then—yes, and then—as we rolled into the outskirts of El Paso, Texas, I spotted the most heavenly blinking red sign, which seemed to illuminate the road for miles. It was not a desert mirage. Oh, no. It was Krispy Kreme doughnuts. No doubt God put that place on my route just for me. He knew I had earned it this day, especially after eating the healthy salad. I had been told I was burning from 4,000 to 8,000 calories a day, so I had permission to eat a doughnut once in a while.

Since it was the first KK I'd seen on this trip, I bought thirteen doughnuts in honor of my thirteen days of riding. I think they call it a baker's dozen. Yes, of course, I ate them all. Don't judge me!

Well . . . I might have let Jeremy have one.

Map 2 of 7 of the Southern Tier Bicycle Route completed.

TODAY'S REFLECTION:

JOHN 3:8

> "The wind blows wherever it pleases. You hear its sound, but you cannot tell where it comes from or where it is going. So it is with everyone born of the Spirit."

When you are riding a bike, the wind is either your friend or foe. One of the first things I did each morning when I got up and right before I went to bed at night was to check the weather. Even on otherwise perfect days, the wind has everything to do with your ride. You never know where or how much it's going to blow even after checking the forecast. It changes constantly throughout the day and every time the road makes a turn. Wind is huge to a biker.

"The wind blows wherever it pleases." Jesus is speaking to Nicodemus, who had come to inquire about the new birth, salvation in Jesus.

Day 13

Las Cruces, New Mexico to El Paso, Texas

Miles Pedaled: 56.51

A SALAD AND A DOZEN KRISPY KREMES

It was a lazy, hazy Sunday. I worshiped online with my Oasis Church Family and then headed out for what would be an uneventful day. Not many miles ridden since we had 21-mile-per-hour (34-kilometer-per-hour) winds and higher gusts pounding us all day, but no detours, no change of plans, dead ends, or distractions. Just a great day to ride.

With the wind, I did experience something I had never dealt with before. There were miles and miles of farms along the route on the border with Mexico. All day, I breathed in what I assumed was the smell of pesticides and fertilizer. I thought maybe I should have worn those masks I had hardly needed for the dust storms in the deserts of California and Arizona.

Jeremy fixed me the most incredibly tasty salad for lunch. Lunch in the middle of nowhere is wherever you stop the camper. So, on the side of the road, I ate the healthiest thing yet while on this trip. I was definitely feeling good about myself.

visit, I did not know this little town was known worldwide for their Hatch red-hot chili peppers. Before I got to town, my nose began to burn. That's no exaggeration. It was a fun town, and I loaded up on bunches of red-hot chili peppers to take home to family.

Jeremy Higdon and I finished our day by treating ourselves to a steak in the town's world-famous restaurant, Sparky's Burgers. If you ever pass through Hatch, New Mexico, eat at Sparky's and buy some fresh Hatch red-hot chili peppers. You will be glad you did.

TODAY'S REFLECTION:

PSALM 109:26–27

Help me, Lord, my God; save me according
to your unfailing love. Let them know that it is
your hand, that you, Lord, have done it.

"Help me, Lord!" That was my thought, and yes, I prayed this more than once that day as dogs chased me, hoping to shred me into kibble. We have a way of praying without hedging when dogs are snapping at our heels. Even though I know it, I tend to forget that God loves me beyond what I can imagine. His love will not fail me. He wants to protect you and me; He wants to bless us and show us the abundance of His love. But sometimes He's waiting for us to cry out in desperation as David did.

Don't miss what the psalmist said in verse 27: he not only wanted to see God work in his life but also desired for others to see God's mighty power in the incredible things He did for him. May we all desire not only to have prayers answered but that God would get all the credit when they are.

Day 12

Deming to Las Cruces, New Mexico
Miles Pedaled: 43.54

AIR HORNS, RED-HOT CHILI PEPPERS, AND DOGS

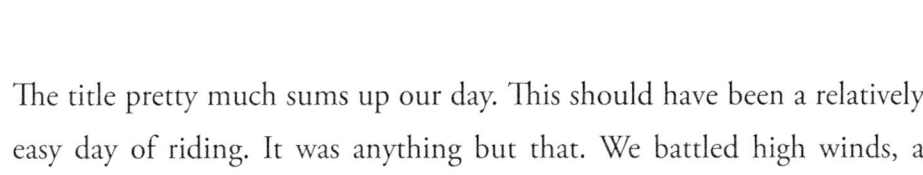

The title pretty much sums up our day. This should have been a relatively easy day of riding. It was anything but that. We battled high winds, a rainstorm, a detour of 100 miles (161 kilometers), and dogs the size of horses.

When you have detours like this one, you are thankful for a support vehicle. I can't imagine what lone bicyclists do out here when this happens.

While training in Tennessee, I bought some very loud air horns for the bears. I never needed them there, but this day, I was glad I had them. Dogs were chasing me all day. It seemed as if every trailer out in the rural areas of New Mexico had a dog. Or several. Thankfully, I was not pedaling up a mountain. I ran from more dogs this one day than during my entire trip up the East Coast of the U.S.

The end of the day made it all worthwhile. We biked into the little town of Hatch, New Mexico, with a population of around 1,500 people. Until this a frontage road to I-10. While expecting a paved street, I got a rocky road of gravel for more than 10 miles (16 kilometers). Skinny road tires aren't made for gravel, but I never took a spill. On another occasion, Google sent me down a road that ended up being a dead end. We had to turn around and ride back to the expressway.

TODAY'S REFLECTION:

PSALM 3:3

But you, Lord, are a shield around me, my
glory, the One who lifts my head high.

Ephesians 6 reminds us that each believer is to put on the full armor of God. While this is extremely important, it is also vital to know that no matter what the enemy throws at us, our God is a *shield* to protect us.

In Psalm 3:4–5, He says He hears us when we cry out to Him, and when we sleep, He sustains us. These are great promises to remember as we go through difficult times. King David wrote this psalm as he ran from his own son, Absalom, who was trying to kill him and steal his kingdom. Hopefully, you aren't facing such a desperate need today, but maybe the mountain you are up against or the valley you're stuck in seems impossible to navigate. During these times the words of the psalmist David can be of comfort and strength. God is our shield. He is our defender, and He is our sustainer. Praise Him with me today.

Day 11

Lordsburg to Deming, New Mexico
Miles Pedaled: 66.79

WHEN MAPS FAIL

On the eleventh day, I rode the easiest 26 miles (42 kilometers) of the over 600 miles (966 kilometers) I'd biked so far. It was another day of new adventures and some surprises. No matter how well you plan, sometimes it just doesn't work out the way you think it will.

I spent the entire ride this day above 4,000 feet (1,219 meters) and crossed over the New Mexico Continental Divide at 4,585 feet (1,398 meters). This altitude would seem small when I reached the West Texas Mountains, which took me up to 6,300 feet (1,920 meters). It was a cool day, with temps below 90°F (32°C). Rain clouds hovered above. You could even smell the moisture in the air.

Because I had changed my bike route map to miss the 8,500-foot (2,591-meter) mountains, we had to ride I-10 for part of the day. Google maps are not very reliable when it comes to biking, so I was thankful I was not relying on them this whole trip. On this day, Google sent me off onto

TODAY'S REFLECTION:

GALATIANS 6:8

Whoever sows to please their flesh, from the flesh will reap destruction; whoever sows to please the Spirit, from the Spirit will reap eternal life.

The principle of sowing and reaping comes from this passage. Those who have not grown up on a farm have a harder time understanding this, but it's an absolute principle whether you are a rural farmer or a city dweller. Feed on the Spirit of God. As we fill ourselves with the things of God and let the Holy Spirit rule us, we will reap the abundant life Jesus offers us. Feed on our flesh—fulfill the fleshly desires that are natural for us as humans—and we will reap its destructive results. Sadly, too many times I choose the flesh to feed.

This ride was definitely an endurance test for a person my age. It was easy to get weary. Seeing all these mountains and deserts during my training caused me to wonder if I'd made the right decision. It would have been easy to give up and find another way to highlight our Haitian partnership. But God called me to this. He made His will clear, so I would not give up. I would not give in. I planned to see the reaping of hundreds and thousands of dollars given to support the beautiful orphans, families, and pastors in Haiti.

Don't give up. No matter how weary you get, don't give in. If God is in you, He will bring you through it. Trust Him and live daily for Him. Feed on the Spirit and not the flesh. In the end, you will reap a harvest of God's blessings. No matter how hard the road is today, keep pedaling.

Day 10

Bylas, Arizona to Lordsburg, New Mexico

Miles Pedaled: 60.78

DETOUR

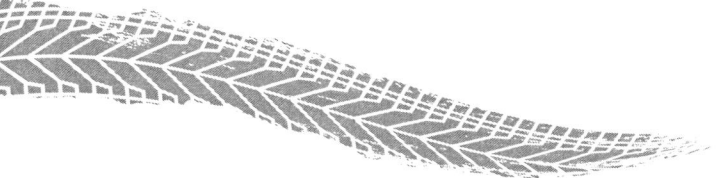

Another climb today to more than 4,500 feet (1,372 meters). At almost 100°F (38°C), the altitude almost got to me. This flatlander's lungs were not accustomed to this type of riding.

The detour a couple of days before outside Superior, Arizona, had been construction related. On this day I took a detour of my own making. It would take us out of the way and create other issues, but during our preparations when we were scouting the mountains, we met two female bikers in a snowstorm. That mountain was over 8,000 feet (2,400 meters) high, with hairpin turns and no shoulders. As part of my recon, I studied maps of the area and decided to take a detour to avoid that mountain at all costs. More on the detour tomorrow. We finished Arizona this day, which took us into our third state in ten days. Hello, New Mexico.

Almost 600 miles (966 kilometers) behind us now; 39,992 calories burned. That's a lot of fat.

Miami! And no, I had not gone home; there is a Miami, Arizona, high up in the mountains. Population 1,936. That's not my Miami!

The long day finished as the sun set in the west. I rode through the San Carlos Apache Reservation. We didn't see many Apache people, but the ones we did see were nice. They no longer live in tepees, although they had some tourist trap tepees along the road in the reservation. We didn't see many tourists out there.

TODAY'S REFLECTION:

PROVERBS 21:31

The horse is made ready for the day of battle,
but victory rests with the Lord.

What an appropriate verse today. There were many horses on the reservation and in the mountains and wilderness where we rode. I could only imagine during my long stretches of no cell phone, no radio, and just peace and quiet how the indigenous people had hidden in the mountains and prepared for battle with the pioneers who came to threaten the land of their ancestors. I envisioned how they must have fought in this valley.

We don't battle on horses today, but most of us understand the struggles we face with our evil thoughts, Satan's temptations, and our fleshly desires. A real war sometimes rages in our hearts and minds.

In a past reflection, we discussed how Paul had to fight to press toward the goal God had for him. He had to battle the evil one just as we do. This is why it's important to remember that God knows our fight and reminds us to put on the full armor of God.

Prepare daily for battle, but also remember that the victory rests with our Lord. Amen.

Day 9

Superior to Bylas, Arizona
Miles Pedaled: 69.2

CRAZIEST RIDING DAY EVER

With the cities of Apache Junction and Superior in our rearview mirror, we set out on what, up to this point, was the craziest day of riding I'd ever experienced. Of course, I didn't know it would get far crazier when I got to Texas and Louisiana. That's for another day, though.

The first thing we saw as we headed up the mountain was a sign saying the road was closed. Yes, Highway U.S. 60 was closed because of major construction on the highway. It would shut down for hours—and sometimes all day. Yikes! Surprised again!

But this was our lucky day; it was closed only a few hours—if "lucky" can be used in this context. For a few miles, the street was so bad, I could not ride. It was all gravel and one-lane roads with large trucks flying past. I alternated between walking and riding in the camper. But between traffic, construction, and crazy steep climbs, we actually rode through Miami! Yes,

TODAY'S REFLECTION:

PROVERBS 20:24

A person's steps are directed by the Lord. How then can anyone understand their own way?

Surprise! Surprise is not just a city in the suburbs of Phoenix; it's what happens in life all the time. I don't know why I still get surprised by God. Most of the time it's a good surprise but not always. I am reminded again today by the verse Nathan shared with me that God is the one who directs my steps—or, in the case of that day, my wheels. This trip had already had some surprises, and it would bring a lot more along the way.

We don't always understand God's ways, but I have experienced many years of His surprises. Please hear me when I say He knows best. It's far better for Him to take the wheel than for us to try to steer this life on our own.

Proverbs 20:18 tells us this: "Plans are established by seeking advice; so if you wage war, obtain guidance."

It's always good to listen to people who are wiser and have been down the road before. The Bible is clear that we should seek the counsel of others in our decisions. However, never forget that the most important person to seek direction from is God Himself. If you don't, the surprises will not always be good ones. Trust me; I've learned the hard way.

Day 8
Phoenix to Superior, Arizona
Miles Pedaled: 73.73

SURPRISE

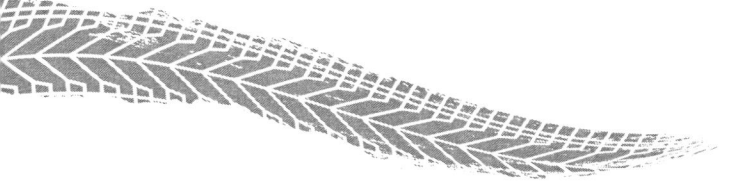

Our second week began what I called the "brutal weeks"—full of desert, mountains, and lots of heat. Most days, I was riding in temps over 100°F (38°C).

Today, we left the valley floor from Phoenix—or actually, you can say "Surprise" (yes, there is a city called Surprise). I loved the names out there. Hope, Surprise, and on day 8 after a long day of climbing mountains, we arrived in Superior. Nothing I saw there was superior, but I guess it was, or is, for someone out there.

Our route took us straight up into the mountains to 2,800 feet (853 meters) and would only get steeper the next day. Amazingly, though, we were able to get almost 74 miles (119 kilometers) in while biking through the Superstition Mountains. Welcome back to my friend Jeremy, who was my everything support that week.

was due to arrive that evening, so I set about doing my "chores"—I had a lot of clothes to wash and supplies to buy, and then I would get a little rest.

Map 1 of 7 of the Southern Tier Bicycle Route was complete.

TODAY'S REFLECTION:

PHILIPPIANS 2:13

For it is God who works in you to will and to act in order to fulfill his good purpose.

PHILIPPIANS 3:16

Only let us live up to what we have already attained.

God has given each of us a purpose in life. Our goal should be to find that purpose and run after it. If you are struggling with finding your purpose, start in prayer and delve into His Word. Then speak to others—not just anyone, though. Speak to those who are living out God's purpose for their lives. They can give you some good advice.

My purpose on this ride was beyond me. It was for the children and people of Haiti, and only God working in me had brought me through this brutal first week.

Philippians 3:16 encourages us to live up to what God expects. In prior verses, Paul wrote about pressing toward the goal, his high calling in Christ Jesus, straining to move forward, and not looking back.

I encourage you to press forward toward your calling, and don't look back. Don't give up. Don't let others discourage you from doing what God has purposed for your life.

Day 7

Phoenix, Arizona

Miles Pedaled: 0

IN THE BOOKS

Within the rhythms of a 3,200-mile bike ride, I needed something God Himself commanded: rest. This was the day.

There was much to do, and the Sabbath is seldom a day of rest, but this was rest from the day-to-day ride. In that way, it was a break from the norm.

Pastor Ricky (our executive pastor) and Jordan (one of our staff members) spent the first week with me—supporting me in everything from fixing flats to driving the camper to setting up camp to cleaning out the sewer hold in the camper. I could not have done this trip without guys like them. I am blessed beyond words.

Pastor Jeremy Higdon was now joining my support team. He had been on our pastoral team for twelve years before planting a church in North Jacksonville, Florida. He also spent a week with me on our ride from Miami to New York City. I was looking forward to this time with him. He

and report the incident. Sadly, the dispatcher acted as though he couldn't care less and blew it off. I am happy to be alive today.

I did get to worship with our Oasis Church family online before my ride since we were three hours behind the East Coast. That was beyond refreshing and emotional. It was Mother's Day—one of the few I had not been with my mom—and I called her from the road. It was hard being so far away, and I knew she worried 24/7 about me when I was riding.

TODAY'S REFLECTION:

MATTHEW 7:14

"But small is the gate and narrow the road that
leads to life, and only a few find it."

In this verse, Jesus reminds us His kingdom is not one everyone will choose—not everyone will spend eternity with Him. In fact, He says few will find it. My mom found it.

What I did not know that day was that this Mother's Day would be her last. She passed away in November, four months after my ride. It's still hard when I think I was not with her for her last Mother's Day.

At her funeral, I read her testimony—the story of her new birth in Jesus. Her story is one of heartache, loss, and pain, but it is also a story of great joy, happiness, and anticipation of eternal life. Even in her last hours, she continued to plead with family members to follow Jesus. She would tell them with passion and urgency, as only a dying person can do, that she wanted to see them again in heaven. She found life, and you can too. If you have never accepted Christ as Savior and Lord, I would encourage you to do it today. Read Romans 3:23, 5:8, 6:23, and 10:9–13. Anyone who trusts Jesus as their Savior can enter the small gate to eternal life.

Day 6
Salome to Phoenix, Arizona
Miles Pedaled: 93.70

HAPPY MOTHER'S DAY!

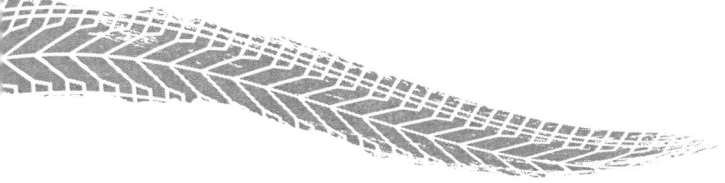

Although it was Sunday, since we had just started our journey on Tuesday, I decided to ride. It was the first and the last time I planned to ride on a Sunday. It was a long day—one that would have had us riding 100 miles (161 kilometers), called a "century" in biking. It got dark as we rode into the suburbs of Phoenix. The busy road was under construction, so it was not safe. While I would have loved to ride my first century of this journey, we continued to remind each other of our priority: safety first. It was time to stop for the day.

On the road, I had been listening to worship music while out on a desolate stretch of road and was almost struck by an 18-wheeler. It sped by a car, whipped across the road to avoid an oncoming vehicle, and came within a few feet of sideswiping me. That was one of the scariest moments I've ever had on a bike—and by far the most dangerous. If I had not swerved off the side of the road, I would not be writing this today. It shook me up, to say the least, and stirred up some anger that rarely surfaces. It disturbed me so much, I had to stop and take a break. I asked Corey to call the truckline

(80 kilometers) going downhill toward Phoenix.

Speaking of *hope*, as the sun set in the beautiful western sky that night, we rode through a little town named Hope. "Little" meaning they did not have even a stoplight or a gas station. But at the edge of town, which couldn't have been more than a couple hundred yards, I saw a sign reading, "Your Now Beyond Hope." That was hilarious. You can google it; I promise it says that.

TODAY'S REFLECTION:

2 CORINTHIANS 12:9

> But he said to me, "My grace is sufficient for you, for my power is made perfect in weakness." Therefore I will boast all the more gladly about my weaknesses, so that Christ's power may rest on me.

Beyond hope. Someone reading this today feels exactly this way. It would be one thing if you were just beyond Hope, Arizona, but you may feel hopeless about life.

You are not alone.

Paul had some type of ailment. It seems he had given up hope of having it healed, but his words in 2 Corinthians 12:9 show that no matter what his circumstance, even though his hope of healing would never be fulfilled, he leaned on God's grace. He acknowledged that in his weakness, the power of God shows off. God's grace and power prove themselves real in our weakest areas. You are *not* beyond hope. Let the words of the prophet in Jeremiah 29:11 ring in your heart and mind:

> "For I know the plans I have for you," declares the Lord, "plans to prosper you and not to harm you, plans to give you *hope* and a future." (emphasis mine)

Day 5

Blythe, California to Salome, Arizona
Miles Pedaled: 58.69

BEYOND HOPE

I love milestones. I live for goals. They keep me going and give me hope.

Today was a milestone for Bike for Haiti. We left California on the worst roads I've ever ridden and began the day in Arizona. We were still in the desert, and my team and I once again found ourselves riding on another interstate, this time I-10. Yes, the same one in Florida that many of us take from Jacksonville to Pensacola if we go east to west. I can't tell you how nervous this made me. I stayed as far away from the lanes of traffic as I could. I'm glad it only continued for 25 miles (40 kilometers). That was plenty.

Today was another day of climbing, from the low desert of 100 feet (30 meters) above sea level to 2,000 feet (610 meters) above. All on I-10. So here I was going 8 miles per hour (13 kilometers per hour) uphill, with semis passing me at 80+ miles per hour (129+ kilometers per hour). I don't think anyone goes 70 (113 kilometers) out west. Up and down, up and down. But there was hope. The next day I would have about 50 miles

Often semi-trucks sped over the hill at 80 to 90 miles per hour (129 to 145 kilometers per hour), which was just a little scary. My support team and gear vehicle (sag wagon) tried to stay close and alert the truckers before they reached me. I was fortunate to have that help. Hundreds of bikers ride this route alone—just them and their bike with all their belongings attached on the back.

We had one special blessing today: it rained lightly for part of the ride. Remember, this is a desert. It never rains there, but today God cooled me off. I had to wear a rain jacket for about an hour.

TODAY'S REFLECTION:

PSALM 92:12, 14

> The righteous will flourish like a palm tree, they will grow like a cedar of Lebanon. . . . They will still bear fruit in old age, they will stay fresh and green.

How ironic that today's verses give a beautiful picture of a righteous person. I rode through a desert with no palms, no fruit, no green vegetation, nothing alive at all that I could see—just beautiful sand dunes painted across the landscape of His creation.

Deserts have a certain beauty about them—especially the one I rode through that day. But one does not live in a desert without certain preparation and supplies. For the believer, we may traverse a desert in our lives. We may feel dry at times, lifeless and without energy. This is not uncommon. If you are human, you will experience these desert times. I love that God, through the psalmist, promises that we will flourish if we live a righteous life. We will bear fruit and have a freshness about us as we get older. Our body might be aging, but our soul and spirit can grow stronger as we draw closer to Him.

Day 4
Brawley to Blythe, California
Miles Pedaled: 87.98

AN AMAZING ARTIST

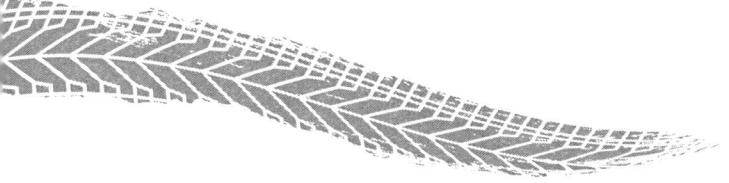

The western United States has an amazing variety of culture and geography. While we continued to ride in the deserts of California, we pedaled through the most unusual place I've ever seen: the Imperial Sand Dunes. Until this journey, I never realized sand dunes like the ones I have seen on TV and in the movies exist in America. They do! They are in one of our national wilderness areas—and wilderness it is. Sand as far as the eye can see. Beautiful dunes that look like something out of a movie. Perfect formations that do not even look real. God is an artist. He amazes me constantly. This day was no exception.

This two-lane road with just me and many sixteen-wheelers seemed to stretch forever, with no cell towers, gas stations, or civilization anywhere in sight. It was beautiful and tranquil. I enjoyed zooming over the hills small enough to coast over. Many times I'd get enough speed down one hill to take me to the next. This went on for miles. There was only one problem: I could not be seen over the slopes.

TODAY'S REFLECTION:

2 CORINTHIANS 4:18

So we fix our eyes not on what is seen, but on what is unseen, since what is seen is temporary, but what is unseen is eternal.

2 CORINTHIANS 5:7

For we live by faith, not by sight.

Once again, the daily verses Nate sent spoke to me. I prefer to ride my bike in safe zones—the paths in my neighborhood and on our beautiful Hollywood Beach. Those are familiar roads. After pedaling along them for almost ten years now, I feel safe there. It's the unfamiliar interstates, deserts, and mountain roads that scare me. They create a lot of stress and anxiety. I wish I could say I enjoyed this first part of my bike ride and the beauty of the new surroundings, but I did not.

If you are like me, you probably prefer to fix your eyes on the things you can see. To travel somewhere without a roadmap or previous experience is unsettling. But this is what God wants us to do. He asks us to trust Him, and we can only do so when we have fixed our eyes on Him even when we can't see where He is taking us.

God is eternal. He wants us to live with eternity in view, not clinging to the safety and security of what we know. He wants us to live by faith and not by sight.

What unfamiliar road is He taking you down today? Follow Him. You will be glad you did.

of the mountain the temperature could skyrocket to 110°F (43°C). This stretch frightened me for sure.

That morning, a short ride gave us the picture of blustery weather and signs warning of high winds on the mountain. My team decided it was too unsafe to ride. Having second thoughts myself, I listened to them.

After 4 or 5 miles, we got out of the camper and rode the last 2,000 feet (610 meters) into total desert. Here, we exited I-8 and had to take the worst road I've ever ridden on. There is no way to describe it. If you have been to Haiti, it was every bit as bad as any road I have traveled there. Here, we encountered our only desert sandstorm of the trip and had to endure about thirty minutes riding with a mask. Yuck! Hot desert and a mouthful of sand. Many bikers have endured sandstorms for days at a time, so I was fortunate.

At the end of the day, our support team—Pastor Ricky, Jordan, and Corey (my youngest son)—stopped at the local Walmart in El Centro, California, to stock up for the next couple of hundred miles. We spent the night in their parking lot. I was now an official Walmart camper. I loved the price, and we had 24/7 security.

By the way, Walmarts around the country offer a free overnight stay for truckers and campers. The next time you're in a Walmart and see a camper in the parking lot, think of Bike for Haiti.

Day 3

Jacumba to Brawley, California

Miles Pedaled: 49

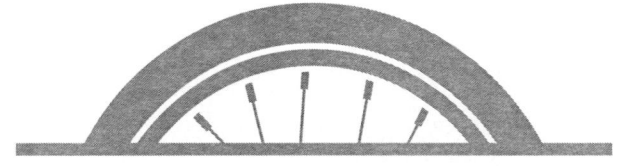

FROM THE MOUNTAINTOP TO THE VALLEY

We started at over 4,000 feet (1,219 meters) as we began our ride in Jacumba and descended to below sea level in only minutes. Mountains frighten me; I've already told you that. But I had never realized going down them can be scarier than pedaling up.

One of the more unique parts of this ride was that in the West we *had* to ride on interstates. In California and Arizona, it is legal to do this because in certain areas there are no roads for bicyclists. Today was my first experience riding on an interstate.

I began the day headed straight down I-8 from the In-Ko-Pah Mountains toward the gorge of the same name. A Customs and Border Patrol agent in Jacumba had told me to be careful going down that stretch of road since the crosswinds can get up to 80 miles per hour (129 kilometers per hour) and literally blow you off your bike. This was going to be a wild ride! Oh, and he also said while it might be 60°F (16°C) in Jacumba, at the bottom

But we survived and ended our second day in the little Mexican border town of Jacumba, California. This was as close as you can possibly get to Mexico without being there. It's the first sight of the walls and fences that would separate our two countries during the hundreds of miles we would ride throughout the southwestern United States.

TODAY'S REFLECTION:

> 2 CORINTHIANS 4:7 (NLT)
>
> We now have this light shining in our hearts, but we ourselves are like fragile clay jars containing this great treasure. This makes it clear that our great power is from God, not from ourselves.

Paul knew what it was to be persecuted, yet he reminded the Corinthians that life is hard. Despite the difficult times and circumstances they would face—and we still face today—God resides in us. We are but fragile pots, imperfect vessels who have the light of God living in us. His power sustains us and carries us through tough times.

Once again, the verse my son had sent was perfect for this day. I had never felt more frail, broken, and needy than I did climbing those first 4,100 feet (1,250 meters). I prayed often when I was not straining for my next breath. I truly felt the only way I could do this was if God filled my lungs and gave my burning Jell-O legs the strength to make the climb. I realized more than ever how fragile I am and how much I need Him.

May we all be thankful for the days when we feel too fragile for the obstacles we face. It is only His great power within us that brings us through those times.

Day 2
Alpine to Jacumba, California
Miles Pedaled: 43.64

FRAGILE—HANDLE WITH CARE

Days 1 and 2 were "in the books." I would use this phrase repeatedly as the days ticked by. The cities became distant memories as we pedaled through the mountains and deserts ahead. I'm so glad those "books" were short. In those two days, I climbed from sea level to an elevation of 4,151 feet (1,265 meters). I thought the first 2,500 feet (762 meters) had been a challenge, but the second day the altitude really got to me.

Headaches, dizziness, and a lot of water—along with many stops—pretty much summed up the day. The scenery was absolutely breathtaking, but I could not enjoy it as I struggled to gasp down the next breath to get to the following hilltop. I am not exaggerating when I say these were the two most physically brutal days I had ever endured in my life. That includes when I was in high school playing football and our coaches would put us through two practices a day in August in the South Florida scorching heat.

for months. But we made it and celebrated with a Starbucks latte in the small, picturesque city of Alpine, where we would begin day 2.

TODAY'S REFLECTION:

ISAIAH 43:18–19

> "Forget the former things; do not dwell on the past. See, I am doing a new thing! Now it springs up; do you not perceive it? I am making a way in the wilderness and streams in the wasteland."

My son Nate had planned to encourage me by sending daily Scriptures—you will read them throughout this book. What a perfect passage he sent me on our first day of riding. Isaiah tells the children of Israel to forget the past. They had made so many mistakes and had messed up so many times, it would be easy to stay defeated, to give up, and to expect God to give up on them. Except He didn't. He gave Isaiah the words to challenge His people. God said, "I am about to do something new, and I have already begun."

God had already assured Israel that when they passed through the rivers, the valleys, and the fires, He would be with them. I put myself in their shoes as I began this new thing God was doing, not just for the children of Haiti but also for my own life. Forget the past and the failures on my first Bike for Haiti ride in the mountains of Gatlinburg. Forget those days I did not finish what I set out to accomplish. As I stood there on that San Diego Beach Park, I was embracing God's Word: it was a new day indeed.

For you too, it's a new day. God is giving you a fresh, new twenty-four hours. Seize it. Accept it, and thank Him for allowing you to begin afresh. Forget the past. You are on a new journey today. Embrace it.

I invite you to join me on this journey. Let's see God do a new thing in our lives.

Day 1
San Diego Beach to Alpine, California
Miles Pedaled: 42.36

GOD IS DOING A NEW THING

We began our 3,200-mile (5,150-kilometer) trek home to South Florida at San Diego Beach Park at sea level. Starting with an immediate incline from the beach through a typical big city area, we wove from bike paths into six-lane traffic along the San Diego River for about 15 miles (24 kilometers). Then the real climb began. This was the part I had dreaded since deciding to complete the ride. Mountains. There was no time to prepare, no gradual slope. Nope. We were headed up an incline that would take us 2,500 feet (762 meters) above sea level in 42 miles (68 kilometers).

My goal was to get as far as possible. I had no idea I could do 42 miles, but my team and I crossed that distance anyway. During the steep climbs, some beautiful little towns like Santee, Lakeside, and Alpine popped up. Being a flatland/beach person, I began feeling the effect of the altitude at about 1,500 feet (457 meters)—something we never give a second thought to when we are in a car driving up mountains. This was the day I had feared

education and meals to hundreds of kids living in the orphanage Oasis Church helps sponsor, digging wells for clean water, further developing the projects and infrastructure that began in Haiti, and providing 250,000 meals after Haiti was severely impacted by Hurricane Matthew. Bike for Haiti's goal was to raise one million dollars for Haiti over the course of ten years and counting. This amount was surpassed at the twelve-year mark in pledges and commitments!

In this 2-in-1 book, you will also learn all about Bike for Haiti 2 in *Devotions from the Road*. While the journal entries contained in it have been revised for smoother reading, they are faithful in their essence. As you read them, you will experience some of Pastor Guy's thoughts in real time during his second Bike for Haiti ride in 2016. In the sections noted as "TODAY'S REFLECTION," he will share with you spiritual insights gained each day through his triumphs and struggles, detours and dangers, reunions with friends, and encounters with rabid dogs—all because of one man's willingness to take a radical step in faith for God's glory.

Throughout his tenure as pastor, Guy Melton has led his church to believe wholeheartedly in the Great Commission found in Matthew 28. Should you ever visit his church, you will witness "Oasisers" living out the church's core mission: worshiping God in word and deed, coming together to live in community, and going on mission to help those in need. While it may be overwhelming to think of the many needs around us, Pastor Guy and Oasis believe they can all be a "drop," one small factor that will make a difference in the lives of others as they advance His kingdom.

Hold fast—it's going to be a wild ride!

to diverse and beautiful landscapes of the United States. He spends his nights with his support team in a little camper, sometimes going days without sleeping in a proper bed. All day long he rides; all night long he contemplates. But every day he flips on the light in a small corner of his RV, opens his journal, and pens his thoughts—the things he's seen, the struggles he's faced, the insights God has shown him while pedaling down the long stretches of road. Sprinkled among these pages are little anecdotes of his band of brothers in the faith who, as you will see in the pages ahead, come and go, rallying up to unreservedly support Pastor Guy's mission and vision.

Guy Melton is the senior and founding pastor of Oasis Church of South Florida and has a passion for improving the lives of those living in Haiti. In 2011, he responded to God's call to serve the people of this beautiful country and to draw attention to its people's needs by developing the Bike for Haiti initiative, biking 1,500 miles (2,414 kilometers) from South Florida to New York City. The money raised went directly to faith-based organizations with whom Oasis Church partners to start churches, build and underwrite schools, construct a seminary and an orphanage, as well as provide nourishment to hundreds of Haitian children and families.

In 2012, Pastor Guy authored *Lessons from the Road: Moving from the Mundane to the Miraculous* (included here as written in 2012). In it, he captures the lessons he learned on his first Bike for Haiti ride. The book raised approximately $158,000 to further support the initiatives in Haiti.

In 2016, Melton again responded to God's call to continue raising funds by biking 3,200 miles (5,150 kilometers) from San Diego, California, to Hollywood, Florida. The money raised has gone toward providing

INTRODUCTION

Imagine, if you will, a pastor climbing the stairs to his pulpit. His heart is racing, palms sweating. His mind is a rush, for he is about to upend his church's point of view.

"The people of Haiti are hurting," he says. "I want you to pledge $55,000." It is the middle of a recession, when many have lost jobs, homes, cars. "I'm going to ride a bicycle 1,500 miles (2,414 kilometers) from here to New York to raise money. Let's do this!" At fifty-five years old—with a heart condition.

His church pledged $150,000.

Imagine with me now, five years later, that same pastor climbs the stairs to his pulpit to propose his riding 3,200 miles (5,150 kilometers) from San Diego, California, to Pembroke Pines, Florida, to continue the congregation's ministries in Haiti. He proposes to raise $250,000.

His church pledges $500,000.

Picture now this sixty-year-old pastor, thousands of miles from home. He is away from his family and his church on this mission in the middle of nowhere, biking through the deserts and mountains of the West Coast

Day 44: Hello, Dixie	109
Day 45: White Sand Beaches and Another Century	111
Day 46: Best Day of the Trip	113
Day 47: Wind at Our Backs	116
Day 48: One Million Dollar Stop	118
Day 49: Mexico Beach	121
Day 50: Another Week, Another Walmart	124
Day 51: Third Century in Three Weeks	127
Day 52: Some Days Just Don't Go As Planned	129
Day 53: Southern Tier Complete	132
Day 54: Map 7 Complete; Week 7 in the Books	135
Day 55: Remembering Mike	137
Day 56: Happy Birthday—Happy Anniversary	140
Day 57: A Bicycle Built for Two	142
Day 58: Week 8 Begins at Camp	144
Day 59: Reunion Ride	146
Day 60: Space and Treasure Coasts' Ride	149
Day 61: "I Can Do This; I Can Do This; I Can Do This . . . "	152
Day 62: **Day 62**	155
Day 63: Final Strokes	157
Day Final: Home	162
Days Ahead . . . One Last Log	165
Final Thoughts	168
Are You Ready?	170

Day 19: Map 3 of 7 Complete	49
Day 20: Being a Kid Again	51
Day 21: Well, This Is Texas	53
Day 22: Texas Hill Country	56
Day 23: Peaches, Jambalaya, and Barbeque	58
Day 24: Television in Austin	61
Day 25: Soaking in the Scenery	63
Day 26: Years Ago	65
Day 27: Three Incredible Women	67
Day 28: My Crazy Friend	70
Day 29: Time to Reconnect	72
Day 30: Memorial Day: The *R* Train	75
Day 31: Worst Two Years of My Life	77
Day 32: Thank God for Backups	79
Day 33: Worst Day Ever	82
Day 34: It's a New Day	85
Day 35: Worship and Wash	87
Day 36: A Century, Cheerwine, and Slim Jim	89
Day 37: Hello, Louisiana . . . Good Riddance, Texas	92
Day 38: Bayous, Crayfish Ponds, and Rice Fields	95
Day 39: Thankful for Air Horns	98
Day 40: Facing My Fears	100
Day 41: Bike for Beignet	102
Day 42: Riding and Worshiping	105
Day 43: Just a Dot on a Map	107

CONTENTS

Introduction		7
Day 1:	God Is Doing a New Thing	11
Day 2:	Fragile—Handle With Care	13
Day 3:	From the Mountaintop to the Valley	15
Day 4:	An Amazing Artist	18
Day 5:	Beyond Hope	20
Day 6:	Happy Mother's Day!	22
Day 7:	In the Books	24
Day 8:	Surprise	26
Day 9:	Craziest Riding Day Ever	28
Day 10:	Detour	30
Day 11:	When Maps Fail	32
Day 12:	Air Horns, Red-Hot Chili Peppers, and Dogs	34
Day 13:	A Salad and a Dozen Krispy Kremes	36
Day 14:	Transitions	39
Day 15:	Flat But Not Out	41
Day 16:	Only in Texas	43
Day 17:	The 12 Gage	45
Day 18:	Boring	47

Devotions from the Road

Copyright © 2023 by Oasis Church of South Florida. All rights reserved. No portion of this book may be reproduced, stored in a retrieval system, or transmitted in any form or by any means, except for brief quotations in printed reviews, without prior permission of the author. Requests may be submitted by email: info@visitoasis.org.

All Scripture verses, unless otherwise indicated, are taken from **THE HOLY BIBLE, NEW INTERNATIONAL VERSION®, NIV® Copyright © 1973, 1978, 1984, 2011 by Biblica, Inc.® Used by permission. All rights reserved worldwide.**

Scripture quotations marked MSG are taken from *THE MESSAGE*, copyright © 1993, 2002, 2018 by Eugene H. Peterson. Used by permission of NavPress. All rights reserved. Represented by Tyndale House Publishers, Inc.

Scripture quotations marked NKJV are taken from the New King James Version®. Copyright © 1982 by Thomas Nelson. Used by permission. All rights reserved.

Scripture quotations marked NLT are taken from the *Holy Bible*, New Living Translation, copyright © 1996, 2004, 2015 by Tyndale House Foundation. Used by permission of Tyndale House Publishers, Inc., Carol Stream, Illinois 60188. All rights reserved.

Editing and formatting services by ChristianEditingAndDesign.com.

DEVOTIONS FROM THE ROAD

BIKE FOR HAITI 2

The road of life twists and turns. Sometimes it's all uphill—sometimes a downhill coast. Ruts, surprises, and curves lie in wait for the weary traveler. We never know what's around the bend. But God does . . .